# Teaching Language as Communication to Children

# Teaching Language as Communication to Children

### Frank B. May
Washington State University

**Charles E. Merrill Books, Inc.**

Merrill's International Education Series under the Editorship of Kimball Wiles, Dean of the College of Education, University of Florida.

Library of Congress Catalog Card Number: 67-16516

1 2 3 4 5 6 7 8 9 10 11 12 - 73 72 70 69 68 67

PRINTED IN THE
UNITED STATES OF AMERICA
Printed in the United States of America

# Preface

Why do students by the thousands in the United States continue to leave school with a negative attitude toward their mother tongue? Why do so many leave school with a dearth of communication skills necessary for self-actualization and constructive citizenship? Part of the blame must be placed upon teaching methods which demonstrate a worship of form more than substance. But could our biggest mistake be that of focusing classroom learning upon the *acts* of reading, writing, speaking, and listening rather than the *serious problems* of communication which human beings have?

Language is far more than the acts of reading, writing, speaking, and listening. Language is the major medium of perception. To a large degree, as we use language, so do we perceive our environment. Language is the medium of discussions, discussions which lead to vast changes in personal behavior, institutional policies, and human welfare. Language is the medium of propaganda, propaganda so vicious and all-pervasive that only the dedication of teachers can prevent man from losing his spark of rationality. It might almost be said that language is man, for no other characteristic so distinguishes man from beast.

Men must communicate with each other more effectively than ever before, or mankind will be erased from this planet. It takes little insight into world affairs to recognize that nearly all of mankind's failures can be attributed to faulty communication and faulty perceptions based on linguistic trappings. Yet, faulty communication and faulty perceptions are not necessary evils. There is little, if any, evidence for supposing that education cannot eradicate, or at least reduce, these communication failures. If we have failed to reduce them so far, we cannot afford to excuse ourselves by pointing the finger at "man's basic contrariness." Our only hope is to try again—this time with a different approach.

The communication approach advocated in this book is a mixture of philosophy and brass tacks. The philosophy assumes that man can learn to communicate with his fellow man and his environment with reasonable harmony. It assumes that the substance of communication is as important as the form of communication. It assumes that students, young and old, should concentrate on the serious problems of communication which confront them every day of their lives—problems involving perception, discussion, propaganda, friendships, and mental health. To deal with these problems students must be taught a number of specific skills—the brass tacks of the communication approach. Students must be taught critical thinking skills needed for combating propaganda, creative thinking skills needed for entertaining or persuading others, and discussion skills needed for arriving at group decisions. They must learn to recognize grammar and usage for what they are—custom, nothing more, nothing less.

The purpose of this book is a practical one—to identify for teachers and prospective teachers some of the communication skills which need to be taught and to suggest methods of teaching them. Although the book is practice oriented, it is also research oriented, because it is the belief of the author that teachers should understand the bases for curricular and instructional practices. Each chapter attempts to provide the reader with reasonably solid information which will permit him not only to understand the suggested classroom exercises but also to create learning experiences for his pupils.

The writing of this book was actually a group project since I have borrowed and revised the ideas of so many others. Most of their names will be found in the list of references at the end of each chapter. It is to be understood, of course, that the originators should not be held accountable for my modifications and restatements, or even the quotations, which must necessarily be taken out of context. However, there are some whose names have not been listed, such as Basil Pillard and Fran Lemcke, who taught me at Antioch College to appreciate the role of language in human behavior. Actually, Antioch College as a whole was partly responsible for this book since it provided me with the most significant opportunities for learning about human beings that I ever had in an educational institution. My thanks go also to my wife for her thoughtful and considerate editing.

*To My Family*

# Table of Contents

# Part I

## Environmental Effects on Language Development

# LINGUISTIC GARDENERS
## (Who Plants the Seeds of Confusion?)

Noises such as crying, cooing, grunting, and groaning are like plants in a jungle, while the noises we call language have been pruned, shaped, and cultivated by gardeners—some much more careless than others. To be more accurate, the child is his own gardener, trimming and fertilizing in a valiant attempt to keep up with his neighbors. His "neighbors", of course, include his parents, siblings, teachers, school peers, and other influential people.

The teacher who does not understand, at least on a general level, the intricately complex matrix of personal relationships which go into the making of a child's language patterns can not hope to gain the rapport necessary for effective language teaching. Language resides on the hub of the self-concept; a teacher who abuses a child's language abuses the personal integrity of the child. A teacher who helps a child *understand* his language helps him move toward self-understanding.

The understanding teacher must comprehend and appreciate the various ways in which the environment of children affects their speaking behavior. He must know intimately the answers to such questions as these:

How influential are parents and siblings in determining a child's oral language patterns?

What effect does socio-economic status have on oral language growth?

Does our culture encourage the speech development of girls more than boys?

Are there any ways in which the school can influence the speech of its captive learners?

To concern ourselves, at this point, with the development of speech is not to ignore the interrelatedness of the language arts but to recognize the primacy of oral language. Not only does the child learn to speak before he learns to read and write, his speech habits greatly influence his competencies in reading and writing. Furthermore, the greatest proportion of a person's communication is in the form of speech. First, then, let us look at the effects of parents and siblings on children's oral language growth.

## Effects of Parents and Siblings

Jamie was raised in an orphanage from infancy. At the age of fourteen, he was adopted into the Clunden family and began to live a more "normal" life. Although his foster parents and new siblings made his life at home quite pleasant, he found school to be a very fearful experience. His vocabulary was so limited he could barely communicate and only when someone was patient enough to listen intently and use the simplest of words. No intensive training was given to Jamie, although it was assumed that his everyday contacts with school peers and his foster family would cause him to improve his speaking and conceptual abilities. The assumption was an honest and understandable one, but after a year's time it proved to be fallacious. For some reason, Jamie was making no progress. Finally, an experimentally minded teacher agreed to tutor him for a short period after school each day, and within two months Jamie had learned several new words and was using a few of them in his daily conversation. But progress after that was pitifully slow and the tutor had to give up the attempt. Jamie is presently sixteen and gardens for the Clundens and two of the nearby neighbors. Because of his inferior linguistic abilities, the Clundens have not attempted to find him a job in town.

Jamie's story is a fictitious one, but it demonstrates the importance of a non-institutionalized childhood to the development of language. In Goldfarb's study (21) of adolescents who were raised in institutions during early childhood, he found that despite later schooling and ordinary family and community life, they generally remained retarded in language and mental growth. Apparently, a critical period for oral language growth exists, which, if passed by without concomitant emotional and linguistic nurturing, generally results in permanent damage.

Moore (40) found that oral language development was slower for a group of orphanage children than for a group of non-orphans, and Brodbeck's study (6) indicates that even in early infancy one can detect the detrimental effects of institutionalization on speaking ability. McCarthy (33) has summarized other studies which show the same sorry plight of children raised in orphanages. It seems obvious, however, that orphanages, per se, are not to be blamed. The most consistent difference between the environment of an institutionalized child and a non-institutionalized one is the relative opportunity of the latter to receive plenty of attention and affection. The orphanage child is competing with dozens of other children for the attention of a few harried adults who may develop little or no emotional attachment for any of the youngsters.

Few teachers have to be concerned with a previously institutionalized child, but, of course, that is not the point. The point is that children come to school with backlogs of emotional-linguistic contacts with adults that range from a symbiotic level to nearly an orphanage level. To expect all children in the third grade to be similar in linguistic comprehension and skill is, at best, naive.

Sandy is an only child. She eats breakfast and supper with her parents and grandmother. During both meals the conversations are fairly lively, and Sandy does at least her share of the talking—probably more. At bedtime her father reads her a story, and her mother has a brief chat with her before turning out the light. Her room contains a desk, well stocked with pencils and paper, and a book case spilling over with her own books and books borrowed from the library. Her parents and grandmother are all avid readers and frequently engage in conversation about mutually read material. Sandy has consistently topped every reading and language test she has ever

taken. Her participation in discussions is enthusiastic, and she frequently volunteers to give reports or to discuss an experience she has
had. Her teachers like her very much!

Sandy has all the cards stacked in her favor—as far as language
maturity is concerned. First of all she is an only child and gets a
great deal of adult attention, which in itself might give her a better
chance for oral language growth than her friends with siblings. In
recording the "share and tell" episodes of 108 private school children
whose intelligence scores and socio-economic ratings were all above
average, Higgenbotham (26) found that only children gave longer
talks, used longer sentences, spoke more slowly, were more easily
heard, and had more correct articulation than children with siblings.
Furthermore, she found, in general, an inverse relationship between
the number of siblings and the quality of oral language. (The fact
that the only children spoke more slowly is readily understandable
when you consider the low level of competition for "air-wave" control.)

Davis (10), in a study of children from five to ten years of age,
found the same linguistic superiority of only children. The only
children were more mature in oral language than children with
siblings, who were in turn, somewhat more mature than twins.

The relative inferiority of twins was also demonstrated by Day's
investigation (11). Day found that a group of "singletons" was
markedly superior in language development to a group of 160 twins.
The relative superiority increased between the ages of two and five.
Since no twins over five were studied by Day, the question arises as
to whether the relative superiority of singletons continues. McCarthy
(33), in answer to this question, found that twins tend to catch up to
singletons in later years.

If young twins are generally inferior in oral language to singletons, holding other factors constant, one would expect triplets to be
even more retarded. Howard (28), in a study of 82 triplets, found this
to be the case. Her group of triplets demonstrated an even greater
oral language deficiency than Day's or McCarthy's groups of twins.
The reason for the retardation of twins and triplets is speculative but
probably straightforward: twins and triplets meet each other's needs
for intercommunication so readily, the need for oral communication
with adults is diminished.

The studies previously cited and research done by Aserlind (4) and Milner (37) make it tempting to generalize that the quantity of adult contacts is the major factor in oral language development. Aserlind examined the verbal skills of children in families of very low socio-economic status. Despite the consistently low status of the families, he was able to differentiate the children on the basis of language development. Those children whose language skills were relatively mature tended to have fewer siblings. Milner selected from among 108 first graders 21 children who scored "high" on the language portion of an intelligence test and 21 children who scored "low." She found that families of high scorers usually had breakfast together, and that children in these families had active conversations with adults at breakfast, before school, and at supper; they also received more affection from the adults. Families of low scorers, however, did not eat breakfast together, and the children in these families had no conversations with adults during breakfast, before school, or at supper. Furthermore, they seldom talked to siblings at breakfast or before school.

It should be noted that no direct relationship has been drawn between language maturity and the number of children in a family. It is the number of adult contacts that seems to make the difference. But this is not to say that the *quality* of adult contacts is not important. The story of Bruce should demonstrate that quantity alone is not enough.

Bruce began to stutter at the age of seven—at least that is when his parents decided that he was a "stutterer." He had been perceived as a nervous child by his mother and father for several years, and they had tried various ways of "calming him down." Sometimes they spanked him, sometimes they scolded, but usually they relied upon threats. Bruce tended to be negligent about most everything that adults consider important—such as getting to bed on time, washing his hands before dinner, and keeping out of the mud. Both parents attempted to "straighten him out" by nagging him and keeping a close eye on him. Sometimes an "evil eye" was enough to keep Bruce in line, however. After the parents decided that Bruce had a stuttering problem, they began to work on it. When Bruce was trying to say something his mother would often supply a word for him, whereas the father insisted that he stop and start over, but "think before you speak!" Bruce is now in college and still stutters. He feels that "my parents have never understood me."

Research on stuttering demonstrates that the hypothetical story of Bruce is illustrative of many stutterers. Moncur (39) matched 48 stutterers and 48 non-stutterers between five and eight years of age on sex, age, school placement, and residential area. By means of structured interviews with the mothers he found that, relative to the non-stutterers, the stutterers were perceived as aggressive and nervous children with definite speech problems. Mothers of stutterers more often reported harsh disciplinary measures such as corporal punishment, threats, or humiliation. Their discipline was less consistent, and they were more often guilty of nagging and over-supervision. Furthermore, the parents more often disagreed on disciplinary matters. Mothers of stuttering children were frequently inconsistent in their eating and sleeping requirements. They reported more often than mothers of non-stuttering children that they had supplied a word to the child, had told him to stop and start over, had called his attention to his speech, had scolded him for his speech, and had told him to think before he spoke. Moncur suggests that the parents' attitudes and behavior contributed to the onset of stuttering, since the stuttering commenced after the parents had had ample time to establish discipline patterns.

Kinstler (29) found that mothers of stuttering boys tended to reject their sons more often than a control group of mothers. Moll and Darley (38) detected a tendency of mothers of articulatively impaired children to maintain higher standards and be more critical of their children's behavior.

Duncan (13) administered a questionnaire to 62 college-age stutterers and 62 non-stutterers from the same college. The two groups were equated for IQ, sex, and socio-economic status. Significant differences between the two groups were found. The stutterers more often felt that their parents did not understand them (56 per cent *vs.* 24 per cent). More of them felt a lack of affection in their home experience (23 per cent *vs.* 2 per cent). The stutterers had more frequently desired to run away from home (34 per cent *vs.* 6 per cent). They more often perceived that their parents were presently disappointed in them (47 per cent *vs.* 23 per cent), and they more frequently considered one or both parents to be very nervous (no per cent given).

A study by Wood (56) may confirm the reader's growing suspicion that the parents may be as "nervous" as the children, if not more so. He discovered that the mothers of 50 articulatory defectives tended to score higher on neuroticism and lower on self-adjustment than women in the norm group for the test. The fathers as a group did not differ significantly from the norm group on neuroticism, but they did score lower on self-adjustment. The mothers of stutterers also tended to have higher social standards than women in the norm groups. Wood found that 96 per cent of the children with articulation problems had one or both parents who ranked below the forty-fifth percentile on the self-adjustment scale.

It is reasonably evident, then, that stuttering and articulatory defects, when not physiologically caused, are related to a mentally unhealthy home environment. Children free of such defects tend to come from homes in which parents have positive feelings toward themselves, accept their children and display affection toward them, maintain consistent but mild discipline, avoid setting impossible standards for children, and provide ample opportunities for them to speak without being under tension. Obviously these criteria of a mentally healthy home environment also apply to the school environment.

Most children readily learn the oral language patterns of the home. But what of children who are expected to learn two languages? Are they able to assimilate them both as rapidly as other children assimilate one language? Carrow (7) compared a group of third grade bilinguals with a group of monolinguals equated for IQ, socio-economic status, age, sex, and hearing proficiency. The bilinguals had been exposed to English and Spanish from infancy, could communicate in both by the age of three, and preferred English by the time of testing. The monolinguals had been exposed only to English. Results of testing showed significant differences favoring monolinguals on oral reading accuracy, oral reading comprehension, hearing vocabulary, speaking vocabulary, and articulation. Smith (48) studied the language of 92 preschoolers, 30 of which had been exposed both to Chinese and English in the home. For the bilinguals the average vocabularies in either language were far below the average vocabulary of the English monolinguals. Many of the bilinguals had combined vocabularies which did not equal that of the average monolingual. Arsenian (2), after examining nearly 100 studies, concluded that monoglots tend to be superior to bilinguals on verbal intelligence, vocabulary, and school achievement; but the discrepancy between monoglots and bilinguals tends to decrease with combined age and education. Nevertheless, it should be pointed out that a bilingual child tends to have a language handicap during the elementary school years.

We have been considering the effects of parental behavior on oral language development. In doing so we have considered only the father and mother and have ignored the modern child's third parent, namely, the television set. What influence does this "parent" have on oral language growth? Unfortunately, no research dealing with this specific question seems to have been done. Witty (55) has been studying the television viewing habits of children and their parents in the Chicago area since 1951. Children in this area tend to watch television about 20 hours per week, although the viewing time varies considerably among children and between grade levels. Sixth graders tend to stare at the box more than second graders; and high school students less than elementary school students. However, Witty has found no evidence that television viewing, per se, either hinders or enhances school achievement. In a random sample of about 2500 seventh and eighth grade students in California, Ridder (44) found no significant relationship between academic achievement and the amount of television viewing. Until further research of a more specific nature has been done, it is doubtful that valid generalizations can be made concerning the relationship between television viewing and oral language development.

## Effects of Cultural Conditions and Expectations

Dennis is a twelve-year-old boy who lives in a large Eastern city with museums, playhouses, art centers, libraries, and inexpensive public transportation. Dennis has never been to a museum, playhouse, art center, or public library; in fact, he has never been more than 25 blocks from his home. His home consists of a two room apartment shared by nine people. Their bathroom is shared by many more. You would look in vain for a book in the apartment; not even a pencil or pen could be found. Dennis has mixed feelings about school. He enjoys getting out of the apartment and "horsing around" with the boys on the playground and in the halls. But schoolwork is frustrating and boring. Dennis can read 30 or 40 words, but he hates reading because the readers "always talk about those rich white kids." His only participation in discussion is to giggle when another boy "pops off." He knows how to write his name and little else. Because of their income and location, the parents of Dennis have lower-class status. Because of their skin color their opportunity for climbing the status ladder is low. Because of his cultural environment Dennis is nearly illiterate.

Dennis is similar to a majority of Negro children in this city (12). Cultural deprivation is prevalent in many parts of the United States, but no group is hit harder by it than the Negro. Riesman (45) estimates that by 1970 fifty per cent of the public school pupils in large cities will be "culturally deprived." Governmental intervention may stem the tide, but the greatest burden of responsibility for helping these children will be placed on the schools. The fact that something can be done to overcome the language deficiencies induced by cultural deprivation will be demonstrated in a later section.

It is axiomatic that cultural deprivation is more likely to occur among families of low socio-economic status. As shown by Eels, *et al.* (15), Coleman (9), and Havighurst and Janke (24), this cultural deprivation results in a level of cognitive ability which is usually lower for children from low-status families than for children from high-status families. It should also be expected that children from low-status families will demonstrate a lower level of oral language proficiency than children from high-status families. Research supports this expectation.

Templin (49) in a study of 480 children between the ages of three and eight, discovered that the oral vocabulary of high-status children was definitely superior to that of low-status children. Gough (22) found that the high-status sixth graders had higher vocabulary scores on an achievement test than low-status pupils. Hill and Giammateo (27) computed a correlation of .84 between vocabulary scores and socio-economic rating.

In other studies the structural components of oral language used by high-status and low-status children have been compared. Barnes (5) studied the oral language of 100 second graders selected randomly from the total second-grade population in a large Midwestern school district. He found that the use of multiple verbs was higher for high-status children. Templin (49) noted that high-status children tended to use advanced sentence structures more frequently.

Loban (31), in his investigation of 338 children between kinder-garten and sixth grade found that high-status pupils generally used more complex grammatical structures. Francis (18) discovered a positive relationship between socio-economic status and the ability to use moveables and subordination elements, in her study of first graders. McCarthy (36) found that children from high-status fam-ilies used longer sentences and more mature sentence forms at earlier ages. Deutsch's study (12) of first and fifth grade children from low-status families indicated that these children had more expressive language ability than generally emerged in the classroom, but that the syntactical organization of their language was quite deficient.

Studies of the articulation abilities of high- and low-status chil-dren have also been made, although the findings are inconsistent on this aspect of oral language growth. Mahon (32), Hall (23), and Healey (25) all found no significant relationship between articulation abilities and socio-economic status. Templin (49), on the other hand, found that low-status children were consistently lower on articula-tion scores. Furthermore, they took about one year longer to achieve adult articulation (eight years of age as contrasted to seven years of age for the high-status children). Weaver, *et al.* (51) administered an articulation test to 594 first graders before they had been given reading instruction. The mean number of errors for children of professional parents was 7.6; clerical, skilled trades, and retail busi-ness, 9.6; day laborers, 13.1.

Research by Smith (47) lends support to the well-known fact that low-status children make more usage "errors" than high-status children. This is easily explained by the fact that "standard" usage refers to the dialect of high-status people. Furthermore, Noell (42) has shown that children tend to make the same usage errors as their parents. Since the dialect of low-status people precludes the possibil-ity of errorless usage, it is hardly surprising that children of low-status parents do not shine in this respect.

As Negroes are often handicapped by cultural deprivation based on both class and racial discrimination, one might expect to find even greater oral language deficiencies among Negro children in low-status environments than among white children in the same type of environment. Thomas (50) selected randomly 50 Negro kinder-garten children from one economically depressed urban area and

50 white kindergarten children from a similar area. Interviews with the children demonstrated that all of the children showed deficiencies in amount, maturity, and quality of oral expression, and the Negro children were somewhat more deficient than the white children.

It appears conclusive that our society presently fosters the language development of children whose parents have high socio-economic status; the opposite seems true for families in the lower socio-economic brackets. In addition to these biases of wallet and skin color, there also appears to be a slight bias in favor of the gentler sex. The differences between boys and girls in language growth is often reported as small and insignificant, but when IQ, socio-economic status, and stimulus are held constant, the differences are consistently in favor of the girls. Winitz (54), Barnes (5), Templin (49) and McCarthy (33) found differences favoring girls on such variables as length of response, number of different words, and structural complexity.

With respect to speech defects, the difference between the sexes is highly significant. Many more boys than girls are victims of stuttering and articulatory disorders in our society. Yedinack (57), for example, found that 75 per cent of those suffering from non-organic articulatory defects were boys. Her population consisted of second graders selected from 43 schools in ten cities. In Moncur's investigation (39) of stuttering, 83 per cent of the stutterers were boys. In explaining such research findings, McCarthy (35) suggests that a boy receives much less satisfaction from imitating the speech habits of his mother, who is around much more than the father; consequently, he imitates less than girls. Also, noisy, energetic boys are sent out to play more often and, thus, are given less linguistic practice with an adult; boys also tend to receive more rejection. It should also be pointed out, moreover, that certain aspects of this anti-linguistic reinforcement are repeated in the classroom.

## Effects of School Environment

A central thesis of this book is that the school can have a very great influence on the development of language skills. But it is readily admitted that many aspects of oral language are, to a large extent, habitual by the time a child enters kindergarten or first grade.

As mentioned earlier, Noell (42) demonstrated that the usage of parents largely determines the usage of the children. Templin (49) found that there was little change after the age of three in the parts of speech used. She also found that the greatest growth in articulation took place between the ages of three and four.

There is little, if any, evidence that children can learn basic oral language patterns from merely listening to the teacher's normal speech, although Gesell (19) found that young children tend to imitate a teacher's speech mannerisms. However, the leadership pattern of a teacher may have a considerable impact on the oral language growth of his students. Christensen (8) discovered that vocabulary growth was significantly greater under teachers whose pupils rated them high on a "Warmth Scale." Lippitt and White (30), in their classic boys club study, found that democratic leadership by the teacher encouraged friendly discussion of personal matters, joking, asking opinions of each other, and making suggestions on group policy. The authoritarian pattern of leadership resulted in either apathetic withdrawal (which would hinder oral language practice) or aggressive resistance (which would channel oral language into narrow, destructive uses). Ryans (46) found that teachers who were understanding and friendly, yet organized and stimulating (similar to Lippitt and White's "democratic" pattern of leadership), encouraged productive and confident participation. Other studies by Flanders (17) and Anderson and Brewer (1) demonstrate the positive effects of supportive teachers on the self-confidence of students and their willingness to participate. It is apparent that certain types of leadership on the part of teachers encourage more practice in oral communication. It is likely, moreover, that such practice would lead to greater facility with oral language.

Of course, the teacher is not the only influential person in the classroom. In general, the older a school child gets the more influential his peers become and the less influential his teachers and parents become. McCarthy (34) suggests that little improvement in articulation can be hoped for if an adolescent's peers do not articulate correctly; the peer influence is generally too strong for training by adults to have much lasting influence. Goldberg (20) points out that Puerto Rican children in large cities often speak Spanish instead of English in order to avoid being taken as Negroes by their school peers. Wilson's study (53) shows that even socio-economic status may be less important than the educational standards set by peer groups. The mean reading achievement score of white collar workers' sons was 106 in a school attended predominantly by children of high-status families. The mean reading achievement score of white collar workers' sons in a school attended predominantly by children of low-status families was only 81. In another study Wilson (52) found that 93 per cent of the sons of professional men in predominantly upper class schools reported that they wanted to go to college, while only 64 per cent of the professional men's sons in lower class schools wanted to go to college. Obviously, aspirations based on peer values have a strong influence on cognitive growth. It is likely that oral language development will be affected by school peer values as much as any other cognitive skill.

Will the administrative structure of the school influence the language development of students? This unanswerable question is often asked in reference to various academic areas of specific skills. It is almost as useless as asking, "Will the seating arrangement at a banquet affect the guests' digestion?" The number of uncontrolled variables related to either question approaches infinity. Research has been done, however, on the effects of such administrative devices as team teaching, multi-age grouping, ability grouping, and non-grading. The results are inconclusive and inconsistent and can be interpreted only by discovering exactly what different teachers did under the different administrative arrangements. If one group of teachers, for example, spends more time on language development under a team arrangement than another group of teachers under a self-contained arrangement, the resulting superiority of the "team students" should not be attributed to team teaching as such.

While it is conceivable that the administrative organization of a school may have some influence on the opportunities which children have for oral language development, research indicates that specific curricular and instructional practices are the main agents of change. Moyer (41), for example, carried on an instructional program with groups of fourth, sixth, and eighth graders in which the written drill on usage was compared with self-selected drill performed with a tape recorder. Improvements in written and oral usage were greater for groups using the experimental ear-training approach. Some individuals also showed improvement in volume, enunciation, and voice quality. Moreover, the differences between the control and experimental groups were even more pronounced the following year. Emerick (16) randomly assigned 47 children to morning and afternoon kindergarten sessions and provided the afternoon session with 26 brief speech improvement lessons. Whereas the articulation errors of the afternoon group changed from 36 to 16, the articulation errors of the morning group changed only from 33 to 29.

Assuredly the schools could have a much greater impact than heretofore on oral language growth if they would spend more time on specific training programs in fluent and articulate speech. More than one educator has decried the paucity of speech instruction in comparison to reading instruction. Yet, as pointed out by Artley (3), several studies demonstrated the importance of oral language growth *before* reading instruction. After all, in the act of reading, we are utilizing our behavioral and oral language experiences as background for attaching a meaning to the printed page.

The principle of oral language competence prior to, or concomitant with, reading instruction is being utilized by several programs for culturally deprived children, as described by the Research Council of the Great Cities Program for School Improvement (43). In these programs teachers spend a considerable portion of instructional time helping children develop oral vocabulary and ease of expression. To ask these children to read prior to such instruction is, and has been, to invite failure. This principle of speech before reading, as applied in programs for culturally deprived, is just as applicable for culturally advantaged—witness the "revolution" in foreign language instruction, in which oral instruction precedes reading of the language. In fact, Dykstra (14) describes an attempt at the Columbia University Curriculum Study Center to develop special materials for teaching English as a *second* language to culturally deprived students. Oral models are provided for the students in the form of plastic records which can be played on inexpensive, manually-operated, playback equipment.

## Classroom Activities

The following suggestions for classroom learning experiences relate only to voice quality, articulation, and oral vocabulary since many activities conducive to other aspects of oral language growth are described in later chapters.

1. The class listens to tape recorded versions of paired statements.

One member of the pair should be spoken by the teacher in a thin, metallic, or muffled voice. The same statement should then be read in a full, resonant voice. After each pair ask the children which one they can understand better.

2. Individual children record the same paired statements as recorded in number one and listen to themselves. "Say it in a bad way and then in a good way."

3. Children who articulate certain sounds incorrectly listen to a tape recording of words using those sounds. After each word the child records his version on the tape. Later he listens to the entire tape which now includes the teacher's pronunciation and his own side by side. (Most children will need assistance from the teacher, cadet teacher, or older child on the mechanical aspects of this exercise.)

4. Small groups of children work with the teacher on improperly articulated sounds, saying each word after the teacher. Avoid words which contain two of these sounds.

5. The class takes a variety of field trips and excursions during which new vocabulary is introduced and after which they describe what they have seen.

6. The children feel, listen to, smell, observe, and taste objects which are new to them. New words are introduced in oral form after the sensual experiences have occurred. The children can make up oral stories about the objects. They can also be asked to describe the objects several days later.

*     *     *     *     *

In working with a child's speech we are working with a significant aspect of his self-concept. If the teacher is to be effective in language instruction he must understand the types of environmental experiences which influence oral language development. In this chapter we have seen how the quantity and quality of oral communication with adults during a child's early years affect his linguistic maturity. We have also discussed the negative impact that cultural deprivation, low socio-economic status, and (to a very small extent) being a boy have on language growth. The author has assumed in this chapter that teachers can have a very great influence on the oral language development of children and has suggested several ways in which this influence might be felt.

# REFERENCES

1. Anderson, Harold H. and J. E. Brewer, *Studies of Teachers' Classroom Personalities, II: Effect of Teacher's Dominative and Integrative Contracts on Children's Classroom Behavior.* Stanford, California: Stanford University Press, 1946.

2. Arsenian, Seth, "Bilingualism in the Post War World," *Psychological Bulletin* 42:65-86, February, 1945.

3. Artley, A. Sterl, "Oral Language Growth and Reading Ability," *Elementary School Journal* 53:321-327, February, 1953.

4. Aserlind, LeRoy, Jr., *An Investigation of Maternal Factors Related to the Acquisition of Verbal Skills of Infants in a Culturally Disadvantaged Population.* Doctoral Dissertation: University of Wisconsin, 1963.

5. Barnes, Margaret D., *An Analysis of the Oral Language of Second Grade Children with Emphasis upon Patterns of Sentence Structure and Verbs, and Their Relationship to Factors of Reading Age, Mental Age, Sex, and Socio-Economic Status.* Doctoral Dissertation: Indiana University, 1962.

6. Brodbeck, Arthur J. and Orvis C. Irwin, "The Speech Behavior of Infants without Families," *Child Development* 17:145-156, September, 1946.

7. Carrow, Sister Mary Arthur, "Linguistic Functioning of Bilingual and Monolingual Children," *Journal of Speech and Hearing Disorders* 22:371-380, September, 1957.

8. Christensen, C. M., "Relationships between Pupil Achievement, Pupil Affect-Need, Teacher Warmth, and Teacher Permissiveness," *Journal of Educational Psychology* 51:169-174, June, 1960.

9. Coleman, Hubert A., "The Relationship of Socio-Economic Status to the Performance of Junior High School Students," *Journal of Experimental Education* 9:61-63, September, 1940.

10. Davis, Edith A., *The Development of Linguistic Skill in Twins, Singletons with Siblings, and Only Children from Age Five to Ten Years.* Institute of Child Welfare Monograph Series No. 14. Minneapolis: University of Minnesota Press, 1937. pp. 131-137.

11. Day, Ella J., "The Development of Language in Twins: I. A Comparison of Twins and Single Children," *Child Development* 3:179-199, September, 1932.

12. Deutsch, Martin, "The Disadvantaged Child and the Learning Process," *Education in Depressed Areas.* A. Harry Passow (editor). New York: Bureau of Publications, Teachers College, Columbia University, 1963.

13. Duncan, Melba H., "Home Adjustment of Stutterers versus Non-

Stutterers," *Journal of Speech and Hearing Disorders* 14:255-259, September, 1949.

14. Dykstra, Gerald, "Columbia University Curriculum Study Center: Materials for Teaching English as a Second Language," *College English* 25:225, December, 1963.

15. Eels, Kenneth; Allison Davis, R. J. Havighurst, Virgil E. Herrick, and Ralph Tyler, *Intelligence and Cultural Differences*. Chicago: University of Chicago Press, 1951.

16. Emerick, Lonnie, "Speech Improvement in the Kindergarten," *Education* 84:565-568, May, 1964.

17. Flanders, Ned A. "Personal-Social Anxiety as a Factor in Experimental Learning Situations," *Journal of Educational Research* 45:100-110, 1951.

18. Francis, Sarah E., *An Investigation of the Oral Language of First Grade Children*. Doctoral Dissertation: Indiana University, 1962.

19. Gesell, Arnold and Frances L. Ilg, *The Child from Five to Ten*. New York: Harper & Row, Publishers, 1946.

20. Goldberg, Miriam, "Factors Affecting Educational Attainment in Depressed Urban Areas," *Education in Depressed Areas*. A. Harry Passow (editor). New York: Bureau of Publications, Teachers College, Columbia University, 1963.

21. Goldfarb, William, "The Effects of Early Institutional Care on Adolescent Personality, "*Journal of Experimental Education* 12:106-129, December, 1943.

22. Gough, Harrison G., "The Relationship of Socio-Economic Status to Personality Inventory and Achievement Test Scores," *Journal of Educational Psychology* 37:527-540, December, 1946.

23. Hall, William F., *A Study of the Articulatory Skills of Children from Three to Six Years of Age*. Doctoral Dissertation: University of Missouri, 1962.

24. Havighurst, Robert and L. L. Janke, "Relations between Ability and Social Status in a Midwestern Community, I: Ten-Year-Old Children," *Journal of Educational Psychology* 35:357-368, September, 1944.

25. Healey, William C., *A Study of the Articulatory Skills of Children from Six to Nine Years of Age*. Doctoral Dissertation: University of Missouri, 1963.

26. Higgenbotham, Dorothy C., *A Study of the Speech of Kindergarten, First, and Second Grade Children in Audience Situations with Particular Attention to Maturation and Learning as Evidenced in Content, Form, and Delivery*. Doctoral Dissertation: Northwestern University, 1961.

27. Hill, Edwin H. and Michael C. Giammatteo, "Social Economic Status

and Its Relationship to School Achievement in the Elementary School," *Elementary English* 40:265-270, March, 1963.

28. Howard, Ruth W., "The Language Development of a Group of Triplets," *Journal of Genetic Psychology* 69:181-188, December, 1946.

29. Kinstler, Donald B., "Covert and Overt Maternal Rejection in Stuttering," *Journal of Speech and Hearing Disorders,* 26:145-155, May, 1961.

30 Lippitt, Ronald and Ralph K. White, "An Experimental Study of Leadership and Group Life," in *Readings in Social Psychology.* Eleanor E. Maccoby, *et al.* (editors). New York: Holt, Rinehart & Winston, Inc., 1958.

31. Loban, Walter D., *The Language of Elementary School Children.* Research Report No. 1 Champaign, Illinois: National Council of Teachers of English, 1963.

32. Mahon, Florence L., *The Relationships of Certain Psychological Factors to Speech Development in Primary Grade Children.* Doctoral Dissertation, Boston University School of Education, 1962.

33. McCarthy, Dorothea, "Language Development in Children," in *A Manual of Child Psychology,* Leonard Carmichael (editor). New York: John Wiley & Sons, Inc., 1954, 492-630.

34. ———, "Language Disorder and Parent-Child Relationships," *Journal of Speech and Hearing Disorders,* 19:514-523, December, 1954.

35. ———, "Some Possible Explanations of Sex Differences in Language Development and Disorders," *Journal of Psychology* 35:155-160, January, 1953.

36. ———, *The Language Development of the Preschool Child.* Institute for Child Welfare Monograph Series No. 4. University of Minnesota Press, 1930.

37. Milner, Esther, "A Study of the Relationships Between Reading Readiness in Grade One School Children and Patterns of Parent-Child Interaction," *Child Development* 22:95-112, June, 1951.

38. Moll, Kenneth L. and Frederic L. Darley, "Attitudes of Mothers of Articulatory-Impaired and Speech-Retarded Children," *Journal of Speech and Hearing Disorders* 25:377-384, November, 1960.

39. Moncur, John P., "Environmental Factors Differentiating Stuttering Children from Non-Stuttering Children," *Speech Monographs* 18:312-325, November, 1951.

40. Moore, Jean K., "Speech Content of Selected Groups of Orphanage and Non-Orphanage Preschool Children," *Journal of Experimental Education* 16:122-133, December, 1947.

41. Moyer, Haverly O., "Can Ear-Training Improve English Usage?," *Elementary English* 33:216-219, April, 1956.

42. Noell, Doris I., "A Comparative Study of the Relationship between the Quality of the Child's Language Usage and the Quality and Types

of Language Used in the Home," *Journal of Educational Research* 47:161-167, November, 1953.

43. Research Council of The Great Cities Program for School Improvement, *Promising Practices from the Projects for the Culturally Deprived*, 228 North La Salle Street, Chicago, Illinois, April, 1964.

44. Ridder, Joyce M., "Pupil Opinions and the Relationship of Television Viewing to Academic Achievement," *Journal of Educational Research* 57:204-206, December, 1963.

45. Riesman, Frank, *The Culturally Deprived Child*. New York: Harper & Row, Publishers, 1962.

46. Ryans, David G., "Some Relationships between Pupil Behavior and Certain Teacher Characteristics," *Journal of Educational Psychology* 52:82-90, April, 1961.

47. Smith, Madorah E., "A Study of Some Factors Influencing the Development of the Sentence in Preschool Children," *Journal of Genetic Psychology* 46:182-212, March, 1935.

48. ———, "Measurement of Vocabulary of Young Bilingual Children in Both of the Languages Used," *Journal of Genetic Psychology* 74:305-310, June, 1949.

49. Templin, Mildred C., *Certain Language Skills in Children: Their Development and Interrelationships*. Minneapolis: University of Minnesota Press, 1957.

50. Thomas, Dominic R., *Oral Language Sentence Structure and Vocabulary of Kindergarten Children Living in Low Socio-Economic Urban Areas*. Doctoral Dissertation: Wayne State University, 1962.

51. Weaver, Carl H., Catherine Furbee, and Rodney W. Everhart, "Paternal Occupational Class and Articulatory Defects in Children," *Journal of Speech and Hearing Disorders* 25:171-175, May, 1960.

52. Wilson, Alan B., "Residential Segregation of Social Classes and Aspirations of High School Boys," *American Sociological Review* 24:836-845, December, 1959.

53. ———, "Social Stratification and Academic Achievement," in *Education in Depressed Areas*, A. Harry Passow (editor) New York: Bureau of Publications, Teachers College, Columbia University, 1963.

54. Winitz, Harris, "Language Skills of Male and Female Kindergarten Children," *Journal of Speech and Hearing Disorders*, 2:377-385, December, 1959.

55. Witty, Paul, "Some Results of Twelve Yearly Studies of Televiewing," *Science Education* 46:222-229, April, 1962 .

56. Wood, Kenneth S., "Parental Maladjustment and Functional Articulatory Defects in Children," *Journal of Speech and Hearing Disorders* 11:255-275, December, 1946.

57. Yedinack, Jeanette G., "A Study of Linguistic Functioning of Children with Articulation and Reading Difficulties," *Journal of Genetic Psychology* 74:23-59, March, 1949.

# Part II

## The Structure of
## American English

# 2

# DIALECTICAL NOISES
## (Whose Usage Is Correct?)

Zoologist Says Dog Yaps Make Sense

LONDON (EPI)—A zoologist from Oxherd University claims to have deciphered the yelps, snarls, and bays of canines. Dr. Feline, who has been studying dog "speech" for years, says that dogs communicate with each other by means of a very elaborate set of noises, which he has dubbed "fanguage."

After traveling through various parts of the world, Dr. Feline has come to the conclusion that there are at least 3000 different fanguages. Furthermore, he states, most dogs understand only one or two fanguages, resulting in a great deal of confusion, misunderstanding, and dog fights.

Not only are there a great variety of fanguages, but each fanguage has a number of "dogalects" (variations within a fanguage). A hound in one part of a large city, says Dr. Feline, may woof a dogalect which differs in many respects from the dogalect woofed in another part of the city. Curs from these two parts of the city can usually intercommunicate to some extent, but they find it either irritating or amusing. Dr. Feline has observed, moreover, that each mutt acts as though his dogalect were superior to all other dogalects.

Dogalects differ not only among geographical regions, says Dr. Feline, but also between canine classes within a region. The upper-class dogs (consisting of pedigreed animals and those who strive to be like them) woof a different dogalect from the lower-class dogs (consisting of mutts, mongrels, and tramps). For example, the upper-class dogs in London will woof, "Grrr rowlf urr yelp," whereas the lower-class dogs will woof, "Grrr rowlf orr yelp." According to Dr. Feline, this slight difference is enough to cause frothing of the mouth by upper-class and lower-class dogs alike.

In this chapter we will analyze one type of structural phenomenon of the English language which often hinders communication—the phenomenon called "usage." The terms "usage" and "grammar" will be defined as words which describe relatively separate aspects of communication. The arguments between descriptive and prescriptive grammarians will be noted and given historical perspective, followed by a brief bow to "functional usage." Social-class differences in usage will then be discussed, and suggestions for handling these differences in the classroom will be offered. Finally, specific techniques of teaching English usage will be described.

## Usage or Grammar?

First we must reach agreement on the definitions of two terms: grammar and usage. These two terms are often used interchangeably by educators, resulting in a lack of clear-cut goals for the teaching-learning process. Notice the three following sentences:

1. John threw his dog some meat.
2. John throwed his dog some meat.
3. John some meat his dog threw.

Which sentence is not grammatical? In which sentence is "proper" usage violated? Modern linguistic scientists (9, 16) would argue that sentence 3 is the only ungrammatical one. They would also argue that sentence 2 contains a verb which is "proper" for some people but "improper" for others. Sentence 2, then, differs in *usage* from sentence 1, while sentence 3 differs *grammatically* from sentences 1 and 2. A native of our country would never use sentence 3, although he might use sentence 1 or sentence 2, depending on his background or motivation. Only a very young child or an adult in the early stages of learning English would use sentence 3.

Grammar, to linguistic scientists, consists of devices used in sentences to signal meaning. The following sentence has several grammatical signals: "The farmer will give his son a horse." One device signals to us that the farmer, rather than the son or horse, is performing the action. Another device signals to us that only one farmer is performing the action. A third device signals that the action will take place in the future, while the fourth device signals that the sentence is a statement of fact rather than a question or request. Notice that many of the meanings in the sentence are not dependent upon the lexical (dictionary) meanings of the words in the sentence.

Grammar, then, is a way of signaling; a way of showing relationships within a sentence; a way of organizing meaning. Grammar is also a collection of subconscious rules—rules of word order (syntax) and word form (morphology)—which guide us in the creation of new sentences.

Usage, on the other hand, is related more to dialect than to grammar. The dialect of some groups of people includes "brung" as the past tense of bring. The dialect of other groups includes "brought" as the past tense of bring. Since these two words have equal signaling power, i.e., they both signal the past tense of bring, they are both grammatically "*correct.*" Yet, to most of us only one of them seems proper and elegant.

## Descriptive vs. Prescriptive Usage

What is "proper" or "correct" usage? For several years this question has served as the battle line between descriptive and prescriptive grammarians. The descriptive grammarians argue that the notion of usage being either proper or correct is prescientific. To the descriptivists, certain words and phrases are used by certain groups of people; the duty of the grammarians is to analyze objectively and describe the manner in which words and phrases are used—not to determine which words and phrases are better than others. If some people say, "He come over to my house," this fact should be recorded rather than berated, according to the descriptivists. Furthermore, they say, the grammarian should be concerned with *who* uses *what* words under *which* conditions. Since a variety of people communicate with each other under a variety of conditions, a variety in usage is to be expected rather than deplored.

What would a descriptivist say about the choice between "brought" and "brung"? Roberts (16) points out that "brought" is used by most "educated" people; consequently it sounds better to those who either consider themselves educated or emulate educated people. The *association* between "brought" and educated people is the only reason for considering it better than "brung."

However, the descriptive grammarians point out that usage differs even within educated circles. Take, for example, the following set of sentences:

1. Who were you speaking to?
2. I will buy it later.
3. He wished to really believe her.

1. To whom were you speaking?
2. I shall buy it later.
3. He wished really to believe her.

Which set is correct? Descriptivists contend that both sets are used by educated people; only a "purist" would insist on the correctness of the second set. The only justification for insisting that the second set is best is that some authors of grammar books say so.

In place of grammar books, descriptive grammarians have developed a Linguistic Atlas of the United States and Canada (13) in which usage is delineated according to region and educational background. Malstrom (13) compared information from the Linguistic Atlas with information from current English textbooks and found much disagreement between the two sources. For example, "dived" is preferred by educated people in some parts of the United States, while "dove" is preferred by educated people in other parts of the United States; yet most grammar books claim that "dived" is correct.

In contrast to descriptivists, prescriptive grammarians feel that the English language will be degraded unless standards of usage are maintained. Prescriptivists indicate that English has already been "degraded" in recent years because of the work of descriptivists:

> Linguistic scholarship, once an encouragement to the most exacting definitions and standards of workmanship, has for some time been dedicating itself to the abolition of standards; and the new rhetoric evolved under its auspices is an organized

assumption that language good enough for anybody is good enough for everybody (8:73).

The relationship between correct usage and a disciplined mind is "obvious" to the prescriptivists:

> Let those who choose to define usage as what a swarm of folk say or write by reason of laziness, shiftlessness, or ignorance; the tenable definition is still what the judicious do as a result of all that they can muster of conscious discrimination . . . the best, whether or not we have it in us to attain it, is not too good to be aspired to (8:76).

A logical way of ending the debate between descriptive and prescriptive grammarians might seem to be that of examining the linguistic habits of those who use English as their primary tool for earning their living. How do authors, editors, and English teachers feel about proper usage? By presenting various usages to such people it should be possible to determine the degree to which they worry about correct and incorrect usage. Lewis (12) sent questionnaires to English professors, authors, editors, high-school English teachers, and other people who work in the medium of words. The questionnaire asked them to respond to each of 19 sentences as to whether or it it was acceptable English in educated circles. The agreement among the different groups of word experts was not very high. The English professors were the least concerned about the supposedly incorrect usage in each sentence. The editors of women's magazines were the most concerned. The high school English teachers were much closer to the latter group than they were to the English professors.

## Historical Perspective on Usage

Evidently, a middle ground position between descriptive and prescriptive usage cannot be found by consulting those who grind and polish words for a living. Let us seek historical perspective instead. Evans (7) tells how Samuel Johnson, in 1747, set out to develop a dictionary in order to purify and fix the English language once and for all. By the time the dictionary was published eight years later, Johnson had become a considerably wiser man. After a futile effort to prescribe usage, he came to the conclusion that lexicographers should only describe it. His conclusion had been reached by philosophers before him (7): Montaigne, in the 16th Century, argued that only a fool would fight custom with grammar; and Horace, long before him, observed that use was the sole arbiter and norm of speech.

Bloomfield and Newmark (2) describe the evolutionary nature of our language and how a particular usage comes in and out of style: "It is real cold" is condemned today, while "It is very cold" is considered correct. Yet *very* was originally an adjective meaning true. Time is kind to "incorrect" usage. But time is sometimes cruel to "correct" usage; consider the demise of *clomb* which used to be the proper way of uttering the past tense of *climb*.

Historical perspective, then, makes this author wary of those who would prescribe how English is to be used by all people in all times.

> Looking at the Western languages objectively, what we find is that those varieties or dialects of each language have developed prestige exactly to the extent that the users of those varieties or dialects have been looked up to by other users of these languages . . . (2:291).

## Functional Usage

Nonetheless, a realistic appraisal of social conditions demands an awareness of the conditions under which usage will be *considered* proper or improper by others. In general a person who wishes financial success and at least middle-class status has little choice in the matter of usage. The usage requirements for membership in the middle class or upper class are illogical and unfair, but they are chiseled in marble. It is probably true, as Evans (7) jibes, that one can *express* himself no better in Outer Mongolian than he can in Inner Mongolian. But obviously, one can *communicate* better in Outer Mongolian if one is speaking to Outer Mongolians.

This is not to say that a truly educated person rigidly guards his usage in every social situation. The man who answers his wife at the breakfast table with "To whom are you speaking?" is probably either jesting or harboring delusions of grandeur. With friends an occasional "ain't" or double negative adds spice to conversation.

With strangers, of course, an educated person is aware of the obstacles to communication which might be built by foreign usage.

## Appreciating Social-Class Differences in Usage

Certainly one function of formal education is that of developing respect for people with various cultural backgrounds. What better way can teachers encourage such respect than through tolerance and appreciation of each student's dialect. How often have teachers been responsible for inculcating a sense of mutual repugnance among classmates because of dialect differences? Surely it is possible to teach one dialect without depreciating all other dialects.

Foreign exchange students are generally treated with great respect in our schools. Pupils and teachers alike show interest in the foreign student's customs and language. Yet, students from the other side of the tracks are often treated as inferior creatures whose use of the English language is abhorrent to sensitive ears.

The number of students who live on the other side of the tracks in our country is probably much greater than most teachers realize. Well over half of our citizens are in the "lower" socio-economic class (10). This is a striking fact, when one realizes that the vast majority of teachers in the United States are in the "middle" socio-economic class (10). To oversimplify the situation, most teachers with a middle-class dialect are teaching primarily students with a lower-class dialect. Of course, the degree of dialect mixture in the classrooms varies a great deal across the country and within cities. It is doubtful, however, that many middle-class teachers in our country will spend their entire career teaching only middle-class children. Thus, most teachers will sooner or later be faced with the necessity of working with children whose dialect may seem "uncultured."

If teachers are to understand and appreciate these children, it would be helpful to be aware of certain facts. First, it has been shown (15) that children make the same "mistakes" in usage as their parents do. Obviously, teachers need to be wary of insulting a child's parents or making him ashamed of them by depreciating his use of the English language. Thus, if a middle-class dialect is to be taught to a lower-class pupil, it should be taught as another dialect which some people use in our country—one which a pupil should know in order to communicate effectively with such people. Just so, the middle-class pupil should become aware of the lower-class dialect and when it might be appropriate to use this dialect. (It is hoped that the reader who is ready to discard this book will read the next section before doing so. In this section the discussion refers to appreciation rather than instruction.) In either case the notions of good *vs.* bad, pure *vs.* impure, intelligent *vs.* stupid, and other similar value dichotomies are irrelevant to classroom discussion of English usage.

A second fact to be aware of is that many teachers have moved into the middle class via the teaching route (10). Those who have made this status jump may be the least tolerant of lower-class dialect. Like a six-year-old who ridicules the "baby talk" of a four-year-old, the person who has just risen to middle-class status may be prone to belittle lower-class dialect.

A third fact is that lower-class children have a special type of difficulty in communicating with middle-class teachers. Bernstein (1) claims that middle-class dialect includes both a "formal language" and a "public language." Public language relies on condensed sentences, rigid syntax, and expressiveness. Formal language is varied and individualized, relying on subtle changes in syntax and vocabulary. As Bernstein explains, a middle-class child can readily understand both "Shut up" and "I'd *rather* you made *less* noise, darling." A lower-class child cannot react adequately to the latter statement until he has first translated it into "Shut up!" The translation is not only difficult for the lower-class child, it is inaccurate, since "Shut up!" is an oversimplified translation. A middle-class child would react quite differently to "Shut up!" and "I'd *rather* you made *less* noise, darling." He can distinguish between the two meanings; generally, the lower-class child cannot. Thus, a teacher who wishes to be of help to lower-class children must become sensitive to such translation problems. He must become skilled in translating his own statements into public language. Even more important, perhaps, he needs to patiently explain to lower-class children, through concrete examples, the subtle differences which exist between formal and public utterances.

We see, then, that helping children to appreciate the dialect differences of their classmates requires a knowledgeable and sensitive teacher. In general, the teacher will set the tone of appreciation; his example may be sufficient. However, special activities might be useful in making children more appreciative of dialect differences. Folk songs might be studied with this purpose in mind. In addition to listening for various dialects in the songs, the children might also write their own songs, using a dialect which seems appropriate for the song.

## Techniques of Usage Instruction

Although one of the functions of public schools (and hopefully private schools) in the United States is to develop appreciation of the various sub-cultures which exist in our country, another function is to provide opportunities for families to advance or maintain their socio-economic position. It should be quite clear, even to the casual observer, that language usage is one of the most influential weapons available to one who wishes to fight for a higher rung on the social ladder or to one who wishes to maintain his footing. Therefore, it appears only fair that children should be instructed in usage which is common to people with middle-class and upper-class status. In a democracy the initiation rites should not be kept secret.

Four stages of instruction seem appropriate for teaching high-status usage. First, the teacher should decide which usage items are worthy of concentrated instruction. Past research on children's usage "errors" will be of some help in this respect. In 1915 Diebel and Sears (6) studied the speech habits of 1400 elementary school children. Teachers of the children recorded the usage "errors" as they were noticed during a four day period. Of the errors which were recorded, 50 per cent were in the use of verbs; 13.5 per cent, pronouns; 11.6 per cent, negatives; 9.7 per cent, syntactical redundance; 8.0 per cent, mispronunciations; 3.5 per cent, prepositions; and 3.3 per cent, adjectives and adverbs. Since this study is rather antiquated, the question arises as to whether children of today have similar difficulties. In 1956 Templin (20) studied the usage errors of 480 children between the ages of three and eight. Templin again found that verbs were the greatest trouble makers; difficulties with pronouns, negatives, etc., were similar in order and magnitude to those found by Diebel and Sears.

Perhaps the most appropriate way of selecting specific usage items would be to administer an oral pretest to the children. This can be done with a tape recorder on which the teacher has recorded a series of sentence pairs—one member of each pair containing the desired usage. The children would number their paper and write an "a" or "b" after each pair had been heard. The pretest should concentrate, of course, on verbs—particularly the irregular forms such as *run*, *come*, and *go*. Such a pretest could be refined gradually over a period of two or three years. The first pretest might contain sentence pairs based on usage items in language textbooks and on the teacher's hunches. As the year progresses the teacher can add or subtract items according to the actual "mistakes" children make in classroom situations, thus refining the pretest according to the particular region in which he is teaching.

The second stage in usage instruction might be to develop a rationale or purpose for learning high-status usage. Before actual instruction in usage begins children should probably be exposed first to the fact that usage varies in real-life situations. To act as though a language textbook adequately represents usage in our society is to assume the role of an indoctrinator rather than a teacher. We have already discussed ways in which a teacher might develop appreciation for the usage of different sub-cultures. How might children become more aware of the usage employed by people who have relatively high status in our society? Although a language textbook might seem to be the easiest and most efficient starting point, a more appropriate starting point might be one or more of the following: newspapers, magazines, radio, television, conversations with adults in the community, library books. These materials offer the pupil an opportunity to carry on his own "original" research and to generalize from his research rather than accept textbook pronouncements on faith. A language textbook should probably be held in reserve for its value as a handy reference and as a source of practice exercises.

Here are some experiences, ordered from simple to complex, which a teacher might arrange for the initial attack on "standard" usage:

1. Scan a story in a reading textbook together. Decide ahead of time which usage to look for. Record on the chalkboard the usages which the children find.

2. Tape record a newscast or other radio program and listen to

the recording together. Decide ahead of time which usages to listen for. Stop the recording whenever a pupil notices one of the usages. Record each usage on the chalkboard.

3. Listen to a newscast or other radio program together. Decide ahead of time which usages to listen for. Have some children record their findings on the chalkboard during the broadcast.

4. Have each child use the first chapter of his current library book as a source of information. Decide on two or three usages to look for. Omit conversations; look only at the author's narration. Determine the number or percentage of authors who preferred each usage.

5. Divide the class into small committees. Each committee can be responsible for reporting to the class on two or three usages. Each member of the committee might use a different source—one person listening to a news broadcast, one person scanning a newspaper article, one person interviewing a public official, etc. Each member should document his findings.

6. Have the pupils canvass a small sample of people in the community, asking them to indicate anonymously their preferences for certain usages. Determine the number or percentage of people who preferred each usage. If possible, repeat the survey with another sample.

The third stage in usage instruction would consist of practice on specific usage items which have been selected on the basis of the pretest and the original research carried on by the children. Which techniques seem to be most effective in teaching particular forms of usage? According to Dawson (5), surveys show that many teachers make several "mistakes" in their instruction on usage. One mistake is covering too many errors in a year. Another mistake is drilling on items which are already known by the children in the classroom but appear in workbooks. These two mistakes can be avoided by individualizing the instruction on usage. Research shows that individualized instruction on usage is more effective than mass instruction. In a carefully designed study by Warner and Guiler (21), for example, control groups taught via mass, workbook practice were compared with matched experimental and check groups. All groups were administered a pretest. Only within the experimental groups, however, were errors diagnosed. If the majority in an experimental group had difficulty with an item, the entire group received practice on the item; if less than the majority had difficulty with an item, only those who needed practice received it. After 12 class periods the students in the experimental groups had made an average improvement of 32 per cent, whereas the students in the control groups had made an average improvement of only 21 per cent. The students in the check groups, who received no usage instruction, had made an average improvement of 6 per cent.

The percentage of improvement might have been even greater for the experimental students if the instruction had been completely individualized—that is, if only those who needed it had received practice on an item. It seems rather pseudo-democratic to insist that all students receive practice on an item merely because the *majority* of students are having trouble with it. Nevertheless, the partially individualized instruction established in Warner and Guiler's study was more effective than the mass instruction.

A third mistake which Dawson mentions is concentrating on "errors" which are quite customary in informal communication. To avoid this mistake there is no substitute for the teacher's own good judgment as to which utterance is inappropriate and which is informal. The child who says, "I brung you an apple, teacher," needs practice (later) in using the past tense of *bring*. The child who says, "Who ya talking to?" is probably using language which is appropriate for an informal situation.

A fourth mistake cited by Dawson is teaching usage only in isolation without having children apply what they have been taught. We're all familiar with situations similar to the one in which a child gets all usage items on his work sheet correct and exclaims, "I done it!" How can teachers avoid such moments of despair in which learning does not transfer from one situation to the next? Educational psychologists (3, 11) agree that for transfer to occur the learner must recognize the similarity between the new situation and the situation in which the original learning occurred. Thus, if we wish to have a child employ standard usage in his speech, certainly the instructional practice should be largely oral. Cutright (4) found that oral instruction was the most effective of seven instructional approaches used with elementary school pupils. About 1800 children were divided into seven treatment groups, matched for intelligence. A pretest in oral and written usage was followed by six weeks of instruction, with practice time and activities carefully controlled. A post-test indicated that the instructional approaches were effective in the following order:

1. Pupils chose the "correct" form among alternatives and wrote it in the blank. Then they practiced saying the correct form in the sentence context.

2. Pupils were instructed with six different methods for one week each.

3. Pupils practiced "incorrect" forms with knowledge of the "correct" form.

4. Pupils chose the "correct" form among alternatives and wrote it in the blank.

5. Pupils proofread prepared paragraphs.

6. Pupils played usage games.

7. Pupils received no special instruction in usage.

The pupils who practiced orally made much greater gains than the other pupils, not only on the oral test but also on the written test. These results are not surprising, since psychologists have demonstrated that subliminal speech occurs during the act of writing (17). In other words, before writing a word the writer subconsciously speaks it. Consequently, oral instruction in usage is very likely to improve both oral usage and written usage.

Cutright's technique of oral instruction probably could be improved by the use of a tape recorder, which would permit an individualized approach. A child (or a small group of children having similar difficulties) could read sentences into the recorder and then listen to the sentences. This method of providing children with immediate feedback is similar to the one employed by students learning a foreign language in a language laboratory. Moyer (14) used listening tapes to teach usage to experimental groups of fourth, sixth, and eighth graders. The experimental groups made greater progress than the control groups.

In Cutright's study the students who received no special instruction on usage showed no improvement. This fact should discourage those who feel that usage will improve without guided practice. Yet, even if one agrees that practice sessions should be largely oral, the specific form of practice exercises employed is crucial. Symonds (19) investigated six different forms of practice with six independent groups and found one form which was more efficient than most of the other forms and more effective than four of them. The reader is invited to predict which one of the following took less instructional time and caused more improvement than most of the others.

1. Repetition of correct forms.
   a. The boy was *almost* killed by an automobile.
   b. My baby brother is *almost* two years old.
2. Repetition of correct and incorrect forms.
   a. Wrong: The boy was *most* killed by an automobile.
   b. Right: The boy was *almost* killed by an automobile.
3. Rules of grammar with minimum examples.
   a. *Most* boats carry life preservers. (*Most* is an adjective and should modify a noun.)
   b. John has *almost* finished his work. (*Almost* is an adverb and should modify a verb.)
4. Rules of grammar along with analysis of the grammatical construction of certain words and phrases.
   a. *Most* boats carry life preservers. (*Most* is an _____ and modifies _____.)
   b. John has *almost* finished his work. (*Almost* is an _____ _____ and modifies _____.)
5. Illustrated rules of grammar followed by choices between right and wrong forms of usage.
   a. Are you _____ over your cold? (*most* or *almost*)
   b. _____ birds build nests. (*most* or *almost*)
   c. Which is the _____ fun? (*most* or *almost*)
6. All five methods combined.

Method 6 caused the most improvement but took the most time. Method 2 was almost as effective as Method 6, but it took less time than all other methods except Method 1. The six methods were effective in the following order: 6, 2, 5, 3, 4, 1.

One implication of Symonds' study is that children should practice saying the incorrect form along with each correct form of usage, *with full knowledge of the correct form.* Such practice without knowledge of the correct form would be psychologically indefensible (3, 11). Again, the use of a tape recorder would permit individualized practice. Another inference which one might be led to make on the basis of Symonds' study is that a variety of instructional techniques in combination would be the most effective way of improving usage.

However, such an inference is likely to be erroneous, since the effectiveness of the "combined" approach was probably due to the *quantity* of practice provided by this approach. Since Method 2 was nearly as effective and far more efficient, this would seem to be the best instructional technique to adopt, until further research demonstrates otherwise.

However, none of the studies discussed has dealt adequately with the importance of rewarded and distributed practice. Educational psychologists have demonstrated the usefulness of certain types of rewards (better classified as reinforcements) in helping children to learn and retain specific facts. An effective reward (reinforcement)— and one that is easily administered—is to inform the pupil whether he is right or wrong (3, 11). Teaching machines, to a great extent, are based on this simple technique. Tape recorded programs on usage which incorporate this technique can be designed by the teacher. For example, a small group of pupils who are having similar difficulties might be given a dittoed list of sentence pairs. The pupils could then listen to a recording of these sentence pairs. After each pair there would be a pause, during which the children would mark either "a" or "b." They would then be reinforced by hearing the correct sentence on the recording. After the reinforcement sentence there would be another pause, during which a pupil would mark the correct sentence on his paper (if he had selected the wrong one). Each successive sentence pair would be handled the same way. Following this session each child would be given an opportunity to record the correct and incorrect forms on the tape recorder. While he listens to himself he should look at the dittoed sheet on which the correct form has been marked. (If it is impossible to have each child record and listen individually, the members of each small group could take turns recording; it is doubtful, however, that this would be as effective as individual recordings, since a child's own voice is probably more reinforcing than another child's voice.)

In addition to reinforcing particular usage by means of tape recorded practice sessions, the teacher would do well to distribute such practice sessions over the entire school year. Research by educational psychologists has shown that distributed practice will generally cause students to retain specific bits of information, whereas massed (one-shot) practice is often a waste of time (3, 11). Furthermore, with nonsense material—usage items could easily be considered "nonsense" by some students—it is important to provide pupils with their first review session shortly after the initial practice session (3, 11).

\* \* \* \* \*

In this chapter we have seen that particular forms of English usage achieve the label of "correct" because these forms are used by people with high social status. The author has demonstrated his bias toward a descriptive approach rather than prescriptive approach to usage instruction. At the same time, however, he has argued for a middle-ground position which takes cognizance of the practical problems of communicating with people of various status levels in our society. Several techniques have been suggested for teaching high-status usage and for developing an appreciation of both high-status and low-status usage. Whose usage is correct? Yours and mine, of course.

# REFERENCES

1. Bernstein, Basil, "Social Class and Linguistic Development: A Theory of Social Learning" in *Education, Economy and Society.* A. H. Halsey, Jean Floud, and C. Arnold Anderson (editors). New York: Free Press, 1961.

2. Bloomfield, Morton W. and Leonard Newmark, *A Linguistic Introduction to the History of English.* New York: Alfred A. Knopf, Inc., 1963.

3. Cronbach, Lee J., *Educational Psychology.* New York: Harcourt, Brace & World, Inc., 1962.

4. Cutright, Prudence, "A Comparison of Methods of Securing Correct Language Usage," *Elementary School Journal* 39:681-690, May, 1934.

5. Dawson, Mildred A., "Summary of Research Concerning English Usage," *Elementary English* 28:141-147, March, 1951.

6. Diebel, Amelia and Isabel Sears, "A Study of Common Mistakes in Pupils' Oral English," *Elementary School Journal* 17:44-54, September, 1916.

7. Evans, Bergan, "Grammar for Today," *Atlantic Monthly* 205:79-82, March, 1960.

8. Follett, Wilson, "Grammar is Obsolete," *Atlantic Monthly* 205:73-76, February, 1960.

9. Fries, Charles C., *The Structure of English.* New York: Harcourt, Brace & World, Inc., 1952.

10. Havighurst, Robert J. and Bernice L. Neugarten, *Society and Education.* Boston: Allyn and Bacon, Inc., 1962.

11. Klausmeier, Herbert J., *Learning and Human Abilities: Educational Psychology.* New York: Harper & Row, Publishers, 1961.

12. Lewis, Norman, "How Correct Must Correct English Be?" *Harpers* 198:68-74, March, 1949.

13. Malmstrom, Jean, "Linguistic Atlas Findings versus Textbook Pronouncements on Current American Usage," *English Journal* 48:191-198, April, 1959.

14. Moyer, H. O., "Does Ear Training Help?" *Research in the Three R's* Clarence W. Hunnicutt and William J. Iverson (editors). New York: Harper & Row, Publishers, 1963.

15. Noel, Doris I., "A Comparative Study of the Relationship Between the Quality of the Child's Language Usage and the Quality and Types of Language Used in the Home," *Journal of Educational Research* 47:161-67, 1953.

16. Roberts, Paul, *English Sentences.* New York: Harcourt, Brace & World, Inc., 1962.

17. Strickland, Ruth G., "Implications of Research in Linguistics for Elementary Teaching," *Elementary English* 40:168-171, February, 1963.

**18.** Strom, Ingrid M., "Research in Grammar and Usage and Its Implications for Teaching Writing." Bulletin of the School of Education, Indiana University Vol. 36, No. 5, September, 1960. (No mention in text.)

**19.** Symonds, Percival M., "Practice *vs.* Grammar in the Learning of Correct English Usage," *Journal of Educational Psychology* 22:81-95, February, 1931.

**20.** Templin, Mildred C., *Certain Language Skills in Children: Their Development and Interrelationships.* Minneapolis, University of Minnesota Press, 1957.

**21.** Warner, Paul C. and Walter S. Guiler, "Individual Versus Group Instruction in Grammatical Usage," *Journal of Educational Psychology* 24:140-151, February, 1933.

# 3

# *GENERATED SENTENCES*
## (What's Happening to Grammar?)

*SIXTH DREAM: Man running from ghouls (14).*

*Ghouls:*   We're after you; we're after you; we'll never let you go.

*Man:*   There's my teacher, Miss Jones; she'll help me. Miss Jones, help me!

*Teacher:*   (In a dead monotone.) What is an adverb?

*Man:*   An adverb? Why an adverb is a . . . is a . . .

*Teacher:*   (In the same dead monotone.) What is an adverb?

*Ghouls:*   She won't help you; she won't help you; yahhhhh!

In the last chapter grammar was defined as a set of rules which we use subconsciously in producing sentences. These rules dictate the order in which words are placed in a sentence and the inflections given to particular words. In this chapter we will examine with scepticism several reasons usually given for including grammar in the formal education of our children. In particular we will investigate the myth that a study of grammar is an aid to composition. As an alternative to traditional grammar a particular form of structural grammar will be "hawked"—namely, generative grammar. Techniques for teaching generative grammar will be suggested, along with several sample exercises for children.

43

## Reasons Given for Teaching Grammar

It is likely that grammar was first studied for humanistic reasons. The first grammarians were probably those who were simply curious about the way in which people ordered and inflected their words for the purpose of communicating with each other. It is also likely that these grammarians were impressed with the probability that language is the most notable distinction between man and the other inhabitants of our planet. The science of grammar probably arose, then, as a study which was intrinsically satisfying to a few people. As so often happens to an elite and basic study, this science has gradually become a "must" for all who wish to be considered educated—and during the last several decades, a "must" even for those who do not wish to be considered educated.

Several justifications for this mass indoctrination have been developed by teachers who have invested considerable effort in learning formal grammar and by citizens who wish the new generation to have the same advantages as the old. One justification is that formal study of grammar will improve a person's usage. This argument may have originated in our country with Seventeenth Century New Englanders who desired to plasticize their language against the abrasive influence of constant immigrants (18). It was shown in the last chapter that this rationale for teaching formal grammar has not endured the test of research; formal grammar does not appear to be an effective medium for learning usage.

Another justification given for the formal study of grammar is its power to discipline the mind. This argument is a perennial favorite of those who perceive that their pet subject is losing its grip on the curriculum merry-go-round. Numerous studies, however, have demonstrated rather conclusively that no subject, per se, has such magical power (15, 27). It may well be true that those who faithfully study and follow the rules of formal grammar are individuals with the capacity to discipline certain attributes of their intellect. It does not follow, however, that those without such capacity will gain it through the study of grammar.

A third justification given for the formal study of grammar is that grammar is a humane subject—one which deserves a place among the liberal arts. This argument has led to the supposition that all students should study grammar in order to appreciate better the nature of man. Such an argument is probably not subject to research. On the other hand, it does have merit as a value judgment. However, if one accepts such a value judgment, one should at least be aware of a possible pitfall: children cannot be expected to appreciate any aspect of human nature which is presented to them in a form which is too difficult for them to grasp. For example, it seems evident that more time in elementary and secondary schools is spent on parts of speech than any other aspect of the language program (10). Yet, research indicates that knowledge of the parts of speech and how they function in a sentence is too much to expect of most pupils —particularly in the elementary grades (17). (It might also be argued that such knowledge is too much to expect of adults. Tovatt (29) asked 150 adults to label the parts of speech in this sentence: "Practically all boys play baseball at a very early age." Only 50 out of the 150 were successful!) The point which I am emphasizing is that grammar can only be considered a humanistic subject when it leads to a greater appreciation of humanity. It is no secret that grammar can easily be taught in a manner which leads to disgust rather than appreciation. Some modern linguists insist, nonetheless, that grammar can be taught in a meaningful and humane way. Some of their ideas will be discussed in a later section.

A fourth justification given for the formal study of grammar is that without such study a child would simply not learn to speak adequately. This argument is grounded more on hope than fact— although the hope is commendable. Numerous studies (7, 16, 28) have shown that by the age of six a vast majority of children have largely mastered the grammar of their spoken language without ever learning a rule or the parts of speech. Furthermore, European and Asian children have little trouble learning three or four languages without the aid of formal instruction in grammar. Nevertheless, it is possible that an improved form of instruction in grammar might result in subtle improvements in speech by some children. A developmental study by Templin (28) indicates that the complexity of children's sentence patterns does increase throughout the school years. This type of improvement might be enhanced through the particular type of grammatical study called "generative grammar," which will be described in a later section.

A fifth justification for the formal study of grammar is that teachers in the higher grades will expect children to know the "fundamentals." A statement heard frequently from elementary teachers is that the high school teachers expect them to provide children with a knowledge of the parts of speech and other grammatical terminology. The high school teachers frequently argue in turn that students need such knowledge in order to get into college. Groff (10) surveyed 43 colleges and universities in California and found that 41 of these institutions gave entrance examinations which required no knowledge of the parts of speech. The other two institutions based a negligible portion of their entrance examination on the parts of speech. If other states are similar to California in this respect, the good old days of "passing the buck" may have to cease.

A sixth justification given for the formal study of grammar is that written composition will be improved through such study. Surveys show that most teachers probably believe that grammar instruction leads to improved writing as well as speaking (7). Many of our schools of education and departments of English should take a large share of the blame for the prevalence of such an erroneous assumption. Surely, a large percentage of teachers would change their minds if they were exposed to the negative evidence.

## Grammar and Composition

What effect does the formal study of grammar have on the written composition of children? The answer to this question, of course, may depend largely on the nature of the formal grammar instruction. Surveys indicate that teachers generally concentrate on semantic definitions of grammatical terms and on description of words, phrases, and sentences according to these terms (7). Labels such as *subject, predicate, adjective,* and *interrogative sentence* are standard equipment. This type of grammar study will hereafter be called traditional grammar.

Studies by Hoyt (13) and Asker (1) have shown that any positive relationship which exists between knowledge of traditional grammar and quality of composition is probably due to the general ability called intelligence. That is, the more intelligent one is the more one tends to do well in both composition and traditional grammar. However, no studies (to my knowledge) demonstrate a significant, positive relationship between composition quality and skill in using grammatical labels—when intelligence is controlled.

The independence of composition and traditional grammar can readily be explained through our present knowledge of transfer of learning. As stated in Chapter I, transfer can only occur when the learner recognizes the similarity between the new situation and the situation in which the original learning occurred. Let's take the following exercise as an example of "the original learning situation."

The red fox jumped lazily over the fence.

In the sentence above, underline the complete predicate. What part of speech is lazily? _____ Which word is a preposition? _____ Explain why "lazy" could not have been used instead of "lazily?" _____

Can a teacher honestly expect a child to recognize the similarity between this type of original learning situation and the situation in which he is to write a composition of high quality?

To see how unwarranted it is to consider the possibility of such transfer, consider the transfer between so-called "formal" and "applied" grammar. Catherwood (5) found that of those pupils who were capable of correcting certain errors in verb forms only eight per cent could provide the grammatical explanations for the corrections. Segel and Barr (24) administered an intelligence test, a formal-grammar test, and an applied-grammar test to about 300 high school students. In the applied-grammar test the students were to choose between two forms, whereas in the formal-grammar test they were to classify words and phrases. Here are the correlations which Segel and Barr found:

| | |
|---|---|
| Formal-grammar with applied-grammar | .56 |
| Formal-grammar with intelligence | .40 |
| Applied-grammar with intelligence | .40 |

It can be seen that intelligence is the major factor contributing to the relationship between applied- and formal-grammar. The relationship would not be very impressive if intelligence were controlled. Asker (1) administered a formal-grammar test and an applied-grammar test to about 300 college freshmen. The correlation between the two measurements was only .23, which is to be expected, since intelligence was more nearly controlled than in Segel and Barr's study.

Another indication that applied and formal grammar are not highly interdependent can be found by examining the average scores of the groups in Segel and Barr's study:

|  | First Semester Sophomore | Second Semester Sophomore | First Semester Junior |
|---|---|---|---|
| Formal | 74.4 | 72.4 | 67.7 |
| Applied | 75.7 | 76.0 | 80.0 |

If applied-grammar were dependent upon knowledge of formal-grammar, formal-grammar scores would not have gone down while applied-grammar scores went up. My point is this: if the relationship between applied and formal grammar is low, how can we expect the relationship between traditional grammar and composition to be high?

On the other hand, several studies have shown that transfer is sometimes possible when teachers make a concerted effort to *help* students make the transfer between school subjects or between a school subject and a particular thought process (15). Unfortunately, even when teachers have tried to assist pupils in making the transfer from traditional grammar to composition, the results have been negative. Frogner (9) studied the results of two methods of teaching composition to 107 pairs of high-school students during a period of one semester. In one method the "thought approach" was used. For example, the following sentence was shown to lack parallel form: "To portage is when you carry provisions from one lake to another." This sentence was compared with a sentence which exemplified parallel form: "To portage is to carry provisions from one lake to another." In the other method the thought approach was combined with the study of traditional grammar. For example, in the previously discussed sentence both the lack of parallel form and the improper use of the adverbial clause was noted. Although, by the end of the semester the students taught only by the thought approach had learned less formal grammar than the other students, the thought approach students did much better on tests of sentence structure. Furthermore, the thought approach students received only 80 per cent as much instructional time on sentence structure as the other students. Benfer (3), in another study, also made a futile effort to have students improve their composition by applying their knowledge of grammar.

In summary, the arguments given for teaching *traditional, prescriptive* grammar—particularly in the elementary grades—do not seem conclusive. Does this mean that any type of grammar study should be omitted from the elementary school curriculum? This question should not be answered affirmatively—at least not yet—since the newer, structural grammar has seldom been tried in elementary classrooms.

## The Case for Structural Grammar

Structural grammar and traditional grammar are based on two different assumptions. The traditional grammarian assumes that grammar is a rational science similar to mathematics—that is, one based on prescribed postulates and logical deductions from those postulates. He may even assume a somewhat mystical rightness of those postulates, and, like other men of magic, guard the postulates as his sacred trust. The structural grammarian, on the other hand, assumes that grammar is an empirical science similar to physics—that is, one based on a large collection of individual observations from which tentative laws are derived. Being human, the structural grammarian may become as protective of his discovered "truths" as the traditional grammarian is of his postulated "truths."

One doesn't have to stand too far back from the fracas to notice that the traditional grammarians and the structural grammarians were bound to come up with two different schemes. The traditional grammarians have been analyzing the English language according to the rules and taxonomy borrowed from the Latin grammarians.*

---

* Newman (18) demonstrates how dissimilar Latin and English are with respect to grammar. Notice the differences in the following sentences:
1. Puella hominem amat. The girl loves the man.
2. Puellam homo amat. The man loves the girl.
The different meanings are signaled in Latin by changes in word form, while in English the different meanings are signaled by changes in word *order*. Fries (8:58) shows how dissimilar even Old English and Modern English are with respect to grammar. Notice the differences in the following sentences:
1. Glaedne giefend lufao God.
2. Cheerful giver loves God.
3. God loves cheerful giver.
Although sentence 2 appears to be the modern English equivalent of sentence 1, sentence 3 is the actual translation. Old English, like Latin, relied primarily on word form rather than word order to signal meaning.

Furthermore, they have been looking primarily at *written* English. The structural grammarians, on the other hand, have been concentrating on the spoken language and the development of a new taxonomy and set of rules which seem to fit present-day English as it is spoken in the United States.

The structural grammarians argue that speech is primary; that writing is a distorted mirror of speech and should not be used as the basis for a grammatical science. According to one modern grammarian, written grammar is also a poor basis for educational practice:

> Traditional grammar has been based, understandably enough, on the literary language, but far too often the prescriptive rules which must be followed to *write* acceptably have been used as a basis for how we should *talk*. The result, I'm afraid has been to inject into our population a sort of mild schizophrenia which has produced many afraid to talk and totally unable to write. (25:173)

An even more fundamental difference between a traditional and structural grammarian is in their analysis of the same utterance, whether it be spoken or written. Look, for instance, at the following sentence:

*The mother bear gave her cub a cuff on its ear.*

The traditional grammarian would first determine the meaning of the entire sentence. Then, he would apply his Latin-based taxonomy to the words and phrases in the sentence, labeling *The mother bear* as the "complete subject," *cuff* as the "direct object," *bear* as a noun, and so on. His justification for labeling *The mother bear* as the subject is that an assertion is being made *about* the maternal beast. In essence the traditional grammarian begins with the total meaning (without analyzing how he arrived at that total meaning) and proceeds to classify the bits and pieces of the meaning—*which is already known*. In contrast to the traditional grammarian's approach, the structuralist examines the various structural signals which *lead* to meaning. The sentence about the mother bear has several structural signals which enable the reader or listener to understand its meaning. The order and form of the words indicate that the mother and not the cub is the cuffer, that only one mother and one cub is involved, that the utterance is a statement rather than a request or question, and that the cuffing took place sometime in the past. All of these notions are derived by paying attention only to structural clues, without regard for the lexical (dictionary) meanings of the words. Without too much additional difficulty the structural linguist could analyze the following sentence, which a traditional grammarian could analyze only after he had first looked for structural clues.

*The pubble lut riked her lup a stoof on its ronk.*

By looking at the structural clues one can say that it is probable that one female lut did some riking in the past to her one lup, and that the riking took the form of a single stoof on one of the lup's ronks (or on its only ronk).

The point of all this is that structural linguists apply grammatical analysis at the point where it is functionally necessary, rather than *ex post facto*. Traditionalists study meaning in order to get at the form. Structuralists study form in order to get at the meaning. From the standpoint of understanding the processes of communication, my money is on the structuralists with odds of eight to one in their favor.

## Types of Structural Grammar

The structuralists, however, have at least three horses in the race. To oversimplify the situation, some people have their money on Phonology; some, on Structure III; and some, on Transformational Syntax. This division in the stalls has come about because structural linguists have developed different types of structural analysis.

Phonology is a type of analysis which truly glorifies the *spoken* word. Phonologists are concerned, for one thing, with the signals which are provided through vocal accents. For example, the following sentence can be interpreted in four different ways depending upon which word is vocally stressed.

He bought a hoúse. (He didn't buy a horse.)
Hé bought a house. (I didn't.)
He boúght a house. (He didn't rent one.)
He bought á house. (He didn't buy two.)

More precise analysis of sentences is possible when four levels of stress are considered. These levels are usually called primary ( ´ ), secondary ( ˇ ), tertiary ( · ), and weak ( ˘ ). Smith (25) provides an illustration of how one's perception of syntax (order) is dependent upon the level of stress for each word:

1. Líght - hoúse - keéper: keeper of the lighthouse.
2. Líght - hoúse - keéper: one who does light housekeeping.
3. Líght - hoúse - keéper: a housekeeper light in weight.

Besides stress analysis the phonologist is interested (among many things) in pitch analysis. English seems to have four distinct pitches ranging from a low tone designated as 1 to a high, excited tone designated as 4. The following set of sentences provide an example of pitch analysis:

$$^2\text{He bought a}^3 \text{ house}^1. \text{ (Factual tone.)}$$
$$^2\text{He bought a}^3 \text{ house}^3? \text{ (Questioning tone.)}$$
$$^2\text{He bought a}^4 \text{ house}^1. \text{ (Shocked tone.)}$$

A second type of analysis which structuralists have developed was facetiously designated by the author as Structure III. Structure III refers to the analysis of the structural signals of word order and word endings. This type of analysis was discussed in the previous section.

A third type of analysis which structuralists have developed is called "transformational syntax" or "generative grammar." Generative grammarians are primarily concerned with the unit which we call the sentence and the rules which people seem to follow in producing sentences. However, generative grammar includes many aspects of the grammar designated as Structure III, such as word-form rules and word-order rules.

Perhaps the major contribution of the generative grammarians is the concept of "kernel sentences." Generative grammarians have discovered that all of the sentences which English-speaking people utter are based on kernel sentences (6, 21). For example, from the kernel sentence,

*The dog bit the boy,*

several other sentences can be generated. These generated sentences are called "transformations." For example,

The boy was bitten by the dog.
Did the dog bite the boy?
The boy wasn't bitten by the dog.

Even more phenomenal is the discovery that kernel sentences fall into a limited number of basic patterns—perhaps as few as ten. In other words, it is probable that nearly all of the English language is based on only ten types of kernel sentences! Roberts (21) describes these ten types of kernel sentences as follows:

| | | | | | | | |
|---|---|---|---|---|---|---|---|
| 1. | (D) N V | (Adv) | | | | | The bird sang sweetly. |
| 2. | (D) N V | Adj | | | | | Her breath smelled sweet. |
| 3. | (D) N V-b | (D) | N | | | | The boy became a man. |
| 4. | (D) N V-t | (D) | N | | | | The man shot the wolf. |
| 5. | (D) N V-g | (D) | N | (D) | N | | The man gave his son a car. |
| 6. | (D) N V-c | (D) | N | (D) | N | | My uncle considered me a fool. |
| 7. | (D) N V-e | (D) | N | (D) | N | | They elected my brother their president. |
| 8. | (D) N be | Adv | | | | | The boy was here. |
| 9. | (D) N be | Adj | | | | | The lions were hungry. |
| 10. | (D) N be | (D) | N | | | | My uncle is my friend. |

D stands for determiner—words like *the* and *his*. N stands for noun or pronoun; V, verb; Adv, adverb; Adj, adjective; V-b, verbs like become and remain; V-t, verbs associated with a direct object; V-g, verbs associated with an indirect object; V-c, verbs associated with an object complement; V-e, verbs like elect, choose, vote; be, any form of be. The parentheses indicate that the word-form does not have to occur to make the pattern complete.

Nearly all English sentences, says Roberts, can be generated from these ten basic patterns. For example, *The mean man hit the boy* is a transformation based on patterns two and four: *The man seemed mean* and *The man hit the boy*.

## The Case for Instruction in Structural Grammar

If structural grammar is to be included in the elementary school, it should first stand the test of two questions:

(1) Is instruction in structural grammar consistent with the general objectives of the elementary school in our society?

(2) Is it easier for children to learn structural grammar than it is for them to learn traditional grammar?

Certainly one of the objectives of the elementary school is to improve children's abilities to speak and write. So far, there is scant evidence as to whether or not instruction in structural grammar can lead to improved speaking and writing. The major reason for the scarcity of evidence is that most teachers—particularly elementary school teachers—have not been exposed to structural grammar and have yet to try it out with children. The small amount of available evidence takes two forms: results of testing structural grammar in the classroom and results of arm-chair speculation.

Suggs (26) taught a 13-week unit on structural linguistics to one group of eleventh graders and a 13-week unit on traditional grammar to another group of eleventh graders, matched for mental age and past grades in English. A comparison between the two groups on the STEP writing test showed that the group which had studied structural grammar made greater gains in composition than the group which had studied traditional grammar. Bateman (2) found that a study of language structure seemed to help a group of eighth graders express more complex relationships in their writing. However, drawing generalizations from these two studies would be foolhardy, since the samples were so small and the Hawthorne* effect so likely.

What are some of the armchair speculations as to the possible effects of instruction in structural grammar on children's communication skills? Hatfield (11) feels that the study of voice signals and written signal words will aid punctuation, oral and appreciative reading, and listening. It is also conceivable, from the vantage point of my own armchair, that the study of kernel sentences and the various ways in which they can be transformed will increase the fluency and flexibility of children's oral and written expressions. This supposition is made with some confidence, since the relationship between such study—kernel sentences and their transformations—and composition seems to meet the requirement for transfer of learning: the probability that the learner will recognize the similarity between the new situation (oral or written composition) and the situation in which the original learning (kernel sentences and their transformations) occurred. (Ways in which the teacher might enhance the probability of such transfer occurring will be discussed in the next section.) It is even possible that reading comprehension might improve with the study of structural grammar, assuming that reading comprehension depends not only on vocabulary but also on a pupil's familiarity with structural signals and patterns.

---

* Achievement tends to increase with nearly any novel method, if the subjects feel more important as a result of their guinea-pig status.

Obviously the case for structural grammar in the elementary school is a hypothetical one, with respect to improvement in communication skills. Years of experimentation are necessary to test the armchair speculations.

On the other hand, structural grammar in the elementary school is much easier to justify if one perceives education as something more than practical training. Roberts (22:333) argues that whether or not instruction in grammar makes one a better writer is irrelevant; we don't attempt to justify instruction in chemistry on the grounds that it will make us better cooks. Furthermore, he states, instruction in structural grammar ". . . can surely assist people who are learning to write by the normal process—that is, by reading and writing—but it has no clever way of making writers out of nonreaders."

Some of us have the notion (perhaps a mistaken one) that educators should be concerned with the affective domain of learning as well as the cognitive domain, that appreciation is as important as knowledge, and that humanistic studies are as necessary for the preservation of mankind as technical studies. This leads us to argue that grammar is a proper study for human beings, since language is probably the chief determiner of our humanness and grammar is a major component of language.

> We want the study of grammar to be a humanistic one, which reminds students at every phase of their work that language is a human institution similar in many ways to other human institutions (20:57).

But, is grammar a proper study for *young* human beings? Evidently not, if traditional grammar is the medium of study; possibly so, if structural grammar is the medium. Structural grammar seems to conform to the manner in which children learn to communicate. Children do not learn to communicate by labeling their parents' speech, according to the eight parts of speech and other traditional classifications. However, it is likely that they learn to recognize and use word signals and word sequence. It is also likely that they learn the few basic patterns of kernel sentences and how to transform the kernel sentences.

> The child somehow learns the basic structure and the transformation rule. This is simpler than learning the two structures separately, as if they were unrelated. It also makes him capable of producing new sentences, correct sentences, which he has never specifically learned (21:60).

Therefore, if grammar has a place in the elementary curriculum on humanistic grounds, structural grammar is more appropriate than traditional grammar.

Is structural grammar easier than traditional grammar for children to study? The answer to this question depends upon the assumption that instruction in structural grammar has the same purpose as instruction in traditional grammar—to learn how to label segments of speech. It will be shown in the next section that instruction in structural grammar has more important purposes. But, if instruction in structural grammar were to include labeling-type exercises, the structural approach would appear to be potentially easier than the traditional approach. Schuster (23) taught structural grammar to a group of twelfth grade students and traditional grammar to a control group. At the end of the instructional period he found that the attitude of the structurally taught group was much more positive toward learning grammar than the attitude of the traditionally taught group. The experimental group felt that structural grammar was easier, more interesting and more logical than traditional grammar. This group also did much better than the control group in learning the parts of speech. An attitude test showed that both groups liked the teacher equally well, but, of course, there was no control of the well-known Hawthorne effect. Because of the nature of the sample studied, the results of Schuster's experiment should not be generalized to elementary school populations.

Yet, there are reasons to expect that elementary students would also find structural classification easier, more interesting, and more logical than traditional classification. Let's take, as just one example, the classification of nouns and adjectives. According to traditional grammarians, a noun is defined as the name of a person, place, or thing (and sometimes quality); an adjective is defined as a word which modifies a noun. These semantic definitions lead to all kinds of confusion for children, since they cannot be consistently applied. In the following sentence, is *farm* an adjective or noun?

*The farm hand went to town.*

A traditional grammarian would say that *farm* is an adjective because it modifies the noun, *hand*. A child is likely to say that *farm* is a noun since it is the name of a place. The structural grammarian would agree that *farm* is a noun (or a Class I word) but for structural reasons rather than semantic reasons. Structural grammarians who follow Roberts (21) and Chomsky (6) define an adjective (or a Class III word) as a word which can occur in this pattern: (D) N V Adj, or as any word that can structurally fit in this frame: The man seems _____. According to this structural definition, then, *farm* can not be considered an adjective. The word *farm* would be considered a noun (or Class I word) since it is inflected like *boy:* boy, boy's, boys, boys'; farm, farm's, farms, farms' and since it fits in the frame: (The) _____ is good. (Actually, some structural grammarians avoid the terms: noun, verb, adjective, and adverb, and substitute: Class I, Class II, Class III, and Class IV.) The advantages of the structural approach to classification are its precision and consistency. Surely, these advantages would make structural classification easier to learn than traditional, semantic classification.

## Techniques of Instruction in Structural Grammar

| Teaching Traditional Grammar | Teaching Structural Grammar |
|---|---|
| *Teacher:* What is a noun? | *Teacher:* What is a Class I word? |
| *Student:* A noun is a word which names a person, place or thing. | *Student:* A Class I word is a word which patterns like *boy* or *woman.* |
| *Teacher:* Very good. What is an adjective? | *Teacher:* Very good. What is a Class III word? |

This facetious comparison should demonstrate the distinct possibility that structural grammar will be misused in some classrooms as readily as traditional grammar has been misused. Classification has a place in any science or humanistic study. Just as children discover ways of classifying rocks in science and numerical relationships in arithmetic, so might they also discover ways of classifying words according to their structural forms and relationships. Yet, structural grammar has much more to offer than mere rules for classification. It is probable that structural grammar, if taught in particular ways, can provide students with tools for appreciating, creating, and communicating.

> We are sometimes told that grammar is dull but useful, a disagreeable medicine we take to cure our writing ills. It is better to look at it differently: properly approached, grammar is an

absorbingly interesting study, and it may even do us some practical good (21:4).

Although this statement probably expresses the possibilities of instruction in structural grammar too modestly, it does provide a useful
motto for the study of this new discipline. How might children be
taught to use this discipline in such a way that they learn not only to
appreciate the English language but possibly to use it more effectively?

## Learning About Sentence Patterns: Sample Exercises

Piaget's study of children and their thought process has led him
to conclude that "The line of development of language . . . is from
the *whole to the part*" (19:133). In keeping with this developmental
learning, the study of structural grammar should probably begin
with a study of our basic communication unit, which we call the
"sentence." Several suggestions for classroom activities follow—
activities which seem to the author to conform to a sequence of
simple to complex. No attempt has been made to define these activities according to grade level. Instead they are offered as experimental exercises for any grade level, with Bruner's hypothesis
(modified by the author) in mind: ". . . [most] any subject can be
taught effectively in some intellectually honest form to [most] any
child at [most] any stage of development." (4:33) Furthermore, the
purpose of these activities is to have fun with the English language,
to appreciate the diverse ways in which English can be expressed,
and to expand children's repertoire of sentence patterns just as we
attempt to expand children's vocabulary. Use of these exercises to
make children ashamed of their own sentence repertoire, to mold
children's sentence patterns according to a teacher's own tastes, or
to keep children busy would violate the spirit in which they are
offered. Above all, the ultimate goal in using these activities is to
develop *not* the ability to classify but the ability to appreciate, create,
and communicate.

Exercises 1-7 demonstrate how one basic sentence pattern and
several transformations might be introduced.

1.  Make up as many sentences as you can which seem like these:
    a. That dog runs fast.

b. Their mother called loudly.
c. My aunts knit beautifully.
d. The cat purred happily.
e. The monkey climbed quickly.
f. The glub felped zepply.

This type of exercise might be done orally, with the teacher or children recording sentences on the board. If a child mentions a sentence which does not fit the pattern, the teacher might simply urge him to try again. *It is doubtful that the pattern should be verbally formalized at this point.* A study by Hendrix has revealed several important ideas about the learning of generalizations:

1. For generation of transfer power, the unverbalized method of learning a generalization is better than a method in which authoritative statement of the generalization comes first.
2. Verbalizing a generalization immediately after discovery does not increase transfer power.
3. Verbalizing a generalization immediately after discovery may actually decrease transfer power. (12:198)

2. Discover whether or not some of the sentences developed in Exercise 1 make sense when the last word in each sentence is left out. Then, make up more sentences which are like these:
a. That dog runs.
b. Their mother called.
c. My aunts knit.
d. The cat purred.
e. This monkey climbed.
f. The glub felped.

3. Discover whether or not some of the sentences developed in Exercise 1 make sense when both the first word and the last word in each sentence are left out. Make up more sentences which are like these:

a. Dogs run.
b. Mothers called.
c. Aunts knit.
d. Cats purred.
e. Monkeys climbed.
f. Glubs felped.
g. He runs.
h. They asked.
i. She saw.
j. It flies.
k. Some grow.
l. They felped.

4. Compare the sentences in set A with the sentences in set B. How are the sets alike and different?

A

That dog runs fast.
Their mothers called loudly.
My aunts knit beautifully.
The cat purred happily.
This monkey climbed quickly.
The glub felped zapply.

B

That dog doesn't run fast.
Their mothers didn't call loudly.
My aunts do not knit beautifully.
The cat did not purr happily.
This monkey did not climb quickly.
The glub didn't felp zapply.

(Have the children observe or listen to the two sets without generalizing verbally.)

Change these sentences in the same way. (Contractions are acceptable.)

    a. My uncle jumped quickly.
    b. Snakes hop slowly.
    c. His sister screams.
    d. The lions roared.
    e. Rabbits bark.
    f. He drank eagerly.
    g. She zups.

5. Compare the sentences in set A (see Exercise 4) with the sentences in set B. How are the sets alike and different?

B

Does that dog run fast?
Did their mothers call loudly?
Do my aunts knit beautifully?
Did the cat purr happily?
Did this monkey climb quickly?
Did the glub felp zapply?

(Have the children observe or listen to the two sets without generalizing verbally.)

Change these sentences in the same way.

    a. Sam ate noisily.
    b. Parrots sing.

    c. His brother swims well.

    d. The squirrels chattered.

    e. Mice fly.

    f. Some sleep easily.

    g. Those fongs nuckered mickly.

6. Compare the sentences in set A (see Exercise 4) with the sentences in set B. How are the sets alike and different?

B

When did that dog run fast?

When did their mothers call loudly?

Why do my aunts knit beautifully?

Why did the cat purr happily?

Where did this monkey climb quickly?

Where did the glub felp zapply?

Change these sentences in the same way.

    a. The birds sang sweetly.

    b. Dogs bark.

    c. Their mother works.

    d. This donkey brayed.

    e. Her grandfather went.

    f. She asked quietly.

    g. He pels flacely.

7. Compare the sentences in set A (see Exercise 4) with the sentences in set B. How are the sets alike and different?

B

Why doesn't that dog run fast?

Why didn't their mothers call loudly?

Why don't my aunts knit beautifully?

When doesn't the cat purr happily?

Where didn't this monkey climb quickly?

Where didn't the glub feld zepply?

Change these sentences in the same way.

    a. The orchestra plays.

    b. Pigs eat greedily.

    c. This ink smears easily.

    d. The elephant drinks.

    e. He drives carefully.

    f. Sharon spoke.

    g. Sadires muff.

Exercises 8-10 demonstrate how another basic sentence pattern might be introduced and then combined with the first pattern to produce transformations.

8. Make up as many sentences as you can which seem like these:
   a. The children seem small.
   b. His car looked dirty.
   c. My wood feels smooth.
   d. This egg smells rotten.
   e. That music sounded terrible.
   f. The moon looks yellow.
   g. The flotter seems taggle.

9. Discover whether or not some of the sentences developed in Exercise 8 make sense when the first word in each sentence is left out. Make up more sentences which are like these:
   a. Children seem small.
   b. Cars looked dirty.
   c. Wood feels smooth.
   d. Eggs smell rotten.
   e. Flasses seem fandle.
   f. It looks green.
   g. She felt clean.
   h. Some appeared broken.
   i. They smell musty.
   j. It looked spoun.

10. Compare the sentences in sets A, B, and C.

| A | B | C |
|---|---|---|
| a. That dog runs fast. | That dog seems old. | That old dog runs fast. |
| b. Their mothers called loudly. | Their mothers appeared angry. | Their angry mothers called loudly. |
| c. My aunts knit beautifully. | My aunts seem friendly. | My friendly aunts knit beautifully. |
| d. The cat purrs happily. | The cat looks clean. | The clean cat purrs happily. |
| e. This monkey climbed quickly. | This monkey sounded noisy. | This noisy monkey climbed quickly. |
| f. The glub felded zepply. | The glub seems rizzle. | The rizzle glub felded zepply. |

Make up new sentences for each pair of sentences in columns A and B.

| A | B |
|---|---|
| a. The boy struck hard. | The boy seemed angry. |
| b. His mother called frantically. | His mother looked worried. |
| c. The choir sang. | The choir seemed large. |

    d. The leaves fall noiselessly.    The leaves feel soft.
    e. Their fap winted fibbly.    Their fap looked swousey.

Exercises 11-12 demonstrate how a third basic sentence pattern might be introduced and then combined with the first and second patterns to produce transformations.

   11. Make up as many sentences as you can which seem like these:
      a. The man was here.
      b. The dog is outside.
      c. The children are there.
      d. His mother was nearby.
      e. His marbles were in his pocket.
      f. These boys were on the roof.
      g. They were out.
      h. He was up.
      i. She is inside.
      j. The sedbogs are here.
      k. The feckle is on the stonk.

   12. Compare the fourth sentence with the first three sentences.
      The boy swims fast.
      The boy seems young.
      The boy is in the river.
      The young boy in the river swims fast.

Make up a new sentence from each of the following sets of sentences:
      a. The man ate greedily
         The man seemed old.
         The man was outside.
      b. The woman waited patiently
         The woman seemed tired.
         The woman was in the railroad station.
      c. The birds fly high.
         The birds look large.
         The birds are from the North.
      d. The fixel stodges gaggily.
         The fixel seems foddey.
         The fixel is on the bodge.

In Exercises 13-15 a fourth basic pattern is introduced along with several types of transformations.

13. Make up as many sentences as you can which seem like these.
    a. The hunter shot the bear.
    b. His sister rings the bell.
    c. Their children threw the stones.
    d. Judy erases the board.
    e. Bobby dug potatoes.
    f. She washes dishes.
    g. They buried the garbage.
    h. It ruggled the span.
    i. The flinters fisp the bongs.

14. Compare the sentences in set A with the sentences in set B.

| A | B |
|---|---|
| Jerry held the cat. | The cat was held by Jerry. |
| The rats ate the cheese. | The cheese was eaten by the rats. |
| He threw the pebbles. | The pebbles were thrown by him. |
| The janitors sweep the floors. | The floors are swept by the janitors. |
| The perks smix the veds. | The veds are smixed by the perks. |

Change these sentences in the same way.
    a. Sam climbed that mountain.
    b. A dog bit my brother.
    c. Those boats cross the ocean.
    d. She drove the car.
    e. That airplane carries passengers.
    f. The chire biffs the yarders.
    g. He worped a smiglin.

15. Compare the sentences in set A with the sentences in set B.

A
Bill throws the ball.
She ate a cookie.
The girl drew that picture.
The hunds flate the bings.

B
The ball is not thrown by Bill.
A cookie was not eaten by her.
That picture wasn't drawn by the girl.

The bings are not flated by the hunds.

Change these sentences in the same way.

   a. They flew the airplane.

   b. A man dropped this money.

   c. The boys scrape the dishes.

   d. The cat licks the platter.

   e. That trod scammed these scours.

16. Compare the fourth sentence with the first three sentences.

   The hunter shot the wolf.

   The hunter seemed angry.

   The wolf was in the forest.

   The wolf in the forest was shot by the angry hunter.

Make up a new sentence from each of the following sets of sentences:

   a. That man painted my house.

     That man looked tall.

     My house is in the country.

   b. Lightning struck that tree.

     That tree is near my house.

     That tree seems beautiful.

   c. The klaus antered the mult.

     The klaus is in the ribbox.

     The mult appears quadden.

Exercises 1-16 have demonstrated how four of Robert's ten basic sentence patterns (21) and several transformations might be introduced. The other six patterns might be introduced in a similar manner. Exercises 17-18 show some of the ways in which the predicates of the basic patterns can be expanded.

17. Compare the sentences in set A with the sentences in set B.

               A

The boy drank eagerly.

Sally looks tired.

They became teachers.

He lost the ball.

The farmer gave his son a horse.

A silvert gave the plad a flinx.

We considered Paul a hero.

The club elected me president.

The boss was away.

He is a farmer.
The flaster is a puddler.

### B

The boy will drink eagerly.
Sally might look tired.
They may become teachers.
He could lose the ball.
The farmer should give his son a horse.
A silvert could give the plad a finx.
We shall consider Paul a hero.
The boss must be away.
They might be dirty.
He will be a farmer.
The flaster might be a puddler.

Change these sentences in the same way.

    a. The donkey brayed.
    b. He appeared worried.
    c. The doctor bandaged her arm.
    d. The package is here.
    e. Cake is a dessert.
    f. The daggs seemed smaddled.
    g. A spigton fidges the tants.

18. Compare the sentences in set A (see Exercise 17) with the sentences in set B.

### B

The boy was drinking eagerly.
Sally is looking tired.
They were becoming teachers.
He was losing the ball.
The farmer was giving his son a horse.
A silvert was giving the plad a flinx.
We were considering Paul a hero.
The club was electing me president.
The boss was being away.
They are being dirty.
He is being a farmer.
The flaster is being a puddler.

Change these sentences in the same way.

    a. A lion roared.

   b. The rose smells lovely.
   c. A truck reached the bridge.
   d. Janice is friendly.
   e. They are neighbors.
   f. His pendol brackles.
Of course, there are many other means of expanding predicates. Here are only a few of the possible expansions for the predicate in *He lost the ball:*
   He tried to lose the ball.
   He avoided losing the ball.
   He has lost the ball.
   He may have lost the ball.
   He had lost the ball.
   He might have been losing the ball.
   He has probably lost my favorite ball in the prickly bushes near
      our unfriendly neighbor's house.
   The possible ways of creating, transforming, and expanding kernel sentences are infinite. The teacher's role, it would seem, is a dual one of making a child conscious of patterns which already exist in his own sentence reservoir and of increasing his capacity to deal with unfamiliar patterns.

*     *     *     *     *

In this chapter it has been suggested that the focus of grammar study in the elementary school should be on the creation of sentence patterns rather than the classification of word forms. The study of word forms can be of considerable interest to some children, especially verbally gifted children in the upper grades. The study of sentence patterns, however, seems easier to justify as an important aspect of the elementary school curriculum. Such a study would probably promote not only an appreciation of the English language but also a greater facility with the language—at least a greater fluency and flexibility of sentence constructions. Whether or not this increased facility is applied only to exercises similar to those described in this chapter or to substantive composition as well is probably in large measure up to the teacher. Research shows that we can be confident of transfer occurring only when teachers show their pupils the relationships which are supposed to exist between primary instruction and secondary application.

# REFERENCES

1. Asker, William, "Does Knowledge of Formal Grammar Function?" *School and Society* 17:109-111, January, 1923.
2. Bateman, Donald R., "More Mature Writing Through a Better Understanding of Language Structure," *English Journal* 50:457-460, October, 1961.
3. Benfer, Mabel C., *Sentence Sense in Relation to Subject and Predicate.* Unpublished Master's Thesis, State University of Iowa, Iowa City, 1935.
4. Bruner, Jerome S., *The Process of Education.* Cambridge: Harvard University Press, 1960.
5. Catherwood, Catherine, *A Study of the Relationship Between Knowledge of Rules and Ability to Correct Grammatical Errors and Between Identification of Sentences and Knowledge of Subject and Predicate.* Unpublished Master's Thesis, University of Minnesota, Minneapolis, 1932.
6. Chomsky, Noam, *Syntactic Structures.* 's Gravenhage: Mouton, 1957.
7. De Boer, John J., "Grammar in Language Teaching," *Elementary English* 36:413-421, October, 1959.
8. Fries, Charles C., *The Structure of English.* New York: Harcourt, Brace & World, Inc., 1952.
9. Frogner, Ellen, "Grammar Approach Versus Thought Approach in Teaching Sentence Structure," *English Journal* 28:518-526, September, 1939.
10. Groff, Patrick J., "Is Knowledge of Parts of Speech Necessary?" *English Journal* 50:413-415, September, 1961.
11. Hatfield, W. Wilber, "Will Structural Grammar Help?" *English Journal* 47:570-572, December, 1958.
12. Hendrix, Gertrude, "A New Clue to Transfer of Training," *Elementary School Journal* 48:197-208, December, 1947.
13. Hoyt, Franklin S., "The Place of Grammar in the Elementary Curriculum," *Teachers College Record* 7:467-500, 1906.
14. Jenkins, Gordon, and his Orchestra, "Seven Dreams," Decca Record Co.
15. Kolesnik, Walter B., *Mental Discipline in Modern Education,* 1958.
16. Lefevre, Carl A., "Social-class Influences on Learning: Linguistic Implications," *Elementary English* 38:553-555, December, 1961.
17. Macauley, W. J., "The Difficulty of Grammar," *British Journal of Educational Psychology* 17:153-162, November, 1947.
18. Newman, Harold, "Case Against Grammar," *High Points* 37:39-50, March, 1955.

19. Piaget, Jean, *The Language and Thought of the Child*. New York: Harcourt, Brace & World, Inc., 1926.
20. Postman, Neil, Harold Morine, and Greta Morine, *Discovering Your Language*, Teacher Edition. New York: Holt, Rinehart & Winston, Inc., 1963.
21. Roberts, Paul, *English Sentences*. New York: Harcourt, Brace & World, Inc., 1962.
22. Roberts, Paul, "Linguistics and the Teaching of Composition," *English Journal* 52:331-335, May, 1963.
23. Schuster, Edgar H., "How Good is the New Grammar?" *English Journal* 50:392-397, September, 1961.
24. Segel, David and Nora R. Barr, "Relation of Achievement in Applied Grammar," *Journal of Educational Research* 12:401-402, December, 1926.
25. Smith, Henry Lee, Jr., "The Teacher and the World of Language," *College English* 20:171-178, January, 1959.
26. Suggs, Lena Reddick, "Structural Grammar Versus Traditional Grammar in Influencing Writing," *English Journal* 50:174-178, March, 1961.
27. Symonds, Percival M., "What Education Has to Learn from Psychology—Transfer and Formal Discipline," *Teachers College Record* 61:30-45, 1959.
28. Templin, Mildred C., *Certain Language Skills in Children: Their Development and Interrelationships*. Minneapolis: University of Minnesota Press, 1957.
29. Tovatt, Anthony L., "Parts of Speech Beyond the Classroom," *School Review* 59:481-484, November, 1951.

# Part III

# The Impact of Language on Behavior

# 4

# *DISTORTED PERCEPTIONS*
## (General Semantics vs. General Confusion)

> My cat is a fortunate animal. He is continuously curious about
> his environment, which to me seems rather dull. Each object
> which comes before his Scotland Yardish nose is evidently con-
> sidered to be different from all other objects he has sniffed. Not
> so with "mature" human beings: a cursory sensing usually
> results in a single word, which ends all further exploration.

If all beings were suddenly to perish, thus leaving no creature in
the Universe to perceive our planet, what would the Earth look like?
Would the forests and lakes exist as we now perceive them? As
much as it may hurt our egos to admit it, the Earth would no longer
consist of lakes, buildings, plants and other forms which we now
recognize. Some say it would consist of nothing more than rapidly
moving molecules and atoms. But even the concepts of "atoms,"
"molecules," and "rapidly moving" are inventions of the human
mind; thus, it is impossible to imagine how the Earth would appear
without beings to perceive it.

The "Earth" is an interaction of external stimuli and internal perception. We may strive to grasp the "real" essence of these external
stimuli, but, alas, we can see no further than our perceptual tele-
scopes permit us to see. However, we can improve our telescopic
lenses, through an understanding of perception and the various
factors, including language, which influence perception.

Social scientists have verified through controlled experiments

73

some of the various and often devious ways in which we humans force the world to come to us. These experiments confirm what many of us have suspected, that seeing is, indeed, believing, that what we see is what we desire to see. To see otherwise is to invite "anxiety," and to avoid this unpleasant state we develop perceptual defense mechanisms or adopt those of influential adults. Obviously, such habits of perceiving introduce a certain degree of distortion into our pictures of the world (unless one knows the wave length of Absolute Reality.)

The mechanisms of perceptual distortion vary with individuals, but some mechanisms seem to be common to nearly all human beings. According to Kirk (11) the method of *tenacity* is the chief mechanism by which we distort our pictures of reality—a mechanism as primitive as that of the moth who insists on committing suicide by continually flying against a bright street lamp. The method of tenacity is simply that of holding on stubbornly to the status quo in beliefs. This method is exemplified by the man in the following limerick:

> There once was a man who was sure
> That smoking was truly impure.
> Indian captive he awoke,
> But he passed up a smoke.
> And then there was one man fewer.

The method of tenacity and, for that matter, any other method of perceptual distortion is developed in order to satisfy a basic need of the human organism—stability. The need for stability has been demonstrated by the experiments of Ames and his followers (2). Perhaps the most famous of these experiments is the "cockeyed room." Let us suppose that two people of the *same* height enter this room and you and I are asked to observe them through a window. The two people will almost inevitably be perceived by us as a "dwarf" and a "giant." Why do we insist on such distortions? Probably because in order to see the two people as they are—of equal height—we would have to see the room in its actual shape—"cockeyed." Naturally, we're not used to seeing rooms of such irregular shape; the rectangular prism is the most common shape for rooms. Thus, we perceive the room as a rectangular prism, which forces the people inside our "rectangular prism" to take the forms of "giant" and "dwarf," even if we're informed differently. ("Don't tell *me* they're the same size; I saw them with my own eyes!")

Another common mechanism of perceptual distortion has been labeled by Festinger (4) as "reducing cognitive dissonance." Cognitive dissonance is a type of anxiety which occurs in many situations, but it is particularly strong after a decision has been made. ("Did I make the right decision. Suffering catfish, maybe I should have taken the other one!") Cognitive dissonance, being a form of instability, is insufferable to most of us, and, consequently, we search for ways of regaining stability. One way is simply to avoid any new information which might conflict with the decision we've made. Festinger has found, for example, that most people, after purchasing a particular brand of car, avoid information which might be complimentary to other brands or derogatory to the chosen brand. While reading our newspapers or watching television, we're quick to notice the wonderful things that are said about "our car" but our eyes grow dim when a rival brand is hawked. Another way of reducing dissonance is to decrease the importance of the original decision: ("O.K., so I could have got a better buy at Reliable Motors. A car is a car. As long as we have decent transportation, what difference does it make.") Of course, an even simpler way of reducing dissonance, according to Festinger, is to *misperceive* new information: "Boy, am I glad I got a Hupmobile. I was just reading in *Consumer Facts* that the new LaSalles are uneconomical."* (Actually, *Consumer Facts* had reported that the LaSalle model this year was uneconomical compared to last year's model. It also reported that the new Hupmobiles and LaSalles were equally uneconomical.)

Another cause of perceptual distortion is that of temporary mood. All of us have experienced days when everything *seems* to go wrong. On another day when our mood is brighter, everything *seems* to be going our way. Leuba and Lucas (15) demonstrated the effects of temporary mood on perception through a hypnosis experiment. The subjects of the experiment were individually hypnotized and directed to be in a happy mood. Under this condition they perceived ambiguous pictures as "fun," "wonderful," etc. When the subjects were directed to be in a critical mood, they used such terms as

* Unless a page number is given, all illustrative dialogue is the author's own.

"horrible" and "nothing good about it" to describe the same pictures. When the subjects were directed to be in an anxious mood, their comments about the same pictures included "something may happen" and "I wonder if it's safe."

An experiment by Murray (19) also illustrates the effect of temporary mood on perceptions. A group of children were individually shown a set of photographs and asked to describe the personalities of the people depicted. Then the children played an exciting game of "Murder." After the game they were shown a similar set of photographs and again asked to describe the personalities of the people depicted. This time the children attributed many more malicious characteristics to the people in the photographs.

Frequently people distort the information they are receiving by the process of "supplementing" (20:90). Rather than omit, ignore, or misperceive information, details are added unconsciously in order to maintain the stability of one's beliefs. Horowitz and Horowitz (7) demonstrated this phenomenon by showing several southern white children a picture of an attractive southern home. Many of the children reported immediately after viewing the picture that they saw a Negro in the picture performing a menial task. Actually, no people were shown in the picture!

The process of supplementing is essential in the development of "stereotypes," a term which Lippman (16) invented in 1922 and one which has become a household word. It is true, perhaps, that the use of stereotypes often makes our behavior more efficient. But because of the process of stereotyping we are constantly making errors which are due to perceptual distortion. That is, we are continually seeing too much, or too little, or both.

Supplementing and other mechanisms of perceptual distortion are often stimulated by our normal need to be considered a bona fide member of particular groups. If we wish to be "one of the gang" we have to learn to perceive as other "gang" members do, i.e., to develop "group-sight." Group-sight seems to be normal behavior for some people even if they are merely casual, temporary members of a group. Sherif demonstrated this phenomenon in two different laboratory situations. In one situation (25) a group of subjects were asked to compare the length of a standard line with the length of several other lines in succession. All but one person in the group had been instructed to make errors of judgment and to agree on those

errors. The single naive subject soon began to perceive the lines as
the rest of the group did. This procedure was replicated with several
naive subjects; most of them showed the same tendency to throw
aside their own judgments and see the lines as they *thought* the
others saw them.

In another experiment by Sherif (25) subjects were placed individually in an absolutely dark room and asked to judge how far a
pinpoint of light had moved each time it was exposed. Each subject
developed an individual norm; a norm for one individual might be
three to five inches; for another individual, ten to twelve inches.
(Actually, the light was quite stationary.) After individual norms
had been developed the subjects were grouped and asked to make
their judgments aloud as they observed the light again. No matter
how divergent the individual norms were, a group norm gradually
evolved; the individual norms were thrown aside and "reality" became a group invention.

A humorous story by Rogers (23) illustrates most of the mechanisms of perceptual distortion which we have been considering:
Sometime before the evolution of modern man, a tribe of "Gonks"
roamed a certain portion of the Earth. The particular Gonks who
had survived the harsh environment of Pre-Paleolithic days were
those whose reaction time was approximately zero. Such reflexes
were necessary in order to escape from the Gonk-eating tigers. The
slightest rustling of bushes caused the Gonks to scamper to the top
of the nearest tall tree. Things were going reasonably well for the
Gonks, even though they had to spend much of their time climbing
up and down trees. But, much to their dismay, a severe climactic
change destroyed their chief staple, namely, bananas. Actually, the
cold weather also drove off the tigers, but the Gonks were unaware
of this exodus. Just before starvation set in, rabbits appeared on the
scene, and the Gonks soon learned to capture and eat them. *But* (the
best laid plans of mice and men and Gonks) the rabbits began to
hide in the bushes and make *rustling noises*. With the first quiver
of a leaf, the Gonks were off to the trees, their meal safely out of
reach. Of course, starvation became a serious threat again. This
time the Gonks were saved by a fluke. For some reason a few of the
Gonks began to have a mental picture of "Rabbit" rather than
"Tiger" whenever they heard rustling noises in bushes. These Gonks
became the hunters for the tribe; *now* when the bushes rustled most

of the Gonks would still nervously dash up the nearest tree, but at least they could watch an exciting chase from their tree-top seats. The rabbit chasers gradually began to suspect the exodus of the tigers, but they kept it a trade secret, thus maintaining their high status among Gonks. Finally, the secret leaked out, but the tiger avoiders refused to alter their perceptions. Instead, they fortified their mental pictures by inventing new symbols for tigers; in addition to rustling leaves, the roaring thunder became a signal for taking to the trees. (Modern-day "Gonks"—everyone but you and me— have created so many "tiger" symbols, they spend most of their waking hours dashing for the "trees.")

## Language and Perceptual Distortion

While we are still in the position of outside observers, let us look through the one-way mirror at another interesting tribe called "homo-sapiens" or, as they call themselves, "modern man." The most distinguishing characteristic of modern man is his language. And one of the most interesting aspects of language is its effects on man's perceptions of his world. Most men appear to make the unconscious assumption that their language conforms to their thoughts. Yet, in most instances the exact opposite occurs: Men think in certain ways because their vocabulary and language structure force them to think in those ways. "Language is not a cloak following the contours of thought. Languages are molds into which infant minds are poured (1)." From infancy, a human being is taught to perceive his world according to the noises (words) and sequence of noises (grammatical patterns) which older humans are using. Either he learns to perceive in their way or face the prospect of isolation. A normal child chooses the former alternative. As Chase (2) reminds us, "No human is free to describe nature with strict objectivity; for he is a prisoner of his language."

Of course the original "inventors" of a language had a bit more freedom than the present users of a language. It was more possible for their utterances to conform to their thoughts, *but* these utterances would necessarily have a short life unless others would agree to use them in a similar way. Once usage was established the next generation had little choice. This is not to say that human language is not changed by succeeding generations. Indeed it is; but the changes are often superficial, and the more basic, structural changes evolve very slowly. Thus, Sapir (24:210) reminded his fellow humans that "we see and hear and otherwise experience very largely as we do because the language habits of our community predispose certain choices of interpretation." And Whorf (28:311), a student of Sapir, spelled it out in more detail:

> We dissect nature along lines laid down by our native languages. The categories and types that we isolate from the world of phenomena we do not find there because they stare us in the face; on the contrary, the world is presented in a kaleidoscopic flux of impressions which has to be organized by our minds— and this means by the linguistic systems in our minds. We cut nature up, organize it into concepts and ascribe significance as we do, largely because we are parties to an agreement to organize it in this way—an agreement that holds throughout our speech community and is codified in the patterns of language . . . We cannot talk at all except by subscribing to the organization and classification of data which the agreement decrees.

On the other hand, a man *acts* as if his language describes the external world. He might say, for instance, "that cheese is tangy," thinking that he is describing the cheese. It will be shown, however, that he is describing nothing more (and nothing less) than one of his linguistic habits. Generally, this type of self-delusion is harmless; yet its harmful effects, which will be discussed later, can be severe.

## Words and Distortion

Let us now look at a few ways in which *words* influence man's perceptions. An amusing example is the case of the "Coon Cats" (a type of Persian Cat). According to Whorf (28) these cats were brought over to the United States by Captain Coon; thus the name, "Coon Cats." However, many people who are introduced to Coon Cats, without knowledge of Captain Coon, assume that these cats must be a "cross" between coons and cats (which is biologically impossible). So powerful is the linguistic label, some people will try to convince others of the hybridization by pointing out the "obvious" coon traits of the cats such as long hair and bushy tail.

Linguistic labels also influence humans in their perceptions of each other. A word often acts as a telescope or, as Newcomb (20)

calls it, "a frame of reference" for viewing other people. If A is introduced as a "psychiatrist" to B, for example, several pictures flash
across B's mind. B notices that A has "penetrating" eyes, asks
"crafty" questions, and "tries to play" a "fatherly" role. As another
example, consider Jim Hales and Joe Forester who are neighbors. Joe
has often used the word "careless" for describing the manner in
which Jim backs out of his garage. Joe has decided that he will never
patronize Jim's drugstore: "He's so 'careless,' he'd probably give me
rat poison instead of cough syrup."

In an experiment performed by Rice (22) three groups of subjects
were individually shown photographs of nine men and asked to
judge the men on "intelligence" and "craftiness." Before the subjects
judged the photographs, they were told that one man was a labor
leader, another a bootlegger, and so on. In one group each subject
had to decide who the labor leader, etc., was before he judged the
intelligence and craftiness of the man. In the second group the
photographs were labeled "labor leader," etc., before judgments
were made, but the labels were false. In the third group, the photographs were labeled correctly. With each group, it was evident that
the men were judged according to the verbal labels and not the facial
characteristics. For example, one man was judged much more intelligent when labeled "labor leader" than he was when labeled
"bootlegger." Thus, it can be seen that verbal labels evoke certain
attitudes which in turn influence men's perceptions of each other.

While words influence men's *visual* perceptions, it seems likely
that words even influence their auditory perceptions. Lotz (17) describes a study in which three staccato beats of equal intensity were
presented individually to a Czech, a Pole, and a Frenchman. The
Czech, whose language often stresses the first syllable of a word,
said the first beat was the loudest. The Frenchman, whose language
often stresses the last syllable of a word, reported that the third
beat was the loudest. The Pole, whose language often stresses the
next to last syllable of a word, claimed that the second beat was
the loudest!

## Grammar and World View

Although it has been shown that words have a definite effect on
man's perceptions, the grammatical *structure* of his language influ-

ences his perceptions even more profoundly. Why do English-speaking people say: "The Eskimo is carving a miniature seal out of rock."? Is such an occurrence actually happening in the external world, or do they see it that way because their language structure forces them to see it that way. The Eskimo might insist that he is not carving a seal; he is humbly trying to permit the seal to be seen more clearly; it was in the rock all the time. The English-speaking man is almost forced by his linguistic habits into asking: "What is that Eskimo doing?" (rather than "What are the man and rock doing to each other?"—which is probably closer to reality); "What is he carving?" (rather than "What does the rock tell him?").

In general, people look for things in their environment which will satisfy their sentence patterns. The English-speaking people look for subjects and verbs because it would be nearly impossible to think about their environment without them. The Hopi Indians, on the other hand, can have verbs without subjects (27). While the English-speaking person might say, "it flashes," the Hopi Indian would probably say a word translated as "flash" (2), thus describing a process rather than cause and effect. As a matter of fact, the Hopi approach may be much more useful in scientific investigation. Most physicists today would argue that looking for processes or inter-actions is a more fruitful way of perceiving the world than looking for causes and effects (2). But the English language divides up nature into discrete entities such as cause and effect, means and ends, actor and action; and the interactions, the steady flow, the wholeness of nature is ignored. In effect, the phenomena of nature are made to represent the components of a sentence pattern, rather than the sentence pattern representing the natural phenomena. The linguistic symbols are given more reality than the natural events which they are supposed to represent.

Let us briefly compare the English language with the Hopi language and the Wintu language to see how grammatical patterns influence the world view of those who use these three languages. Whorf (29) has studied and described the Hopi language and Lee (14) has reported on the Wintu language. While the English language uses plurals for both real duplication and imaginary duplication, the Hopi language has no imaginary plurals. The English-speaking people say "ten rocks," which are real, and "ten days," which have to be imagined. Instead of saying, "They stayed ten days," the Hopi Indian says "They stayed until the eleventh day" or

"They left after the tenth day." Instead of saying, "Ten days is greater than nine days," the Hopi says "The tenth day is later than the ninth." Thus the English language often treats time as if it were a set of objects, while the Hopi language treats time as an orderly flow, with only one instance of it ready to be experienced.

This different perception of time is also seen in the Hopi verb (28). While the English verb includes time as a major element of description (past, present, future), the Hopi verb differs according to the type of validity of a statement. One form of the Hopi verb indicates that the statement is a report of an event; another form indicates expectation of an event; a third form designates that the statement is a generalization about the event. Obviously the English and Hopi verbs lead to different perceptions of the natural environment.

The Wintu language does not include the sentence pattern, A is A, a highly popular pattern in the English language. The Wintu Indian would say, "We call this bread," rather than, "This is bread." The latter pattern causes English-speaking people frequently to confuse words with actual objects. The Wintu language has a built-in protection against such deception. The Wintu language also includes suffixes which indicate *how* information has been received: eyes, other senses, inference, hearsay. The English language is deficient in this respect; only through probing can such qualifications be discovered. The Wintu's language draws attention to form rather than action. Instead of saying, "He plays the piano," the Wintu might say, "He makes a braying noise." The English name "automobile," is based on its action, whereas the Wintu classify it in the same class as a turtle, because the *form* of an automobile is similar to that of a turtle. These two types of classifications—action and form—are built into the language patterns and thus into the perceptual habits of the English-speaking and Wintu cultures.

## Language and Mental Illness

Language patterns not only influence our ordinary, everyday perceptions, they also act as a catalyst in the development of mental illness. Mental illness is ". . . the slow hardening over the course of years of habits of response, habits that hinder a person's adequately knowing or dealing with his world" (30:324). It has already been indicated that certain linguistic habits can prevent a person from "adequately knowing his world." Whorf (27:182) went so far as to say that "the commitment to illusion has been sealed in western Indo-European language . . ." On a more optimistic note Whorf (27:182) suggested that "the road out of illusion for the West lies through a wider understanding of language . . ."

Although Whorf's suggestion is a valuable legacy to the West, the type of understanding he recommends needs to be buttressed with an understanding of neurosis. Linguistic habits seem to be a major factor in the evolution of neurosis, but they are not the only factor. For our present purposes, it is important for us to comprehend the particular role which language plays in neurosis development. As a model of neurosis, let us take the experiment on rats performed by Maier (5). Each rat was first trained to jump through one of two doors; if he jumped at one door it opened and the rat could obtain food; if he jumped at the other door he bumped his nose and fell into a net. After the rats were well trained, the conditions were reversed. Some of the rats adjusted to the change but many did not; after many nose bumps the latter gave up; rather than make a choice they were resigned to starvation. These rats were then forced to jump by means of air blasts or electric shock. Under these conditions the rats became *fixated* in their response, always jumping at the same door no matter whether food was available or not. If a rat's response became fixated on the left-hand door, he would never jump at the right-hand door even if the door were left open and the food was made visible! When the experimenter persisted in forcing a rat to make a choice, he eventually went "mad," racing around wildly and finally falling into a coma.

This pattern is typical of many human neuroses: habit, change, failure to adjust to change, forced response, fixation, forced response, nervous breakdown. How does language fit into this pattern? As explained earlier, we are dependent upon language for the processes of perception and thinking; and, unfortunately, most of us, most of the time, confuse language with external reality. With rigid linguistic patterns serving as a perceptual screen it is difficult to adjust to changing conditions or new information. But we are usually *forced* to make decisions related to the changing conditions or new information. Thus, if we are not aware of linguistic distortion, our responses (usually in verbal form) become fixated and mental illness is only a step away. An example of this pattern can be seen in the following story:

> Alyce was brought up to believe that "petting is evil." This exact statement was made many times by her mother and repeated dutifully by Alyce. When Alyce was a young teenager in high school, she was often confronted with the choice of "to pet or not to pet." Each time the choice came up she remembered the right door, "petting is evil," and she was rewarded by an unsullied reputation and a strong sense of self-righteousness. But time passed and conditions changed. Alyce was now a college senior eagerly seeking a husband before it was "too late." She was still jumping at the right door and receiving nothing but a bruised nose. The "reality" of the situation included the necessity of petting, since a young man is generally interested in whether or not his wife will be a "good lover." Alas, whenever she was forced to make a choice, she was confronted with a linguistic distortion of reality: "petting is evil." Sad to say, this response became a fixation and a mild form of neurosis developed. Alyce is presently the chairman of C.B.L.B.S.L., the Committee for the Banishment of Lewd Books from School Libraries. She's unmarried, but knows that "the right man will come along some day."

## General Semantics

So far "general semantics" seems to be the best antidote developed for the treatment of mild linguistic neurosis. General semantics may also be an excellent potent for preventing the onset of individual or societal neuroses. "General semantics" means the study of the effects of language on human behavior. Its modern pioneers have included Korzybski (13), Sapir (24), Whorf (27), Chase (2), Johnson (9), and Hayakawa (5), as well as many others.

> For the general semanticist, communication is not merely words in proper order properly inflected . . . or assertions in proper relation to each other . . . or assertions in proper relation to referents . . . but all these together, with the chain of 'fact to nervous system to language to nervous system to action.' (21:14)

According to Hayakawa (6) the central concern of general semanticists is the effect of the "linguistic unconscious" on human thought and behavior. This "linguistic unconscious" causes us to develop "neuro-semantic compulsions." In other words, our linguistic habits become so much a part of us, they act in a manner similar to the autonomic nervous system, causing unconscious, involuntary reactions. However, general semanticists have found that once the linguistic habits are understood and brought to the conscious level, they can be controlled. With this control comes the ability to interpret and evaluate our complex environment with greater precision, to communicate with others more effectively, and to maintain a higher level of mental health.

## Word Worship

There are two general rules which general semanticists have developed to help people maintain a conscious control over their linguistic habits. The first of these is that *words are not things.* Amazingly simple, isn't it? Yet, a careful observation of our own behavior and the behavior of others will show how often the rule is ignored. Consider the following example: "In modern India, a large animal called the 'blue cow' was renamed the 'blue horse' so that its name would not remind people of the sacred cow and it could be killed to protect the crops (17:15)." Could this happen in our sophisticated society? "State Senator John McNaboe of New York bitterly opposed a bill for the control of syphilis in May, 1937, because the innocence of children might be corrupted by a widespread use of the term . . . " (5:35) Could this happen today? For political reasons, American soldiers in Vietnam were called "advisors" even though they fought as actively as their "advisees."

The examples just given are illustrations of the fact that modern man still believes—*albeit* unconsciously—in "word magic." Cartoonists and writers often make use of this fact by exaggerating our weakness in this respect. The musical comedy "High Button Shoes," for example, contained a scene in which one character had a sneezing fit every time the words "ragweed" and "fresh country air" were mentioned. It's a rare comedian who has not occasionally relied upon the word magic gag.

What causes this unconscious belief in word magic? It arises out of our very natural tendency to make associations between two adjacent phenomena. If I were suddenly to plunge into quicksand (never having heard of it) and my friend who pulled me out made the noise "quicksand," a strong association between the word and my horrible experience would be "printed" on my brain. The next time I heard the word I would undoubtedly experience to some extent the same feelings I had when I was trapped in the actual substance. The word has become magical to me. This same chain reaction of experience—feeling—word—feeling is a natural, unavoidable part of man's environment. The danger lies in not being conscious of our magical associations.

Word magic takes many forms and is not always easily discernable, even when one is searching for it. A rather obvious example, nonetheless, occurred in the early 1930's when certain people repetitiously used the phrase, "Prosperity is just around the corner." Under certain conditions this slogan might enhance the confidence necessary for conditions to improve. At the time the slogan was used, however, it was an expression of magical thinking. Another example might be the campaign that occurred in the early 1950's in a midwestern city we'll call "Penton." Penton's reputation for crime and corruption had been worsening steadily and there was evidently great concern by prominent citizens and businessmen that a mass exodus might begin, or at least that new citizens and businesses would be scared away. The obvious remedy for this situation was quickly utilized: in dozens of shop windows a sign was displayed which read: "Penton is a Wonderful Place to Live."

In Andrew Jackson's day dueling was still a popular way of counteracting word magic of a detrimental nature. If someone threw the magic noise, "liar," at you, there was only one thing to do: destroy his magic by killing him in a duel. Today we "politely" ostracize those who make use of disagreeable word magic such as "damn," "hell," and other dangerous expletives. (And boys try to grow up faster by using such magic words.)

Sometimes words neither frighten nor anger us but provide us rather with a false sense of security. As a fire insurance analyst, Whorf (29) found many examples of this problem. In one factory it was necessary for a group of men to work around gasoline drums. When the drums were full of gasoline the men were extremely careful with matches and cigarettes. When a drum was labeled "EMPTY" they thought nothing of lighting a cigarette near the drum or tossing their stubs close to it. After all, the word "EMPTY" was written right on it. Unfortunately, the word magic was not strong enough to prevent the gasoline vapor from igniting.

Both words and word users are generally held in awe by our society. The person who is verbally fluent and knows how to make appropriate noises is often considered "sharp," "intelligent," "brilliant." A current television program which has been popular for many years glorifies the college student who has a vast reservoir of verbal knowledge, regardless of whether or not he has a substantial repertoire of experiences. This worship of word users has deep historical roots, penetrating the layer of time when religious and political leaders were the only ones who could read or write or understand big words. These leaders had power, and the association between power and words must have been enhanced by their masterful use of language.

Our heritage of word worship makes it difficult for us to realize that words are nothing more than noises or marks or, as Chase (2) says, "abstractions of abstractions." Many of us are satisfied, though, when our environment is explained through words alone. Take the egg in the bottle experiment, for instance. A piece of paper is set afire and placed inside a milk bottle. Immediately a "peeled" hard-boiled egg is placed over the opening of the bottle. The burning paper inside heats and expands the air and forces some of it to leave the bottle, making the egg perform a gentle dance (which is often not seen by naive observers). The air pressure is now greater on the outside of the bottle than on the inside, and the egg is pushed into the bottle. This experiment has been performed many times in front of college students who have already been shown that air exerts pressure and expands when heated. The most common answer to "What made the egg go into the bottle?" is the word "Suction." Most of them are completely satisfied with this *word* as an explanation of the phenomenon they have witnessed. When asked what the word "suction" would mean in this case they are stymied. If they had a dictionary available, some of them would probably find another magic word to replace "suction." When asked the facetious question, "Who's doing the sucking?" they are forced to make the ridiculous assertion that "The air inside the bottle is sucking in the egg."

The magic word "suction" is harmless enough, but there are other magic words which ought to be locked up. As Chase (2:9) so aptly put it, "The quarter inch of cortex has created, along with the plays of Shakespeare and the abatement of yellow fever, a jungle of contention and a dreadful zoo of verbal monsters." One of these monsters is the word "real." "Give us the *real* story." "What's he *really* like?" "He's lost touch with *reality*." As Meyers (18:265) says, "Such is the magic that inheres within the terms 'real' 'realness', and 'reality' that, once assured of the appropriateness of their use in connection with an ideology, men . . . have engaged one another over and over again in mortal combat." Other verbal monsters are such words as "democratic," "communistic," "progressive," and "patriotic." These and other verbal monsters have the capacity to change form instantaneously, making it impossible to "really" capture and tame them. Because of their elusiveness they can be very useful for purposes of slander and deceit (discussed in Chapter 6).

Some verbal monsters are favorites of teachers: "grade level," "third grade," "second grade." These monsters help us to make inaccurate statements such as, "That's a fifth-grade library book," "You can't expect a second-grader to learn that," and "He's reading well above his grade-level." Many of us catch ourselves in the act of perceiving a group of children as "fourth graders" rather than as individuals with a remarkable range of capacities and degrees of competence. Moreover, we often expect a child to conform to the labels we have given them: "After all, he *is* a fourth-grader, isn't he?"

Our tendency to treat words with reverence is bad enough, but our reservoir of words makes it even more difficult not to confuse words with things. A great portion of English words are used as metaphors, hence, if we wish to speak fluently, we are committed to the pretension that words are as objective as things. In the following sentence, for example, there are eight metaphors: My *point* is that it is *hard* to *see* why the *level* of education is so *low* when it is *clear* that a *lot* of money has been *pouring* into the country. A metaphor allows us to make an analogy between a physical aspect and a non-physical aspect of our environment. Without metaphors much literature would seem colorless; thus consciousness of their abuse is all that is being advocated. As Embler (3:128) warns us, ". . . those who find their attitudes implicit in the metaphor construe the metaphor to be a statement of . . . fact." Some Nazis, for example, used the metaphor of "ants" to refer to human beings. Many Nazis, judging from the way they treated their fellow men must have taken the metaphor to heart. Southern "gentlemen" and Northern "educated" have referred to negroid people as "monkeys." This diabolical metaphor has obviously been confused with fact by ignorant racists on many occasions. Another metaphorical error is that of thinking that the human brain actually *is* a computer and the human body actually *is* a machine. Again Embler (3:137) warns us:

> The moment we say the human being *is* a machine, at that moment we shall believe that the human being can be conditioned to behave in a perfectly predictable way with admirable regularity. Then it is that we shall have made ourselves something less, ever so much less, than we are.

As soon as we fall into the trap of taking metaphorical language literally, we are in danger of *making* something true which is not true. A person who is living in New York City, for instance, is sometimes tempted to use the metaphor, "jungle," to describe his environment. This metaphor is interesting and might even be useful if it causes one to do something about improving the city. On the other hand, the metaphor, when taken literally, can encourage an attitude of distrust and carelessness which indeed fosters a jungle-like atmosphere.

In addition to metaphorical confusion, all of us may sometimes experience the confusion caused by the assumption that there is a definite connection between words and what they stand for. Witness what occurs in this "dream":

*Mrs. Snod:* Look at that lovely little table!
*Mrs. Grass:* My dear, you're looking at a bench.
*Mrs. Snod:* Don't be silly. You can see it's a table.
*Mrs. Grass:* I see no such thing. It's clearly a bench.
*Salesman:* (Overhearing their argument) That, ladies, is a *snoff.*
*Ladies:* (Sniffing at his snoff in derision) Well!
*Salesman:* We're having a nice little special on snoffs this week.
*Mrs. Snod:* Call it a snoff if you will. I still say it's a table.
*Mrs. Grass:* Obviously, it's a bench.

| | |
|---|---|
| *Linguist:* | (Entering melodiously from an adjacent room) And I am right, and you are right, and all is right as right can be. |
| *Mrs. Snod:* | Nonsense! |
| *Mrs. Grass:* | How could all of us be right? |
| *Linguist:* | My dear, as Lord High Linguist I am aware of things of which you have never even dreamed. |
| *Mrs. Grass:* | My dreams are my own business. I still say that *that* is a bench! |
| *Mrs. Snod:* | A table! |
| *Linguist:* | Madams, in France you would call it "table" or "banc." In Germany you would call it "tisch" or "bank." In Spain you would call it "tabla" or "banca." |
| *Mrs. Grass:* | No matter what *they* call it, it's still a bench. |
| *Mrs. Snod:* | A table! |
| *Salesman:* | A snoff! We're having a nice little sale on snoffs this week. |
| *Linguist:* | I'll take one. Please have it delivered. |

In another dream (same night) you are an anthropologist studying a tableless culture called the Nontablans. As an experiment you have asked the United States Department of the Interior to send you a table. The table has just arrived and you have unveiled it in front of three natives. One of the natives becomes ecstatic, turns the "table" upside down, utters the Nontablan word for "raft," and shoves it into the water. He is flabbergasted when the "raft" sinks. Another native rescues the "table" from the waves, turns it "right side up," crawls under it and begins worshipping one of his gods. The third native rushes into the woods, returns with branches and large leaves which he places near the "table," and commences to build a "gonk cage" (the Nontablans are gonk eaters). Just before you sail away to study the Nonbancans, you notice that the three natives have ripped off the "table legs" and are presently attempting to club each other with them. Suddenly you sit up in bed and shout, "The connection between words and things is arbitrary!" Fortunately, no one hears you.

The various types of confusion caused by word worship can all be described with the term used by semanticists: *intensional orientation*

—"the habit of guiding ourselves by *words alone,* rather than by the facts to which words should guide us (5:253)." To be freed from this habit, say the semanticists, one must develop an *extensional orientation*—an awareness of the extreme limitation of words to describe the relationships and processes in the natural world and an awareness of the need for operational definitions. What is an *operational definition?* An operational definition "tells *what to do* to experience the thing defined (21:10)." If you wish to find out what "democracy" means to another person, you must discover the specific behavior he has in mind. For a Nontablan to understand the meaning of "table," he must observe how people in our culture *use* a table. For one physicist to understand another physicist's notion of *length,* he must understand *how* length was measured.

> For an extensionally minded person, words that cannot be defined by operations and statements that do not by implication contain predictions of experience, are like checks on non-existent accounts (21:13).

Thus an extensionally minded person checks his own assertions or the assertions of others by asking: Does the statement have predictive validity? Can I test it? If I perceive that "the world is round," is there some way of testing this notion? (If the notion has predictive validity, I should be able to reach the Far East by sailing west.) If I perceive that "democracy is the best form of government," can I operationalize the words "democracy" and "government" so that I might test the predictive validity of my perception?

To counteract "word magic," then, the following ideas should be kept in mind:

1. Words are not things; the connection between a word and a thing is arbitrary.

2. Words can be best defined operationally.

3. Metaphors are analogies and not statements of fact.

4. Words are inadequate representatives of the natural environment.

## Hyper-generalization

The second general rule which semanticists have developed is that $A_1$ is not $A_2$. This rule is in direct opposition to common modes of thinking and to Aristotle's first principle of logic: A is A; a thing is what it is; a stick is a stick. For hundreds of years Aristotle's principle was considered a basic assumption regarding reality. However, scientists of the past few centuries have pointed out the now obvious weakness of this assumption by showing that in nature no two things are exactly alike. Therefore only in one's mind can two things be the same. Semanticists (13, 5, 2) have further criticized Aristotle's assumption by claiming that his principle, rather than describing nature, describes merely one structural characteristic of the Greek language. This structural characteristic is the sentence pattern described in Chapter 2 as N be N, or as semanticists call it, "the is of identity." In short, Aristotle overlooked the fact that language greatly influences perceptions, and assumed that the words and grammatical patterns of the Greek language were accurate representations of physical reality.

The *is of identity* pattern is perhaps the strongest trap which the English language sets for unwary wanderers on this Earth. This pattern clouds perceptions and fogs discussions, and even accounts for occasional amusement:

> *Cat-lover:* Cats are beautiful animals.
> *Cat-hater:* Ever try to remove their beautiful hairs from an angora sweater?
> *Cat-lover:* And cats are so quiet.
> *Cat-hater:* Try quieting one at two o'clock in the morning!
> *Cat-lover:* And they're so neat.
> *Cat-hater:* Who cleans up the kitty litter in your house!

Obviously, $Cat_1$ is *not* $Cat_2$.

If one compares the cat-lover's first statement with observations of the "natural" cat, it can be seen that this particular *is of identity* statement has many weaknesses:

1. The beauty of the cat is in the mind of the beholder.
2. Some cats seem beautiful; some do not.
3. There are various degrees of beauty, ranging from "ugly" to "beautiful."
4. A single cat may be beautiful on one occasion and ugly on another (after falling in the mud).
5. Beauty varies with the mood of the beholder.

The point is not that we should completely avoid *is of identity* statements, nor that we should exhaustively qualify such statements, but that we should be conscious of their frailties. The three basic faults of *is of identity* statements seem to be these: (1) They may help us to assume that the abstractions in our heads describe the specifics in our environments. (Both "cat" and "beautiful" are abstractions of innumerable specific observations.) (2) They may cause us to ignore the many characteristics which we have not described. (The word "beautiful" cannot describe all there is to know about cats.) (3) They may encourage us to ignore the "fourth dimension" of our environment—time. (The beauty of a cat *changes* with time and events.)

Korzybski (13) suggests three devices which can be used (or kept in mind )to avoid the *is of identity* trap.

1. The symbol, *etc.*, to remind one of omitted characteristics. (Cats are beautiful, etc.)

2. *Index number* to break up false identifications. (Cat$_1$, Cat$_2$, Cat$_3$)

3. *Dates* to remind us that natural objects are constantly changing. (Cat$_{1964}$, Cat$_{1965}$, Cat$_{May 7}$, Cat$_{May 8}$)

By keeping in mind the frailties of *is of identity statements* and the devices suggested by Korzybski, we can avoid some of the possible results of identity thinking: soothsayer complex, institutionalized attitudes, and mental illness. Are you acquainted with anyone who frequently uses *is of identity* statements, who seems quite "dogmatic," and who often uses the word "truth" as if it's his personal possession? If you don't like this person, a "sophisticated" method of aggressing against him is to tell others that he has a "soothsayer complex." (Feel free to use the term, since your author has not been able to obtain a patent on it.) If, on the other hand, someone uses the term to describe *you*, here are some ways of getting rid of the complex.

First, keep in mind that an individual ". . . regards as 'true' those systems of classification that produce the desired results" (5:217). If a man combined a business trip with a vacation, how would he classify his trip for purposes of paying his income tax—"business expense" or "pleasure"? Second, remember Hayakawa's dictum (5:292) to "distinguish at least four senses of the word 'true' "?

1. Some mushrooms are poisonous. (If we call this "true," it means that it is a *report that can be and has been verified . . .*)
2. Sally is the sweetest girl in the world. (If we call this "true," it means that *we feel the same way towards Sally . . .*)
3. All men are created equal. (If we call this "true," it means that this is *a directive which we believe should be obeyed . . .*)
4. $(x + y)^2 = x^2 \times y + y^2$. (If we call this "true," it means that this statement is *consistent with the system of statements possible to be made in the language called algebra . . .*)

"Institutionalized attitudes" (5:303) are another possible concomitant of identity thinking. Here are some institutionalized attitudes: "Democrats are for the common man." "What's good for business is good for the country." "Boy Scouts are trustworthy." With the use of Korzybski's semantic devices, these institutionalized attitudes can be modified: $Democrat_1$ is not $Democrat_2$; $country_{1950}$ is not country $_{1965}$; $Scout_1$ is not $Scout_2$; $Scout_1$ is trustworthy, *etc.*

Identity thinking can also foster various degrees of mental illness. Weiss (26) tested 516 adolescents and young adults to determine the state of their mental health and the extent to which they relied on *is of identity* statements in their thinking. His findings indicated that those who habitually used identity thinking were more "maladjusted" than those who avoided this type of thinking. A replication of this study with 387 individuals confirmed the results of his earlier study.

Kelley (10) and Korzybski (12) have found that specific training in non-identity thinking has been helpful to war veterans whose identity thinking was making it difficult for them to adjust to civilian life. One veteran, for instance, would become terrified whenever he heard a civilian airplane. By constantly reminding himself that $airplane_1$ is not $airplane_2$ he was able to overcome his fear.

## Abstractionitus

A special type of hyper-generalization might be called "abstractionitus." The symptoms of this disease are rather common: circular thinking, mistaking inferences for facts, and perceiving judgments as reports. Mr. Blue has a bad case of abstractionitus:

*Mr. Blue:* I think Jones is an atheist.
*Mr. Green:* What makes you think so?
*Mr. Blue:* Well, he never goes to church, does he?
*Mr. Green:* Yea, but he still might believe in God.
*Mr. Blue:* Nah, he's an atheist all right; said he didn't have any interest in whether God existed or not.
*Mr. Green:* He's an agnostic then.
*Mr. Blue:* Same thing. Must be a communist, too.
*Mr. Green:* How come?
*Mr. Blue:* Why else would he be an atheist?

Perhaps the cure for abstractionitus is to develop a keener awareness of what Hayakawa (5) calls the "abstraction ladder," shown in the diagram on the next page. The diagram demonstrates that one way in which our classifications (words) differ is in the degree to which they are removed from specific instances. The statement, "Jones is an atheist," is at a much higher level of abstraction than the statement, "Jones hasn't gone to church since I've known him." Furthermore, the latter statement is much easier to verify.

One way of making use of our knowledge of the abstraction ladder is in defining words. Sometimes we attempt to define words by moving *up* the ladder:

> What's a bush?
> A bush is a type of plant.
> What's a plant?
> A plant is a form of life.
> What's life?

This approach is not often successful. Sometimes, however, we try to define a word by staying on the *same rung* of the ladder: "a bush is a shrub." Not too helpful, either. Generally, the most helpful way to define a word is to move *down* the ladder: "we use the word 'tree' to stand for anything that looks like this (tree$_1$) or this (tree$_2$) or this (tree$_3$); or "that thing you climb on in the back yard is a tree."

To demonstrate how "abstractionitus" affects some people who are attempting to arrive at a meaningful definition, let us examine a few replies given to the question "What is a Communist?" This question was asked by the *Capital Times* reporters in Madison, Wisconsin (2:134).

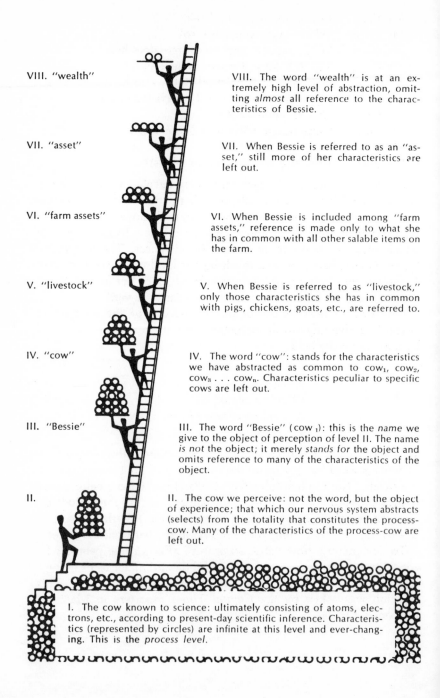

VIII. "wealth"

VIII. The word "wealth" is at an extremely high level of abstraction, omitting *almost* all reference to the characteristics of Bessie.

VII. "asset"

VII. When Bessie is referred to as an "asset," still more of her characteristics are left out.

VI. "farm assets"

VI. When Bessie is included among "farm assets," reference is made only to what she has in common with all other salable items on the farm.

V. "livestock"

V. When Bessie is referred to as "livestock," only those characteristics she has in common with pigs, chickens, goats, etc., are referred to.

IV. "cow"

IV. The word "cow": stands for the characteristics we have abstracted as common to $cow_1$, $cow_2$, $cow_3$ . . . $cow_n$. Characteristics peculiar to specific cows are left out.

III. "Bessie"

III. The word "Bessie" ($cow_1$): this is the *name* we give to the object of perception of level II. The name *is not* the object; it merely *stands for* the object and omits reference to many of the characteristics of the object.

II.

II. The cow we perceive: not the word, but the object of experience; that which our nervous system abstracts (selects) from the totality that constitutes the process-cow. Many of the characteristics of the process-cow are left out.

I. The cow known to science: ultimately consisting of atoms, electrons, etc., according to present-day scientific inference. Characteristics (represented by circles) are infinite at this level and ever-changing. This is the *process level*.

| | |
|---|---|
| *Farmer:* | They are no good to my notion. I can't figure out what they are. |
| *Stenographer:* | If a person didn't have a religion I would be tempted to believe he was a Communist. |
| *Housewife:* | I really don't know what a Communist is. I think they should throw them out of the White House. |
| *High-school student:* | A Communist is a person who wants war. |
| *Office worker:* | Anyone that stands for things that democracy does not. |

If those dead-end definitions seem to lack polish, let us examine instead the definition by a fictitious sophisticate:

What is a Communist?
A Communist is one who doesn't believe in individual freedom.
What do you mean by freedom?
The opportunity to take advantage of God-given rights.
What rights?
The rights which we have in a democratic country.
What is a democratic country?
One that isn't governed by Communists.
What is a Communist?
I've already answered that!

This *circular thinking* is as fruitless as the previous dead-end definitions. In either case abstractions were floating about in the air and the respondents were high on the abstraction ladder catching a good case of abstractionitus.

Another cure for abstractionitus is to develop skill in differentiating three common forms of information: reports, inferences, and judgments. A report is a fact which can be verified (if we wish to make the effort). "Jones hasn't been to church since I've known him" is a report. An inference is an "educated" guess—an extension of a report to cover unknown territory. "Jones doesn't care for church" is an inference based on the previous report. A judgment is an expression of acceptance or rejection. "Jones is a lousy atheist" is a judgment based on one or more reports, one or more inferences, and one or more prejudices.

It is quite common for most of us to accept judgments or inferences as reports. Suppose I made the following statement: "I saw that little thief, Jimmy Smith, steal the milk off our porch this morning!" Am I merely reporting what I saw? Or am I inferring that Jimmy knew he shouldn't take the milk but took it, anyway? Or am I judging Jimmy as a person who will habitually take objects which don't belong to him even though he knows that he shouldn't. Actually, I'm reporting, inferring, and judging in one fell swoop. Notice, however, that the three forms of information can be separated:

*Report:* I saw Jimmy Smith take the milk off the porch.
*Inference:* Jimmy *stole* the milk.
*Judgment:* Jimmy is a *thief.*

There are many words similar to "thief" which, though used as reports, are actually judgments in disguise—words like "progressive," "radical," "patriotic," "socialistic," "capitalistic," "doublecrossed," "sneaked," "lied," "politician," "tramp," "dictator." You can be certain that before these words are utilized, they will be dipped in prejudice. Korzybski (13) recommends the use of quotation marks for such words to remind us that they are "loaded" and high on the abstraction ladder. The basic remedy, of course, is to keep in mind that words can do no more than describe man's internal state; they cannot describe external reality, a fact which is particularly true with "loaded" words.

To summarize (in inverted fashion) what has been said about abstractionitus, we will use this Soviet definition of semantics (8:347):

Semantic philosophy: a fashionable subjective-idealist movement in bourgeoise philosophy which has been particularly widely spread in the U.S.A. in recent years by reactionary ideologists. It is a characteristic form of the decadent philosophy of the age of imperialism.

## Two-Valued Logic

Another type of hyper-generalization has been labeled by semanticists (2, 13, 5) as "two-valued logic." This type of thinking is as old as man, if not older. When a cave man was fighting for his life, either he killed or he was killed; the food which he ate was either edible or not edible. If he brought home some meat the hunt was good; if he came home empty-handed the hunt was bad. If the rain came, his behavior had been right; if the rain did not come, his behavior had been wrong. The habit of thinking in bi-polar ruts is tightly woven into the human fabric. Man is used to paddling up and down a river with no tributaries; upstream is "good" and "right"; downstream is "bad" and "wrong." By now, of course, these grooves of thought are locked into our language, and modern man tends to perceive according to linguistic opposites.

Aristotle encouraged this process by supposing, again, that his linguistic patterns represented reality. According to his water-tight logic, "everything is either A or not-A; nothing is both A and not-A" (6:28). Yet, as scientists have discovered, nature refuses to cooperate with the followers of Aristotle. Consider the Aristotelian-type statement, for example: Every living thing is either a plant or an animal; nothing is both plant and animal. Under the microscope, however, the distinction between "plant" and "animal" often becomes meaningless. The organism called "euglena," for instance, can be called either a plant or an animal—or both (2). Examine another Aristotelian-type statement: "Every human being is either masculine or feminine; no human being is both masculine and feminine." Today it is common knowledge that many of the "masculine" and "feminine" characteristics are based on cultural expectations—thus making a masculine trait in one culture seem feminine in another culture.

With respect to nature, then, our linguistic inheritance demands two-valued perceptions and our scientific inheritance demands multi-valued perceptions. To compensate for our linguistic inheritance, Korzybski (13) urged that we reject Aristotelian logic and make our language conform to the fact that events in nature flow into one another by "insensible gradations." To remind ourselves of this fact, he suggested the use of hyphens between certain words to show the interconnectedness of nature, e.g., "masculine-feminine characteristics." (Hyphenated words have indeed become more common lately, e.g., "geo-political boundaries," "socio-economic factors," "racial-economic tensions.")

Korzybski's advice to the contrary, Aristotelian thought, with its two-valued syllogisms, is still the prevalent mode of thinking among political speakers, lawyers at court, and any of us who ever get emotional (Did I leave anyone out?). Pretend for a moment that you are switching from one channel to another with the hope of finding a television program you will enjoy watching. This might be what you would hear:

> Anyone who talks that way doesn't deserve to be called a Repubocat. In fact, he doesn't even deserve to be called an American. Either he's going to be *for* America or *against* America; he can't be both! And I say . . .
>
> John, either you love me or you don't. Now which is it?
> I'm not sure—I need to ask my psychiatrist.
> But, John, you know I love you, and I didn't even ask my psychiatrist.
> You've told me that before, but . . .
>
> . . . Back to our early, early show:
> Whoever is an enemy of the National Democratic Socialist People's Party is an enemy of Berbandy.
> But, sir, surely we have no enemies left in Berbandy.
> Of course we have, you fool. Not everyone has joined the N.D.S.P.P. yet. Obviously those who have not joined our party must be liquidated. How would you suggest . . .

At this point you give up on TV and turn on the radio:

> Here's an oldie. Remember this one sung by Georgia Fibs? They're either too young or too old. They're either too grey or too grassy green . . .

Switching off the radio, you mumble, "Blasted TV and radio! It's either that sickening puppy love or those windbag politicians. We never get any decent programs!"

Is there any way we can avoid a two-valued orientation toward life? Again our basic remedy lies in the recognition of linguistic tyranny—of realizing that our two-valued statements describe our feelings and our language habits and nothing more. To augment this understanding, however, it would be useful to carry around in one's mind a picture of a normal frequency curve, described in any introductory book on statistics or testing. By keeping such a picture in mind, we might remember that the great majority of human characteristics vary a great deal among a random group of people. As a simple example of this phenomenon, let us select a random sample of one hundred Americans and administer an intelligence test to each of them. Would the test score indicate that "Americans are intelligent people," or that "Americans are ignorant oafs"? Obviously, this is a nonsense question based on two-valued thinking. The test results would indicate, rather, that Americans vary a great deal in intelligence (as defined by the test). One of our subjects might have an IQ below 35, while another subject would have an IQ above 165. About sixty-four of our subjects would have an IQ ranging from 85 to 115. Approximately eighteen would have an IQ below 85 and eighteen above 115. Our frequency curve, then, would look something like the following:

### APPROXIMATE DISTRIBUTION OF IQ's IN A RANDOM SAMPLE OF 100 AMERICANS

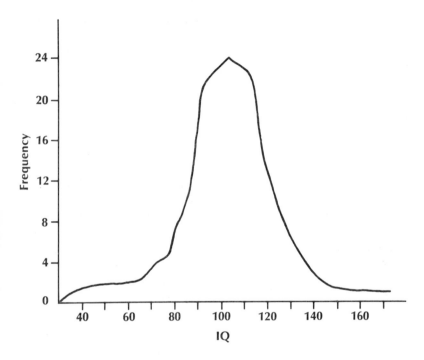

To be sure, not all human traits have as normal a distribution as intelligence seems to have. Yet all characteristics vary among a group of people, whether these people be politicians, sponsors, landlords, principals, teachers, or even school superintendents. Of course, it might spoil our fun to keep the frequency curve in mind

(One can receive a lot of satisfaction from saying, "those superintendents are all alike!"). But if we are interested at the moment in
being objective, a mental image of a frequency curve would make it
possible. Even physical scientists have found the frequency curve to
be a useful concept, for they have discovered that the movements
and relationships of atoms and molecules can be described more
accurately with a frequency curve than with a static formula.

To counteract hyper-generalization, then, the following ideas
should be kept in mind:

1. $A_1$ is *not* $A_2$.
2. Abstractions exist only in our heads and not in nature.
3. Words have different levels of abstraction.
4. Reports, inferences, and judgments are different kinds of information.
5. A frequency curve is generally a better model for describing
our environment than a two-valued syllogism.


## Semantic Exercises for the Classroom

The author's experience has made it clear to him that even very
young children can grasp the two basic laws of semantics: (1) *a
word is not a thing*, and (2) $A_1$ *is not* $A_2$. Naturally, the subtleties of
these laws can be introduced only as maturity warrants. The following exercises may serve as examples of the types of activities which
might be effective in teaching children to avoid some of the snares
of the English language. Probably the earlier in life one recognizes
those pitfalls the better; nonetheless many of these exercises could
be utilized at any level of the school program. At any rate, no attempt has been made to designate grade level for each activity.

1. Words are not things; the connection between words and
   things is arbitrary.
   a. Give several objects in the classroom a new name, e.g., call
      the chalkboard "wumpa" (or if this is too hard for the chil-
      dren to remember, "scribble-slate"). Let the children make
      up names for other objects. Have everyone use the new
      names for a few days.
   b. After a week or so of using the new names given to class-

room objects, make up different names for the same object used in exercise *a*; use these names for a few days.

c. Same as *a*; use a foreign language for purposes of naming objects.

d. Look for "word magic" such as "Prosperity is around the corner" in newspapers, library books, basic readers, and advertisements.

e. Compare the socio-economic status of "word users" and "thing users." Speculate together on why "word users" are still held somewhat in awe.

f. Discuss the words "damn" and "hell" (if you're brave enough). Speculate together on why they have acquired "magic."

g. Study some of the famous duels in history and the relationship between "word magic" and "honor."

h. Look up a word such as "run" in a large dictionary. Why does it have so many meanings? Does a word have meaning in itself, or does something *give* it meaning?

2. Words can be best defined operationally.

a. Have a few children perform a spontaneous skit about a group of Nontablans (from a tableless culture) confronting a table for the first time. Have the rest of the class define the word "table" according to the Nontablans' viewpoints. Then have them define "table" according to their viewpoint.

b. Same as *a*; use objects other than a table.

c. Have one child define the word "length" to the teacher who pretends not to understand the words "inches," "feet" and other words related to linear measurement. Have a yardstick within view so that he might see the necessity of showing you how he *measures* length.

d. Ask the children to define the word "freedom" by explaining how they would "measure" freedom.

e. Same as *d*; use abstractions other than "freedom," such as the present slang terms which they are using.

3. Metaphors are analogies and not statements of fact.

a. Make up metaphorical statements about man similar to the following: "Men are machines which must be constantly provided with fuel and lubrication in order to operate efficiently." After the statements have been shared and ap-

preciated for their literary value, have each author point out the distorted perceptions which his metaphors might cause. (The teacher should take care to distinguish between the literary and informative values of metaphors.)
b. Look in newspapers, books, and television programs for instances in which people accept metaphors as facts.
c. Examine the following dialogue together. Discuss the metaphors of Mr. X and Mr. Y and the resulting limitations of their thinking.

> *Mr. X:* Americans are sheep. They follow anyone that comes along.
>
> *Mr. Y:* Yea, and each of them tries to bleat louder than the next one.
>
> *Mr. X:* This country is doomed. Can you imagine what would happen if a real dictator got in power?
>
> *Mr. Y:* They wouldn't raise a finger—just keep chewing their cud and getting fat.

4. Words are inadequate representatives of the natural environment.
   a. Have two pairs of children leave the room for a few minutes. Call one member of the first pair in and hand him a piece of cotton, asking him whether it is soft or hard. Then hand him a piece of rubber hose, asking him the same question. Have him take his seat and call in the second person of the first pair. Hand him a piece of steel, asking him whether it is soft or hard. Then hand him the identical piece of rubber hose, asking him the same question. Call in one member of the second pair and hand him an ice cube, asking him whether it is warm or cool. Now hand him an empty tin can and ask him the same question. Call in the other member of the second pair and have him touch a steel rod heated by a candle, asking him whether it is warm or cool. Then have him touch the identical tin can, and ask him the same question. Discuss the relativity of the words "warm," "cool," "soft," "hard," and other words of this nature.
   b. Use Korzybski's analogy of "map *vs.* territory" to describe the relationship between words and the things they represent. Discuss the limitations of ordinary maps; what aspects of the territory do they omit? Discuss the word "table"; as

an imperfect "map" what are its limitations? Discuss the word "freedom"; what are its limitations as a "map"? Discuss the word "splash"; is this a better "map" than "freedom" or "table." Are there other words like "splash" which serve as fairly accurate "maps"?

   c. Try to describe with words how you feel when you are walking home alone late at night. Are your "maps" very accurate? Can you describe your feelings again with more accurate "maps"? (For example, "my heart beats faster, the scrunch, scrunch, scrunch of my shoes on the gravel road is almost deafening, etc.")

   d. Same as *c*; describe other types of feelings.

   e. Read descriptions of feelings with appropriate "mood music" for background. Does the combination of words and music provide a better "map"?

5. $A_1$ is not $A_2$.

   a. Play a game called "Find the Referent." The leader thinks of something about a particular person, place, or thing. He then states aloud a broad generalization in the form of an *is of identity* statement. For example, the leader thinks of his little brother who wouldn't give him any candy this morning. The leader's statement might be "People are stingy!" The rest of the class tries to guess the particular person, place, or thing he is referring to. The person guessing asks, "are you referring to _____?" The one who guesses correctly becomes the leader or chooses a new leader. After three incorrect guesses the leader reveals his referent and chooses a new leader. (Before this game begins it might be wise for the teacher to be the leader for three or four statements; then give the children a few minutes to think of their own statement and write it down before the game begins.)

   b. Have the children find *is of identity* statements in newspapers, magazines, books, or television programs. Bring them to school, read them aloud, and have the class criticize them; try to guess the referent, think of instances when the statement would be false, and think of instances when the statement might appear to be true; what characteristics of the subject of the sentence are omitted?

   c. Criticize together the following statements:
- (1) Dogs are friendly. (Under what conditions, etc.?)
- (2) Boy Scouts are courteous. (Is this a fact or a goal, etc.?)
- (3) The weather is lovely. (What about those suffering from hay fever, etc.?)
- (4) A good Christian is a churchgoer.

   d. Which of the following are "nonsense" questions, i.e., questions which encourage *is of identity* answers?
- (1) Was Lincoln the tenth president?
- (2) Are monkeys intelligent?
- (3) Do women work harder than men?
- (4) Are you going on your vacation in March?
- (5) Is he hard of hearing?
- (6) Is a democracy better than a dictatorship?
- (7) Is Mars farther from Earth than Venus?

   e. Select three boys in the class. Have other members of the class make up *is of identity* statements about "boys" on the basis of their observation of the three boys. Then have the class criticize the anonymous statements as the teacher reads them aloud. The criticisms should indicate how the three boys are different.

6. Abstractions exist only in our heads and not in nature.

   a. Make a statement similar to the following: "No one in the room has ever seen an animal!" When a child challenges this statement, ask him to describe the "animal" he has seen. Then say, "But you haven't described an 'animal'; you've just described a bear (or whatever he has described). Has anyone else seen an animal?" Carry on this form of dialogue until many of the children have "caught on" intuitively to the idea that "animal" is only an abstraction—a verbal classification.

   b. Have children draw pictures of verbal abstractions such as the following:
- (1) "animal"
- (2) "danger"
- (3) "fun"
- (4) "wealth"

Before they draw, discuss the need for including many different specific ideas in order to portray an abstraction, e.g., "animal" will have to look like "bear," "snake," etc., all put together. Display and discuss the pictures, pointing out the different ways in which these abstractions have been portrayed, asking them why they are so different. Ask such questions as "Does danger mean the same thing to John and Mary?" "How is Jim's idea of fun different from Bill's idea?"

7. Words have different levels of abstraction.
   a. Draw a vertical "abstraction ladder" with five rungs on the chalkboard. On the bottom rung write the word "Lassie." Going up the ladder write the words "Collie," "dog," "mammal," and "animal." Draw another abstraction ladder and write these words on the rungs from bottom to top: "Sally's rocker," "chair," "furniture," "household goods," and "assets." Ask the children to discover how an "abstraction ladder" works.
   b. Draw a vertical abstraction ladder with five rungs on the chalkboard and write these words horizontally above it: clothes, Roberta's sneakers, possessions, shoes, footwear. Have the children place the words on the appropriate rungs.
   c. Start with the following word and go *up* the abstraction ladder: "Buffalo-head nickel." Do the same with other words.
   d. Start with the word "people" and go *down* the abstraction ladder.

8. Reports, inferences, and judgments are *different* kinds of information.
   a. Decide whether the following statements are reports, inferences, or judgments. (Sometimes a statement could be any of these three.)
      (1) Telling a lie is always wrong.
      (2) Mary doesn't like ice-cream.
      (3) He is a dirty stool pigeon.
      (4) Albert told me something yesterday which I discovered today was not correct.
      (5) Dennis didn't eat his spinach.
      (6) He's a nice guy.
      (7) She told the teacher that I did it.
      (8) He's a Communist.

b. Hand each child in the class a card with a single fact (report) written on it. Have the children write an inference based on the fact, and a judgment based on the inference. Encourage them to make their inferences and judgments as wild as possible. Have each child then read aloud his three successive statements and invite the rest of the class to criticize the inference and judgment which he invented. A typical trio of statements might be:

*Given Fact:*  Timmy kicked a dog.
*Inference:*   Timmy likes to kick dogs.
*Judgment:*    Timmy's a mean kid.

c. Have a few children put on a mock argument and fight in front of the class. Then each child should write a report of the event, attempting to use no inferences and no judgments. Exchange papers and criticize each other's paper.

9. A frequency curve is generally a better model for describing our environment than a two-valued syllogism.

a. A classroom or grade-level group can provide ample data for producing sample frequency curves: test scores, reading rates, running time for a 100-yard dash, height in inches, weight. A sample frequency chart follows:

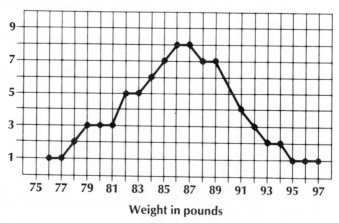

After making several frequency curves, ask the children what they have learned about people from the frequency curves.

b. Make frequency curves of natural phenomena: daily temperatures, yearly rainfall, number of grass blades in a two-inch square of grass, length of dandelion stems. After making several frequency curves, ask the children what they have learned about nature from the frequency curves.

c. Criticize these statements together. What kind of frequency curve might you make for some of them?

(1) Children are lazy.

(2) The weather is dreadful in .

(3) A person is either for America or against America.

(4) Roses are red
Violets are blue
Angels in heaven
Know I love you.

(5) Thinking people prefer Pell-mell Cigarettes.

(6) Doctors make a lot of money.

d. Before the children have learned about the frequency curve, tape record a discussion or a show and tell period. After they have learned about the frequency curve, listen to the tape together and count the number of times these words appear: all, every, always, only, never, same, merely. Discuss the disadvantages of these words.

\* \* \* \* \*

In this chapter we have examined some of the conditions which make perceptual distortion a continuous process for human beings. It was shown that our repertoire of words and grammatical patterns greatly influence our world view and our behavior. It was hypothesized, on the other hand, that wider use of the non-Aristotelian thinking encouraged by general semanticists would make it possible to control both our linguistic impulses and our subsequent behavior. To develop greater awareness in children, several classroom activities were suggested.

# REFERENCES

1. Brown, Roger W., "Language and Categories" *A Study of Thinking* edited by J. S. Bruner, *et al.* New York: John Wiley & Sons, 1956, 247-312.

2. Chase, Stewart, *Power of Words.* New York: Harcourt, Brace & World, Inc., 1954).

3. Embler, Weller, "Metaphor and Social Belief" *Language, Meaning and Maturity,* edited by S. I. Hayakawa. New York: Harper & Row, Publishers, 1954, 125-138.

4. Festinger, Leon, *A Theory of Cognitive Dissonance.* Evanston, Ill.: Row, Peterson, 1957.

5. Hayakawa, S. I., *Language in Thought and Action.* New York: Harcourt, Brace & World, Inc., 1949, reproduced by permission. By permission of George Allen & Unwin, Ltd., London.

6. ———, "Semantics, General Semantics, and Related Disciplines" *Language, Meaning and Maturity,* edited by S. I. Hayakawa. New York: Harper & Row, Publishers, 1954, 19-37.

7. Horowitz, E. L. and R. E. Horowitz, "Development of Social Attitudes in Children" *Sociometry* 1:301-338, 1938.

8. Jameson, Fenton (translator) "A Soviet Account of Semantics" *Language, Meaning and Maturity,* edited by S. I. Hayakawa. New York: Harper & Row, Publishers, 1954, 347-349.

9. Johnson, Wendall, *People in Quandaries: The Semantics of Personal Adjustment.* New York: Harper & Row, Publishers, 1946.

10. Kelley, Douglas M., foreword to an article by Alfred Korzybski *Language, Meaning and Maturity,* edited by S. I. Hayakawa. New York: Harper & Row, Publishers, 1954, 69-70.

11. Kirk, John R., "Communication Theory and Methods of Fixing Belief" *Language, Meaning and Maturity,* edited by S. I. Hayakawa. New York: Harper & Row, Publishers, 1954, 112-121.

12 Korzybski, Alfred, "A Veteran's Readjustment and Extensional Methods" *Language, Meaning and Maturity,* edited by S. I. Hayakawa. New York: Harper & Row, Publishers, 1954, 70-83.

13. ———, *Science and Sanity: An Introduction to Non-Aristotelian Systems and General Semantics.* Lancaster, Pa.: Science Press Printing Co., 1933.

14. Lee, D. Demetracopoulou, "Linguistic Reflection of Winteu Thought" *ETC* 5:174-181, 1948.

15. Leuba, Clarence and G. Lucas, "The Effects of Attitudes on Descriptions of Pictures" *Journal of Experimental Psychology* 35:517-524, 1945.

16. Lippman, Walter, *Public Opinion.* New York: Harcourt, Brace & World, 1922.

17. Lotz, John "Linguistics: Symbols Make Man" *Psycholinguistics,* edited by Sol Saporata. New York: Holt, Rinehart & Winston, Inc., 1961.

18. Meyers, Russell, " 'Reality' and 'Unreality' " *Language, Meaning and Maturity,* edited by S. I. Hayakawa. New York: Harper & Row, Publishers, 1954, 264-279.

19. Murray, H. A. "The Effect of Fear Upon Estimates of Maliciousness of Other Personalities," *Journal of Social Psychology* 4:310-329, 1933.

20. Newcomb, Theodore M., *Social Psychology.* New York: Holt, Rinehart & Winston, Inc., 1950.

21. Rapoport, Anatol, "What is Semantics" *Language, Meaning and Maturity,* edited by S. K. Hayakawa. New York: Harper & Row, Publishers, 1954, 3-18.

22. Rice, Stuart A., *Quantitative Methods in Politics.* New York: Alfred A. Knopf Inc., 1928.

23. Rogers, Raymond, "The Gonks and the Tiger," reprinted by permission of *ETC: A Review of General Semantics,* Vol. III, No. 2; copyright 1950, by the International Society for General Semantics.

24. Sapir, Edward, "The Status of Linguistics as a Science" *Language* 5:209-210, 1929.

25. Sherif, Muzafer, "A Study of Some Social Factors in Perception" *Archives Psychology* No. 187, 1935.

26. Weiss, Thomas M., "Additional Experimental Evidence Supporting Korzybskian Principles" *Science Education* 45:114-118, 1961.

27. Whorf, Benjamin Lee, "Language, Mind, and Reality" *ETC* 9:167-188, 1952.

28. ———, "Science and Linguistics" *Readings in Social Psychology,* edited by E. E. Maccoby, *et al.* New York: Holt, Rinehart & Winston, Inc., 1958, 1-9.

29. ———, "The Relation of Habitual Thought and Behavior to Language" *Language Meaning and Maturity,* edited by S. I. Hayakawa. New York: Harper & Row, Publishers, 1954, 225-251.

30. Young, Adrian "How Sane is 'Sane'?" *Language, Meaning and Maturity,* edited by S. I. Hayakawa. New York: Harper & Row, Publishers, 1954, 320-335.

# 5

# Thwarted Discussions
## (Group Dynamics vs. Group Dramatics)

> The face-to-face group working on a problem is the meet-
> ing ground of individual personality and society. It is in the
> group that personality is modified and socialized; and it is
> through the working of groups that society is changed and
> adapted to its times. (17:3)

Do you remember that first childhood gang or club you joined?
You know, the one in which you unblushingly vowed to keep all the
secrets, and defend each other to the death. Actually, that was your
introduction to adult society. For our society, along with nearly all
human societies is largely group-oriented. We might even say that
most of us never progress beyond the gang age, and this is often to
society's advantage. Social scientists and literary artists continually
provide us with the needed reminder that men are extremely inter-
dependent creatures, who owe their identity and very existence to
each other. Furthermore, it is fairly obvious that when men *do* cooperate in groups they can usually achieve far more than isolated
individuals.

Montague (13) cites several examples of how cooperation among
animals is quite common: White mice, if living with groups, will
grow stronger and faster than they will in isolation. Chimpanzees
will often pass food to each other through the cage bars. Goldfish
survive better in groups, and man generally cannot maintain mental

health without the feeling that he is a member of a group. Montague contends that since human relations are so important to man's health, it ought to be taught as the fourth "R" in school.

This chapter supports Montague's contention, and deals with one aspect of human relations: group problem solving. We will first discuss the need for group problem solving and some of the mistakes which groups make as they attempt to solve problems together. We will then examine a three-pronged attack on these problems: through the development of a listening attitude, through the encouragement of constructive roles which members can play in a group, and through following crucial steps in the problem solving procedure. Finally, some classroom activities, designed to encourage effective group-problem solving skills will be suggested.

## Need for Group Problem Solving

The question of the need for group problem solving can be disposed of quickly. Whether we like it or not, a good proportion of the problems in our society are tackled by committees. Those of us who spend several hours each week working with committees may wonder how such a Hydra-headed procedure could have evolved. We may even wonder if the survival-of-the-fittest theory really applies to social institutions. Nevertheless, under certain conditions small groups of people, working together on a common problem, are often capable of generating intelligent and useful solutions. It would be difficult to find a corporation or any other large institution which does not rely heavily on small-group conferences or committees. For some people, solving problems by themselves is a dull, meaningless, sometimes impossible task. Put these same people in a group and they frequently bubble forth with ideas. Exactly why this is so is difficult to say, but we do know that the group interaction has triggered the desirable response. Osborn (14) cites several studies which demonstrate the power of a group to stimulate ideas, providing the group is functioning harmoniously.

Harmonious functioning within a group is no easy task. The word "committee" has become a derogatory term to many people because of their disappointing experiences with group problem solving. The discussion terrain is pocked with craters, each one of which is capable of blocking progress toward agreement. Just consider the number of interconnections possible in a group discussion. With three people we have three different pairs or connections; with five people, ten connections; with fifteen people, 105 connections. The potential for short circuits is very great!

But let us agree at the outset that some short circuits are desirable —those which are caused by true disagreements based on differing values and experiences. Such differences are both inevitable and useful—useful in achieving balance in a decision, in stimulating thought, and in challenging unfounded prejudices. What we're going to talk about now are the unnecessary short circuits caused by inappropriate habits acquired by years of untrained group problem solving involvement.

## Mistakes Groups Make

One of the most energetic attempts to study people involved in group discussions has been performed by Irving J. Lee (10). Over a ten year period Lee observed over 200 groups in action, most of which were engaged in staff, board, and committee meetings in private businesses, military organizations, and community agencies. He and his co-workers categorized the difficulties which occurred in these meetings and found that some of them were rather consistent. In the following scene your writer will attempt to portray some of these difficulties in exaggerated form.

*Principal:*　All right now, I've got something I want you to make a decision on, and it's got to be done soon or we'll all be in trouble.

*Sam:*　I didn't do it! (rest of faculty laughs.)

*Principal:*　OK now, this is serious business. We've got to decide once and for all how we're going to punish these kids who smoke on the school grounds.

*Mary:*　This is the same problem we had last year. Why don't we just expel them and get it over with.

*John:*　Don't be silly. You know the parents would be up in arms if we did that.

*Alice:*　If you ask me we should just ignore them. They're not hurting us by smoking.

*Principal:* I suppose you think I'm an old fuss-budget, Alice, but I might remind you that the people have given us the responsibility for educating these kids, and we have a moral duty to punish them for wrongdoing.

*Pete:* You bet!

*Albert:* Now, people, before you get all steamed up over this, let's consider this problem in a rational, logical way. Now, you know as well as I do why these kids like to smoke on the school grounds. The truth is that they're trying to get even with us for all the restrictions placed on them. We also know that we're a bunch of fools if we let them get away with breaking our smoking rule. If they get away with this one, they'll try to break them all. It's also quite clear that we can't expel them. There's only one alternative. What does a cop do when he catches you guys speeding? He socks you with a fine. And that's the only logical thing to do with these kids. Fine them two or three bucks every time we catch them.

*Jim:* Al might have a good idea there, although the fine may be a little stiff.

*Joan:* Maybe the students should decide on the fine in a democratic way.

*John:* That's not democracy, that's anarchy!

*Phil:* Did you hear about the fine that Mary got yesterday?

*Mary:* How'd you hear about that? (Laughter from rest of faculty)

*Principal:* Let's stick to the problem. How are we going to punish these kids?

*Alice:* I still don't see why we have to punish them.

*Jim:* Maybe Alice has a point we should consider.

*Bob:* I think that two or three bucks isn't enough of a fine. Some of these rich kids carry a billfold fatter than . . . than . . .

*Leona:* What about the poor kids. Where are they going to get two dollars?

*Bob:* They can earn it like I did when I was a kid.

*Sam:*       How often did you have to pay the fine? (Laughter from faculty)

*Bob:*       I didn't smoke then and I don't now. I say the fine should be at least five dollars.

*Albert:*    Now folks, let's talk about this in a reasonable manner. We all know that some kids couldn't afford five dollars and some could afford a lot more. Let's keep the fine reasonable. As I said before two or three bucks would be about right for most kids.

*Ted:*       Do we have any information on allowances or earnings of our students? This might help us decide.

*Janet:*     I just did a study with my class the other day. We're studying economics and the students are making a budget. The average allowance in our class was $1.65, but the range was all the way from nothing to ten dollars a week.

*John:*      I don't see how that helps us very much. That's only one class. Besides I don't think a fine would work anyway. We're just giving ourselves bookkeeping problems.

*Principal:* Well, we've got to find some punishment. This violation of the rules has gone on too long already.

*Mary:*      Same old problem as we've always had. If you'd expel a few kids we'd be rid of this problem once and for all.

*Ted:*       I wonder if this isn't a new problem. Has it always been this bad? Maybe something's going on which we haven't noticed.

*Fred:*      I think five dollars is too much. I think three is the most we should take from them.

*Phil:*      (to person next to him) Did you see that wild tie Fred's wearing today? (rest of faculty overhears and looks at Fred's tie)

*Sam:*       Where are you going to spend the money you take from them, Fred? (laughter from faculty)

*Principal:* We're getting nowhere this way. Now who has another idea. Or do you want to vote on the fine? (chorus of no's and yes's from faculty followed by an embarrassing silence.)

| | |
|---|---|
| *Fred:* | (filling the gap) I'm sure we can think of something that's fair to the children. |
| *John:* | Who cares about being fair? That's just appeasement! Are they fair to us—sneaking around here disobeying rules. |
| *Fred:* | I'm not trying to appease anyone! |
| *John:* | Of course you are when you talk that way! |
| *Fred:* | All I said was let's be fair! |
| *John:* | But you meant appeasement! |
| *Fred:* | I most certainly did not! |
| *Albert:* | Now, ladies and gentlemen, let's go about this in a logical and non-emotional way. We all know . . . |
| *Principal:* | We've got to solve this problem now or we're . . . |
| *Alice:* | I don't see what the problem is. These kids are just . . . |
| *Mary:* | There's only one way to . . . |
| *Principal:* | (Everyone talking at once) Quiet!! |

What kinds of mistakes do people make in group problem solving situations? Undoubtedly you were reminded of several of them while observing the preceding scene. In Lee's study he found that groups who were having difficulties made these mistakes:

1. Not really listening to each other. (Notice how Bob's first comment indicates that several contributions went by him while he was preparing his statement. John, on the other hand, listened only to words and not feelings. He made the untenable assumption, as demonstrated in Chapter 4, that other people use words exactly the same way he does.)

2. Assuming that another person is a fool if his opinion differs from yours. (John made this assumption several times. Albert actually stated that they were all fools if they did not agree with him.)

3. Jumping to solutions before carefully analyzing the problem. (The principal made the first error in this respect by introducing a solution in his problem. His problem was the violation of the smoking rule, not the punishment of the students; punishment was only one type of solution. Moreover, none of the other group members asked for analysis of the problem, preferring instead to latch on to a ready solution.)

4. Arguing over whether the problem is an old one or new one.

(Mary saw the smoking problem only in the light of past experience with it. She wasn't interested in examining any new elements.)

5. Ignoring the possibility of compromise. (Albert was the only one willing to compromise on the size of the fine, but only because a compromise would coincide with his previous bias.)

6. Labeling other people or their ideas. (John was a master at this. His "silly" and "anarchy" labels received no violent reactions, but his "appeasement" label broke up the meeting.)

7. Leader telling others what to think and do. (The principal made it clear several times what *he* wanted them to do and that *he* thought the students should be punished. Only one brave non-punisher spoke up.)

8. Leader acting too business-like, discouraging amusement or expressions of seemingly irrelevant feelings. (Sam tried to bring in a little light-heartedness, but "Princ" was too princely to enjoy it.)

9. Perceiving difference of opinion as a personal attack. (The principal treated the first remark by Alice as a personal insult.)

How can these types of mistakes be avoided? Are there any ways of insuring against such short circuits in the group communication process? Students of group dynamics, general semantics, and client-centered psychotherapy seem to think so. Examination of their reports and classroom experimentation lead the author to suggest three interrelated approaches toward improvement of group problem solving. One of these is the development of a "listening attitude." A second approach is the encouragement of constructive roles, and a third one is the use of systematic steps in the solution of a problem.

## Listening Attitude

It is not difficult to agree with Chase (5:165) that "Americans are not very good listeners in face-to-face groups." But what are the reasons for this inability? Chase blames it on the competition which pervades our culture, making self-expression a virtue even if nothing worthwhile is expressed. As an antidote, he suggests an active form, or what might be called a creative form, of listening. As one listens to another he asks these questions of himself:

What is he trying to say?
What can I gain from what he is saying?
How does he know what he says?
What has he left out?
What are his motives?

Chase's notion of competition in the United States conflicts with that of Lloyd's notion (11:104) of the "quietmouth American." "The quietmouth American avoids intellectual friction and seeks agreement. Where he has opinions, he drifts into the company of those who agree, and out of the company of those who differ." Such people listen only to those with similar views and consider disagreement as a personal affront. If they can't withdraw from the scene they attack the other person with emotional arguments and generate a good-sized hatred for him in the process.

Probably the observations of both Chase and Lloyd are valid for certain people in certain situations. One can very likely find both types of listening inhibitors in most any group, and perhaps the best defense against them in ourselves is to recognize and compensate for them. But are there other reasons for our listening difficulties? Roethlisberger (15) thinks that the problem lies in our faulty perception of communication. One view of communication, call it View A, contends that the goal of discussion is to reach agreement. The other view, call it View B, is that the purpose of discussion is to express and accept differences of opinion. View A leads to explaining and telling, whereas View B leads to expressing and accepting differences. View A assumes that you understand the other person, but he simply does not understand you. View B assumes that you may *not* understand the other person and that the only way to achieve understanding is to identify with him. Only the rational side of man is considered in View A; View B is concerned with both rational and emotional aspects of man. View A leads to defensiveness; View B, to tolerance. Certainly, View B is the more difficult frame of reference, but it seems likely that it is a more fruitful one— one which could generate not only good feelings but also a type of agreement which View A could never achieve.

Rogers (16:83) suggests another cause of poor listening: ". . . the major barrier to mutual interpersonal communication is our very natural tendency to judge, to evaluate, to approve or disapprove, the statement of the other person, or the other group." In other words, we tend to respond to other people's statements in terms of "good" or "bad." Whether or not this tendency is a "natural" one, however, is a moot point; probably it is a trained tendency beginning with the rejection and acceptance of early childhood behavior. And if it is a trained tendency, it can probably be untrained. Rogers, himself, has trained his own behavior in psychotherapeutic sessions to conform to a non-judgmental figure, empathizing with the patient, accepting him as a valuable person, and listening for his feelings rather than his words. Such empathy requires great courage, because our own views may be changed in the process. But such empathy can be learned, and Rogers has demonstrated this by training many of his students to listen in a non-evaluative way. In a normal, group problem solving situation, of course, it is doubtful that anyone would have enough energy to empathize completely with everyone in the group. But a pervasive, non-judgmental atmosphere would surely alleviate much of the tension and misunderstanding which can occur in a discussion.

Both Lee (10) and Hayakawa (6) feel that language confusion is a major barrier to adequate listening. The listener is often not aware, for example, that a speaker may be using a word which has both a factual and judgmental meaning. The speaker, for instance, may use the word "Negro" to describe the racial heritage of an individual. A "listener," however, may assume that the speaker was using the word in a derogatory sense. Thus, having ears, he hears not.

Hayakawa reminds us that some words are almost totally affective in their connotations—filthy, sly, nice. Yet we sometimes act as though these words were informative in nature. "He's a sly one," says Charlie. "On the contrary," says Benny, "he's perfectly straight-forward." And they're off on a verbal tussle which can only be stopped by a referee with a device for measuring precise degrees of slyness. If Benny had listened for Charlie's feelings rather than his words, if he had listened for what *Charlie* meant rather than what his *words* meant, the useless verbal scuffle could have been avoided.

Another language trap in discussions is the hyper-generalization phenomenon mentioned in Chapter Four. Benny begins the conflict this time by asserting that "Those guys in the Phixel Department can't be trusted!" (Benny hasn't read Chapter Four yet.) Charlie (who hasn't read *this* chapter yet) parries with something like "They're the most trustworthy guys in this outfit." Charlie and Benny, of course, are failing to recognize that each person has a different set of details in mind. But even if Benny is not up on his general semantics, Charlie could have saved the day by listening to Benny's feelings and by then responding with something similar to "What particular incidents make you feel they can't be trusted?" In other words, when faced with hyper-generalization, the listener who is intent on understanding can ask for details.

Suppose, however, that you have been a good listener and now feel that you understand another's point of view. But you don't like his view and wish to express your disagreement. How should you go about disagreeing with him? One way would be to attach a stigma to him or to his idea; labels such as "communistic, silly, appeaser, irrational, woolly thinking," are handy for this purpose. But of course the results of labeling are usually disastrous. The subject of discussion is usually changed to whether or not the label applies, sides are taken, side conversations flourish, and the flow of blood to the brain is cut off, thus creating an aggregate of sub-humans grunting and gesticulating at each other.

Obviously if one wishes to criticize another's point of view it is best to avoid labels. And it is also best to avoid a lordly posture. As Lee (10:109) says, "A man's resistance to criticism will be inversely proportional to the critic's assurance that he is not trying to show his superiority by making the criticism." Lee recommends an interrogative statement such as "There's a great deal to be said in favor of your view, but don't you think . . . ?" (Ben Franklin recommends this same technique in his autobiography.) Lee asked several groups to try this technique whenever they wished to criticize each other; he found that the resulting harmony was remarkable.

Lee also found several patterns of disagreement in his study. The five major patterns were these:

1. The inquiry-investigative attitude, e.g., "No, I don't believe that, but will you explain why you do?"

2. The air of incredulity—listens grudgingly to another, e.g., "I can't see how you could possibly disagree, but I'll let you talk."

3. The inclination to laughter—listens for amusement only.

4. The expression of suspicion and distrust, e.g., "What's in it for you?"

5. The mood of dismissal, e.g., "I refuse to listen to any more of this nonsense."

The inquiry-investigative pattern usually led to reasonably harmonious discussion, whereas the other patterns produced discord.

The listening role, then, is a very responsible one, requiring empathy, tolerance, and tact. Uniformity is not the goal of fruitful discussions. Our concern should not be to discourage disagreement but to get people to listen to each other well enough to know what they are disagreeing about.

## Needs and Roles of Group Members

A second approach toward improvement of group problem solving is to encourage those roles of group members which facilitate open discussion. What roles are needed? This question can be best answered by looking at the needs which a problem solving group has.

In addition to Lee's study several studies of group processes have been carried on since 1947 at the National Training Laboratory in Group Development, sponsored by the National Education Association and the Research Center for Group Dynamics.* Bradford (2), Chase (4), and Jenkins (9), among others, have reported on these studies. Their findings will be summarized in the following paragraphs.

Problem solving groups are both task oriented and personnel oriented. This is necessarily so since they are composed of human beings, who naturally have both intellectual and social-emotional needs.

The task orientation of a group requires one or more individuals who establish directions, that is, there is need for one or more *goal setters*. A group is quickly frustrated if they lack a sense of direction. This sense of direction is enhanced if one or more members perform the role of *clarifying* the goal and of *summarizing* the progress of the group. As solutions are sought someone needs to take the role of *interrogator*—asking for information or clarification. Others need to perform the role of expert—providing information or

---

* The Research Center is now located at the University of Michigan.

opinions based on experience. Keeping a group moving in a task-oriented direction requires the services of a *standard-setter*—one who reminds the group of its goal and urges a high-quality decision.

The personnel orientation of a group requires at least one person who *provides recognition* to group members by supporting their contributions and encouraging participation of those who have not yet contributed to the discussion. This person might also encourage members by asking for more details or by reflecting their feelings. The need for security and tension relief may demand both a *pacifier* and a *wit*.

All of these necessary roles cannot be handled by a single individual. Perhaps the ideal setting is one in which every group member is aware of all necessary roles and performs that role which is presently being ignored. A more realistic setting would be one in which the chairman asks individuals to take those roles which are being ignored.

Unfortunately some group members play roles which are far from helpful either in the process of developing group morale or in the process of solving a problem. Some play the role of *distractor* or *playboy,* making side comments or otherwise displaying their lack of interest in the discussion. In our scene of a faculty discussion, for example, Phil veered the group off its course by calling attention to Mary's fine and Fred's tie. The role of distractor, however, should not be confused with that of the conciliatory wit (such as Sam), who strives to distract the group temporarily from its emotional tension.

Another common role is that of *dominator* or *dictator.* Both Albert and the principal played this role, although each had his own special techniques. The principal used his authority as "boss" to rigidly establish the question to be discussed and the manner in which it was to be discussed. Albert tried to dominate in a slightly more subtle way by insinuating that anyone who disagreed with his solution must be illogical, unreasonable, and foolish. He also managed to speak the most number of words in the play, although the principal was a close second.

An even more disruptive role, perhaps, is that of *sniper* or *aggressor.* This person shoots from the hip with a pistol loaded with scorn. He finds nothing good about any idea and makes it his duty to inform individual contributors or the group as a whole that their ideas are useless, silly, communistic, etc. Like John, they tear down rather than support; they listen for words that can be used as ammunition against the enemy—which appears to be nearly everyone who expresses a thought.

All of us have seen people play these destructive roles, at least in a mild form; and occasionally we may even play them ourselves. No doubt these roles would add spice to a Broadway play, but they're hardly helpful in solving problems. But how can a group diminish the occurrence or effects of such destructive behavior? One way is to counteract it with constructive roles such as pacifier and recognition giver. These roles can be taken by the group leader, or other members who naturally play them whenever they are in a group; or they can be assigned to members by the chairman.

Another way is to agree as a group that the destructive roles are undesirable and people playing them should not be rewarded. Studies at the National Training Laboratory indicate that group members, once they discover the source of dominating and disruptive behavior, develop a variety of ways of discouraging it. Naturally, this course of action requires a group that is conscious of group dynamics and one which is willing to examine and improve its behavior.

The following table summarizes the types of roles which can often be seen in a group discussion. This table was derived from a study done by Heyns (8) of several conferences in industrial plants.

## PROBLEM-SOLVING PATTERNS

| Role | Description |
|---|---|
| Reality tester | Sets goals |
| | Proposes problems |
| | Clarifies |
| Expert | Gives information |
| Interrogator | Seeks information |
| | Seeks clarification |
| Idea man | Proposes solutions |
| Goal reminder | Sets goals |
| | Seeks summary |
| | Gives summary |
| Distractor | Behaves in non-problem-directed ways |
| Passive participant | Opposes |
| | Supports |

### INTERPERSONAL PATTERNS

| Role | Description |
|------|-------------|
| Rejector | Dismisses and ignores contributions |
| Supporter | Reacts in positive way to contributions |
| Social oiler | Reduces frictions |
| | Aids cooperation |
| Isolate | Says nothing |
| | Is ignored |
| Dictator | Tries to dominate others |

## Problem-Solving Steps

A third approach toward improvement of group problem solving is to attempt to follow certain steps in a fairly systematic fashion. Barnlund and Haiman (1) suggest the following steps in a full-fledged discussion:

1. Ventilating feelings; warming up to problem and group.
2. Clarifying problem to work on.
3. Finding information.
4. Proposing solutions.
5. Evaluating solutions and their implications.
6. Making a decision.

Bradford's experience (2) with the National Training Laboratory in Group Development leads him to recommend similar steps:

1. Stating problem.
2. Clarifying problem.
3. Keeping discussion on the beam.
4. Summarizing.
5. Testing consequences of emerging decision.
6. Checking commitment of group.
7. Making a decision.

Brilhart and Jochem (3) made a careful study of the effects of systematic steps in group problem solving. In their study 135 college students were randomly assigned to groups of five and led by trained leaders who used three different discussion patterns. These patterns, rotated in order to avoid sequential bias, were as follows:

*Pattern A:*

1. Clarified the problem—five minutes.

2. Brainstormed for solutions (judgments withheld)—ten minutes.

3. Suggested criteria by which the'best solution could be selected —five minutes.

4. Rated each idea on a four point scale—ten minutes.

5. Selected best solution—maximum of five minutes.

*Pattern B:* inversion of steps two and three (criteria developed before brainstorming for solutions).

*Pattern C:*

1. Clarified problem—five minutes.

2. Discussed solutions without withholding judgments—25 minutes.

3. Selected best solution—maximum of five minutes.

Patterns A and B yielded fifty per cent more ideas than Pattern C, while judges estimated that Pattern A yielded the most "good" ideas. The subjects tended to prefer Pattern B the least and the other two patterns equally well. The optimum pattern, then, would be Pattern A, which is the one which your author recommends, with one modification: the clarification step should be extensive enough to include Barnlund and Haiman's step of "ventilating feelings" whenever this appears necessary.

## Clarification of Problem

A lengthy period on clarification may seem to be a waste of time, but research at the National Training Laboratory (9) indicates that groups who side-step this stage of the discussion must eventually come back to it, after wasting much time considering solutions which do not apply to the problem.

In Lee's study (10) he found that most discussion participants tend to be solution oriented rather than problem oriented. In our faculty scene the "solutions" began to pop immediately after the principal expressed what he thought to be the problem. No consideration was given to whether or not people understood the problem or even agreed that it was a problem. Perhaps you have witnessed scenes similar to that one.

In my own observations of groups, solution orientation has appeared to result in the following types of behavior:

1. Not listening to each other. (I'm so anxious for them to hear my solution.)

2. Insulting each other. (That's the quickest way to dispose of his idea.)

3. Talking about two or three entirely different problems. (If my solution doesn't fit the first problem, I'll make up another problem.)

4. Seeking status. (My solution is better than yours.)

5. Twisting another person's idea to fit one's own solution. (I agree with Harry, because . . . Harry is momentarily flattered until he realizes he's been had.)

6. Over-generalizing. (I know my idea will work because all children are blah, blah, blah.)

7. Interrupting others. (Why waste time listening to him when my idea is much better.)

8. Defending idea on the basis of logic, intelligence, etc. (Certainly the only logical way of handling this is to . . .)

9. Repeating an idea. (They're too stupid to realize the virtue of my idea; I'll have to tell them again . . . and again . . . and again.)

In contrast to solution-centered groups, problem-centered groups tend to begin by asking questions about the problem, rephrasing it, making sure they understand it, sometimes breaking it into smaller, more manageable segments. They are more inclined to listen to each other and ask each other questions. Their voices are softer and show much less emotion. Members of the group support each other even though they are quite frank in their disagreements. Humorous comments are often expressed but the group is not distracted from the problem at hand.

Lee (10) found that the "old-problem" vs. "new-problem" controversy was avoided when groups were problem oriented. Solution orientation, on the other hand, frequently encouraged the "old-timers" to insist that "this is the same old problem we had before" and then to offer the same old solution. The "young bucks" would then insist that "this is a new problem and demands new solutions." Lee recommends that groups develop the habit of first asking "What is it that has gone wrong?" rather than "What should we do about it?" He also suggests that group members first tell what they *know*, before they prescribe remedies. With some groups the chairman may have to ask the members to withhold remedies until he calls for them. In general the group should act as if they were doctors thoroughly diagnosing a "case" before making a judgment on the proper treatment.

According to Maier (12), problems can be located either within individuals, groups, or situations. Although the tendency is to attack the problem from an individual standpoint ("Old so-and-so keeps messing up things by . . .") or from a group standpoint ("Those high school kids just can't be trusted to . . ."), generally a more useful approach is from a situation standpoint ("What does the situation seem to be? What is the evidence?") Having clarified the *situation*, the group is then ready to consider solutions.

Sometimes it is very difficult for a group to become problem oriented because of the nature of the problem presented to them. For one thing the problem may be too broad. A problem such as "How can we achieve better discipline in the classroom?" is difficult for a group to sink its teeth into. When a group is faced with such a broad problem, it should first spend a considerable amount of time breaking up the problem into bite-sized morsels.

Sometimes the very wording of the problem defeats a problem orientation. The solution may be imbedded in the question. For example, "How can we punish these kids who are smoking on the schoolgrounds?" Or even worse, "What kind of fine should we impose on these kids who are smoking on the schoolgrounds?" Questions such as these naturally invite solution orientation. The group must either back up to a consideration of the situation which invoked such a question, or plunge into a solution-centered quagmire.

Barlund and Haiman (1) suggest that open-ended questions are better than yes-no questions. "What is the nature and extent of rule infringement on our schoolgrounds?" is a more useful question than "Is rule infringement on the schoolgrounds increasing?" According to Barlund and Haiman, open-ended questions are more likely to lead to a spirit of inquiry and a creative discussion, whereas a yes-no question often results in an argumentative discussion.

Of course, the question considered by a group should not be devoid of controversy and emotion. One of Thelan's principles (17) of effective group procedures is the "principle of external demand," which simply means that group members should be emotionally involved in the question enough to consider it worthy of discussion. Heisler, Smedling, and Campbell (7) learned this lesson in their attempt to teach principles of group discussion to their junior high students. At first the questions given to them were so academic the students treated the discussion sessions as recitation periods with one student asking questions and the other reciting the answers. When the teachers provided the small groups with controversial questions dealing with comic book reading, brother and sister relationships, etc., the learning of discussion techniques began to take place.

Sometimes the only way to encourage a problem orientation is to agree on discussion procedures before the discussion begins. This agreement may be especially necessary with groups of strangers; it certainly would be necessary with groups who are consistently too solution-oriented.

## Ideation

After the group has remained problem-oriented long enough to define and clarify a problem to work on, the temptation may be to shift gears and become solution-oriented. It appears more profitable, however, to shift from problem orientation to idea orientation. As you recall, Brilhart and Jochem's study (3) demonstrated that the most effective pattern is to move from problem clarification, to idea production *without judging ideas*, and finally to the selection of a solution.

Why is it important to withhold judgment at this point? Osborn (14) uses the analogy of mixing hot water (criticism) and cold water (creative ideas); the result is only lukewarm. If a person's idea is criticized as soon as it is offered to the group, his reaction is usually to defend it or to refrain from making any further comment. If this pattern continues within the group, ideas and thinking soon dry up; emotion, apathy, and timidity take over.

Parnes and Meadow (15) have instigated several studies of groups and individuals in which deferment of judgment was the independent variable. In each study the same results were obtained: When judgment of ideas was deferred until after the "brainstorming" period, not only *more* ideas were generated, more *high-quality* ideas were produced.

Which set of directions do you think would produce the greatest number of high-quality ideas? (Assume the same time limit under each set of directions.)

A. List as many uses as you can for one or more buttons. Do not worry about how good your ideas are. List any idea that comes to your mind. *Quantity* is wanted!

B. List as many *good* uses as you can for one or more buttons. Make sure you list only your *good* ideas, not just any idea that comes to your mind. *Quality* is wanted!

Parnes and Meadow found that set A consistently resulted in more high-quality ideas, as designated by judges who were not informed of the directions given. Your author has frequently made the same comparison with graduate student groups for illustrative purposes and found the same results. (Again the judges were not aware of the directions given.)

What this means for group discussion, then, is that procedural rules will have to be established which will promote deferment of judgment until the ideation session is over. Osborn (14) suggests the following rules for groups to follow:

1. Criticism is ruled out: Criticism is reserved for a later screening session.

2. The wilder the ideas, the better: Even "off-beat," impractical suggestions may "trigger" in other group members practical suggestions which might not otherwise occur to them.

3. Quantity is wanted: The greater the number of ideas, the greater likelihood of winners.

4. Combination and improvement are sought: Improvements by others on an idea give better ideas. Combining ideas leads to more and better ideas.

It might be advisable, though, to add a fifth rule that "side conversations should not be indulged in during the brainstorming period." Side conversations may cause others to think that their ideas are secretly being criticized. Of course, the ideas will have to be recorded on a chalkboard so that the group can select the "best" one later on, and also so that new ideas can be built upon previous ideas. If the group is not familiar with brainstorming, it is advisable to practice first on a brief make-believe problem.

Another method of generating ideas is called "role playing." This child-like game has been used by some very "sophisticated" people and has been found to be quite useful (18). Although it is probably a technique to be used quite sparingly (4), it may be the one which suggests the appropriate solution for a knotty problem. Suppose, for example, the problem is to find an effective way of talking to high school students who are breaking the No Smoking rule. Several people in succession could briefly play the role of adult or student, in that way creating and testing a variety of ideas. (A by-product might be a better understanding of the students.)

Other means of getting ideas include the common but useful devices of calling in experts, hearing reports of studies, and sharing experiences. All of these are probably most effective, however, if utilized within an atmosphere of idea production rather than solution production.

## Selection and Evaluation

Having generated a large number of alternatives, the group is then ready for the sometimes difficult task of selecting the most useful solution. Even now, however, it is doubtful that solution orientation is very useful. It will probably be more fruitful at this point to become criteria-oriented. "What criteria should we develop which will help us select from among the alternatives?" or "What criteria do we now have for this type of problem and solution?" At this juncture creative (original, divergent) thinking becomes somewhat subservient to critical (convergent, analytical) thinking. Agreement must be reached on the selection criteria and these, then, be applied systematically to the previously generated ideas. And here is where the listening attitude and the constructive roles must really be applied! But if the ideas are now on the board and not presently coming forth from the lips of compatriots, it is amazing how much simpler it is to be critical without offending each other. Sometimes, though, it helps to stop the discussion after the brainstorming session and allow a period of time to intervene before meeting again (14). This, of course, allows people to forget who made what contribution and to become more detached about their own ideas.

It is sometimes difficult for people to develop selection criteria with cutting edges. The first attempt at this task may produce fuzzy, non-definitive criteria such as "Must be practical" or "Must be possible." If selection criteria are to be capable of helping the group retain some ideas and throw away others, they must be considerably more specific. The group leader can help things along by suggesting a specific criterion such as "Must not penalize children from economically deprived families more than children from wealthy families."

After the criteria have been developed and agreed upon, the group is ready to select the one solution which they feel should be applied to the problem. This one solution often becomes obvious to the group as they are agreeing upon selection criteria. If the solution is not obvious, however, then the criteria need to be systematically applied to each idea developed during the ideation period. The group may wish to rate each idea individually on a five-point scale or place them in rank order, although reasonable success can be obtained by gradually weeding out the weakest ideas until a consensus is reached. Usually a consensus is more desirable than a vote, since a vote tends to split the group into factions and may even make it difficult to implement the decision. Whether consensus or voting is used depends on the urgency of an immediate decision, the emotional involvement of the group, and other situational factors.

The Quakers utilize consensus almost exclusively as do several industrial concerns (4). They have found that the long-run advantages are such that consensus is worth waiting for even if the expedient procedure would require a vote. If consensus is not reached and anger is creeping into the discussion, the Quakers usually invoke a period of silence. (A wonderful device, but most people seem to be afraid of it.) If the silence interval doesn't work, the discussion is ended and a "cooling-off period" ensues. After people have had time to think some more, the issue is considered again. (Would that all of us could be so patient.)

Whatever device is used to reach a decision, there remains the task of implementing the decision and evaluating the results. If at all possible, contrary to usual procedures, the means of evaluation should be agreed upon before the actual implementation. In other words it is helpful to ask ahead of time "How will we know if we have been successful or not?" This question is quite a common one to natural and social scientists, but it seems to be less often raised among action groups, perhaps because of the hidden assumption that whatever *We* decide to do is bound to work. Sometimes the answer to the question is obvious, e. g., "There should be less smoking on the school grounds." But other times the answer may involve a discussion almost as lengthy—alas, as the preceding one.

Yet, the question must be answered if the group is to avoid the attitude of "throw a life preserver to a drowning man but run away before you see where it lands."

## Classroom Activities

The classroom provides an excellent laboratory for discovering principles of effective group discussion. Whether the following types of activities are used under the guise of "language arts" or "social studies" is not important. What is important is that children begin to learn at an early age—it's much harder later, the listening attitude, the constructive roles, and the problem solving steps which make group decision making an effective procedure.

### *Listening Attitude*

1. Carry on a discussion in which each person has to repeat the essence of the previous discussant's remarks before making his own contribution.

2. Show how people differ on their perceptions of "reality" by asking them to relate what is happening in an ambiguous picture. Discuss the naturalness of differing perceptions; help them learn to expect these differences.

3. Enact a brief dramatic episode (parts can be read) in which differing opinions on a school rule are expressed. Have the audience listen for the different opinions and attempt to describe them after the skit. See if they can explain why people might have these differing views. A partial skit follows:

| | |
|---|---|
| *Mary Fasteater:* | I think we should be able to go out for recess as soon as we're through eating. |
| *Jimmy Sloweater:* | Nah. That's no good. Then everyone would gobble down his food. |
| *Johnny Sportster:* | No we wouldn't. And besides, who wants to sit around in here until twenty after twelve when the sun's shining. |
| *Jimmy Sloweater:* | Yea, but the guys who gobble up their food would get the best playing field. |

*Nancy Stayin:*     I don't see what difference it makes. If people want to gobble their food and run around right away and get all sick, let them.

*Sam Jimmylover:*   I don't think it's fair for some people to get to go out before the rest of us do. We have a right to get the best playing field too.

4. Ask two children to perform the roles of "reader" and "listener." A statement is read and the listener has to decide on the feelings expressed and state them. The reader might say, for example, "Old Johnny Smith is a snake in the grass!" The listener might then say, "You're angry with him." Or the reader might say, "I wonder why Mother's taking so long." The listener might decide to say, "You're tired of waiting," or "You're anxious to get there." Discuss the difference between the words expressed and the feelings expressed.

## Constructive Roles

1. Assign the following roles to seven people:
   a. *Dictator*—be bossy but not mean. Talk more than anyone else. Try to get the group to agree with your idea. Keep explaining to them why your idea is best. (Assign two people to this role.)
   b. *Sniper*—criticize everyone's idea. Use words like "stupid, silly, ridiculous." Keep finding things wrong with what the group is trying to do.
   c. *Expert*—give ideas and facts to the group in a quiet, friendly way.
   d. *Peacemaker*—tell others that you like their ideas. When two people are arguing try to show how they really do agree on some things. If arguments continue try to make a funny remark to make the group laugh and relax.
   e. *Organizer*—help group understand the problem. Explain what people are saying when they are not clear or ask them to explain. Summarize what has been said every few minutes. Try to find out what other people know.
   f. *Clown*—try to draw attention to yourself by saying or doing silly things. Pay no attention to the discussion.

Have each actor keep his role a secret. Write the names of the roles on the board and explain each one. Then let the group of seven actors discuss a controversial subject in front of the room. (For further reference it would be best to tape record the discussion.) After about ten minutes let the audience guess each actor's role. Discuss the effects of each role on the progress of the discussion.

2. Same as number one with a different topic and a different set of actors. Eliminate clown role. Discuss effects of omitting clown.

3. Same as number one with a different topic and a different set of actors. Omit clown and sniper. Assign two dominators, one peacemaker, two experts, and two organizers. Discuss the effects of this composition.

4. Have five to eight students carry on a discussion over a lively issue in front of the room. Do not assign roles. Assign two or three observers for each one of the discussants. After the discussion see if the observers can agree on the role or roles which each discussant naturally played.

5. Break the class into several groups of six each. Put six roles numbered from one to six on the board. (Exclude Clown and include two Dictators.) Have the groups count off so that each person has a role. Assign the same controversial issue to each group and have them begin their discussions. In two minutes give a signal which indicates that each person is to shift roles— role 4 to role 5, role 5 to role 6, role 6 to role 1, etc. Give the signal to change every two minutes until everyone has played all of the roles.

## Problem-Solving Steps

1. Assign a small group to discuss a controversial topic in another room, using this set of instructions:

### Technique A

A problem that is carefully defined is almost solved!

Step 1: Spend about half of your time defining your problem; change it if necessary; reword it; make sure everyone agrees on the nature of the problem.

Step 2: Discuss several different ways of solving the problem.

Step 3: Summarize your areas of agreement and disagreement.

Tape record the discussion. Assign another group to discuss the same topic in a private room, using this set of instructions:

Technique B

Step 1: Don't beat around the bush; get to some answers immediately.

Step 2: Develop your own solution and plug for it vigorously.

Step 3: Try to get others to agree with your solution.

Tape record the discussion. Have the entire class listen to the two recordings and discuss the effects of the two different sets of instructions. Discuss the need for problem orientation rather than solution orientation.

2. Have the class define and clarify such problems as these: (break them up into sets of smaller problems, reword them, etc.)
   a. How can we improve the lunch room?
   b. How can we earn money?
   c. What should we do for a Christmas party?

3. Ask the class to criticize such discussion topics as these:
   a. How can we punish children who run in the hall?
   b. What is the best source of information for a report?
   c. Should those big, bossy sixth graders be allowed to use the swings when the third graders want them?

4. When conflict arises in the classroom or on the playground try to get the children involved to describe the *situation* to the entire class. Then ask the class to think of ways of changing the *situation* so that the conflict does not arise again. Establish the rule that anyone who joins the discussion cannot take sides; only details and ideas are accepted. Train them to be situation-minded. (This will not be easy at first.)

5. Establish rules for brainstorming and practice with such questions as these:
   a. How can we make the room more attractive?
   b. What are some games which can be played outdoors during recess?
   c. What are some ideas for an ideal school?

d. What are some ways of stopping wars?
e. What are some sources of information we could use for our study of the Spanish explorers?
f. How can you help a child who seems to have no friends?
6. Use role playing to get ideas for such problems as these:
   a. One child has been monopolizing a favorite piece of playground equipment. How can you get him to share it?
   b. You have broken something which belongs to someone else. How should you tell him about it?
   c. You would like some information from the Mayor. How should you ask him for it?
7. Develop selection criteria which will be used after a brainstorming session to select the best idea. Suggest a specific criterion in order to provide them with a good example.
8. Try to reach consensus on solutions to some of the classroom problems. Discuss the relative values of reaching consensus and voting.
9. Carry on several full-scale discussions in which all steps are utilized. Then divide class into small groups for this purpose. Ask each group to report back on their success or difficulties. Have the rest of the class offer suggestions to a group having difficulties.

\*　\*　\*　\*　\*

In this chapter we have shown that although it is no easy task for human beings to work together in discussion groups, the opportunities for improving group problem-solving skills are abundant. Having analyzed the mistakes which occur in discussions, and having assumed that people are not inherently bad discussants, we can consciously instruct ourselves and our students in the art of group problem solving. Three inter-dependent methods of improving problem solving discussions have been suggested: developing a listening attitude, encouraging constructive roles, and following systematic steps in the discussion process. No miracles should be expected of course. Until that day when computers carry on our discussions for us, some degree of group dramatics is bound to occur. Hopefully education can reduce it to a minimum.

# REFERENCES

1. Barnlund, Dean C. and Franklin S. Haiman, *The Dynamics of Discussion*. Boston: Houghton Mifflin Company, 1960.
2. Bradford, Leland P. *et al. Explorations in Human Relations Training: An Assessment of Experience: 1947-1953*. Washington, D.C.: National Education Association, 1953.
3. Brilhart, John K. and Lurene M. Jochem, "Effects of Different Discussion Patterns on Outcomes of Problem-Solving Discussion," *Journal of Applied Psychology* 48:175-179, June, 1964.
4. Chase, Stuart in collaboration with Marian T. Chase, *Roads to Agreement*. New York: Harper & Row, Publishers, 1951.
5. ———, *The Power of Words*. New York: Harcourt, Brace & World, Inc., 1954.
6. Hayakawa, S. I., *Language in Thought and Action*. New York: Harcourt, Brace & World, Inc., 1949.
7. Heisler, Walter; Marion Smedling, and Clyde M. Campbell, "Group Dynamics: A Junior-High Class Experiment," *Clearing House* 24:151-154, November, 1949.
8. Heyns, R. W., *Effects of Variation in Leadership on Participant Behavior in Discussion Groups*. Doctoral Dissertation, University of Michigan, 1948.
9. Jenkins, David, "Research in Group Dynamics," *Social Educatio* 12:347-350, December, 1948.
10. Lee, Irving J., *How to Talk with People*. New York: Harper & Row, Publishers, 1952.
11. Lloyd, Donald, "The Quietmouth American," *Harpers* 227:101-10£ September, 1963.
12. Maier, Norman R. F., *Problem-Solving Discussion and Conferences: Leadership Methods and Skills*. New York: McGraw-Hill Book Company, 1963.
13. Montague, Ashley, *On Being Human*. New York: Henry Schuman, 1950.
14. Osborn, Alex F., *Applied Imagination*. New York: Charles Scribner's Sons, 1963.
15. Parnes, Sidney J. and Arnold Meadow, "Effects of 'Brainstorming' Instructions on Creative Problem-Solving by Trained and Untrained Subjects." *Journal of Educational Psychology* 50:171-176, 1959.
16. Roethlisberger, F. J., "Barriers to Communication Between Men," *ETC.* 9:89-93, Winter, 1952.
17. Rogers, Carl R., "Communication: Its Blocking and Its Facilitation," *ETC.* 9:83-88, Winter, 1952.
18. Thelen, Herbert A., *Dynamics of Groups at Work*. Chicago: University of Chicago Press, 1954.

# 6

# *MESMERIZED MASSES*
## (Thought vs. Propaganda)

"At last, a nasal spray that thinks like a doctor!"

"Preserve your freedoms under God and the United States Constitution. Vote for Mark R. Savior."

A friend of mine recently remarked with facetious anger, "I think it's unfair for advertisements to take up more than forty percent of the television broadcasting time!" I have never dared to check his percentage—its proximity to truth would be too depressing. Certainly many of us have been shocked (or perhaps numbed) by the growing forces of miseducation sponsored by commercial and political manipulators. Not only is more time devoted to such manipulation, but the blatant quality of the manipulation has become progressively worse in the past two decades. As one educator views the situation, "it appears quite obvious that forces which profess no educational objectives dominate the cultural climate of our society and are far more influential than the duly constituted agencies of enlightenment" (28).

If rational man is not to wither on the tree of evolution, teachers have a war to wage. It's not too certain they can win—it would appear that the odds are against them—but they have the best position on the battlefield for fighting the commercial and political manipulators of the mind. Many of the religious organizations are ill equipped to fight the battle, as they have often led the way in thought control and manipulation. Most businessmen won't fight it and it seems unlikely that any labor union will. The schools are very imperfect models of objectivity, but they have more opportunity than any other formal agency to expose the manipulators' attempts to degrade man and vulture upon his weaknesses.

The main purpose of this chapter will be to discuss the means of waging war—through analysis of the techniques used by propagandists, through study of human needs, and by training in critical thinking. But first let us define propaganda and discuss briefly some of its ill effects.

Most writers on this subject tend to agree that propaganda is an attempt to persuade people by means of one-sided arguments. But they disagree on whether propaganda is good or bad; the majority of them appear to believe that it is either good or bad depending on the goals that are accomplished by using it. One writer (16), for example, illustrates our indebtedness to propaganda by reminding us that Franklin used propaganda to get the French to come to our aid in the Revolutionary War. Now, obviously if Franklin used propaganda, it must be a good and patriotic technique. Many will point to the usefulness of advertising in "spurring the economy," which might be translated: "encouraging us to buy things we don't need." Hayakawa (9:104) however, fears that much advertising serves to "break down that mutual trust that makes cooperation possible and knits people together in a society."

The question of whether propaganda is good or bad is quite unanswerable. A question which *can* be answered, at least partially, is "what effects do certain types of propaganda have on people?" Can propaganda influence our self image, our attitudes toward self? In 1956 it was estimated that twelve million dollars were spent by commercial concerns on motivation analysis, much of which dealt with encouraging self attitudes that would be beneficial to producers (23). Can it influence our attitudes toward love? Part of the twelve million was confidently spent with that assumption in mind. Can it influence our buying habits? In 1962 over thirteen billion was spent on advertising in the United States (31), demonstrating that producers of goods and services have great faith in propaganda, a faith which is no doubt based on the upward turn of sales graphs. Can it affect our political decisions? Many politicians think so. In fact, since 1956 they have wholeheartedly adopted the methods used by business to merchandise goods and services (23)—which creates the very real danger, as Hughes (11) points out, of disarmament being discussed on the level of deodorants. No one knows how many millions of dollars are spent on propaganda during a political campaign; the costs are too well hidden.

What about children? Do propagandists aim their arrows only at the adult population? Packard (23) quotes one ad man who advocates an all-out assault on children:

> It takes time, yes, but if you expect to be in business for any length of time, think of what it can mean to your firm in profits if you condition a million or ten million children who will grow up into adults trained to buy your product as soldiers are trained to advance when they hear the trigger words 'forward march.'

But some merchandisers are not content with conditioning children for the future. They want Junior and Little Miss in the act right now, even though the youngsters may have to play their roles behind the stage. One company offered a 60 piece model circus, a magic ray gun, and a space helmet to any child who brought his parents to view a display of new refrigerators (23). Parents and children spent $300,-000,000 on Davy Crockett products, which was a manipulated rather than a spontaneous fad (23). On television recently, an advertisement showed a very jealous girl about nine years old peeking around a corner at a boy, her age, who was talking to another girl—a rival, of course. The jealous girl's. mother wisely purchased a particular brand of shampoo, scrubbed the head of her *gleeful* daughter, and fostered her narcissistic tendencies by helping her gaze fondly in the mirror. In the final scene, the nine-year-old princess was happily sitting on the porch swing with Him, and the rival had disappeared.

A survey reported by Newsweek (10) showed that children are very attentive to commercials and tend to feel a loyalty to the advertised product similar to their loyalty to the program. (Pavlov's conditioning experiments would explain this.) A study done by Bateman and Remmers (1) demonstrated that high school students can be influenced quite easily by propaganda. A passage unfavorable to labor unions was read to the students after a pre-test dealing with attitudes toward labor unions had been administered. A post test showed a significant shift toward a less favorable attitude toward labor unions. A second passage, one in *favor* of labor unions, was read and a second post test was administered. There was a significant change this time toward a more favorable attitude.

Research by Collier (2) illustrates that merely informing students of propaganda techniques is not enough to counteract the influence of propaganda. A group of college students were given two lectures on propaganda techniques and then told to read some Nazi propaganda in the library on their own. Compared to a control group, these students tended to become more favorable toward the Nazi viewpoint, as shown by pre and post tests.

It appears likely that *intensive* training is necessary to counteract propaganda and allow students to develop the ability to make decisions on a more objective basis. Furthermore, it would seem advisable to provide such training early in life rather than wait until high school or college. Wolfe (31) and Kottmeyer (14) were both successful in teaching intermediate grade children to analyze the techniques of advertisers. My own experience with children suggests that such analysis can begin, on a very limited scale, as early as the first grade.

## Analysis of Propaganda Techniques

Although there are dozens of thought stopping techniques that commercial and political propagandists have invented, only ten which seem most predominant will be discussed. These have been culled from personal experience and from writings of propaganda analysts (8, 9, 11, 12, 15, 17, 18, 22, 23, 27, 29). The techniques will be discussed in the order which appear to be appropriate for analysis by children.

Perhaps the most widely used technique is that of *appealing to authority*. This may have always been a favorite device of mankind. A child engaged in argument will often refer to Mom or Dad or Teacher. Orators of the Middle Ages usually covered their argument with a quote from Aristotle or from the Bible. It is second nature today for many politicians to quote Lincoln or F. D. R. or John F. Kennedy. And advertisements often begin with such clinching phrases as "Doctors agree" or "Four out of five witches say."

As pupils study examples of fallacious appeals to authority they might be taught to ask these questions:

1. Is it good for *me?* Even if a thousand doctors or husbands or policemen think it's good, is it something that *I* should have? If two out of three doctors smoke Llama Cigarettes, does that make them good for me?

2. What was the sample? Which experts were interviewed—the experts working for the company that makes the product? How many "doctors say?" Does two out of three mean two out of *every* three or two out of *the* three who were given a year's supply of Llama Cigarettes? Did the company do the asking or did an independent organization carry on the research?

3. Does it apply today? Do Wilson's sentiments about war apply to the hydrogen-packed present? Do Calhoun's beliefs about states rights provide us with a suitable philosophy for today's international situation?

4. Does it fit the argument? If a famous president said that "all men are created equal" does that fit the argument that all of us should pay the same rate of income tax? Is a famous golfer an authority on shaving creams?

A second technique, somewhat similar to the first, is often referred to as the *bandwagon approach*. Like appeals to authority this gimmick also has primitive roots. Have you ever been a participant in an argument similar to this one:

"No, you can not go to the Red River Slob Dance."
"But, Mother, every kid in school is going to be there."
"Not the kids from respectable families!"
"Susie's going. And so are Alice and Bob and Jerry and Lucille.
And they all live in our neighborhood."
"Well, I suppose if they're all going . . ."

It is conceivable that this type of argument goes far back into the history of man. However, it probably occurs much more often today, if Riesman (24) is correct in his observation that the past few decades have seen a rapid rise in other-directedness. Riesman contends that most Americans are far more concerned today about doing what others are doing and believing what others are believing.

A study by Marple (19) illustrates the strength of other-directedness in our society. Several hundred adolescents and adults were asked to express agreement, disagreement, or uncertainty toward 75 controversial statements on a variety of topics. One month later the same subjects were asked to respond to the statements again. But this time one-third of the subjects were first shown how the majority had responded previously (bandwagon technique); one-third were shown how 20 "experts" had responded to the statements, and one-third were used as controls. With the bandwagon technique one-half of those responses which were previously not in agreement with the majority were changed to correspond to the response of the majority. About the same results occurred with the "expert" approach, with very little change occurring among the control group.

This tendency toward other-directedness is grist for the propaganda millers. Their pet serpents are all trained to say, "Everybody's doing it!" The propaganda hacks expend their energies thinking of different ways of saying "Jump on the bandwagon!" But it all sounds the same: "More people buy Hupmobile than any other make." "More choose Village Life Insurance: millions more than any other company." "Vote for a winner!" "Forty million people can't be wrong." "Why do so many want Fatz Beer?" Occasionally someone tries to use the bandwagon technique in a more subtle and devious way. One car manufacturer—let's say the maker of Hupmobile— has been running ads on television in which a supposedly "successful" suburbanite buys a Hupmobile, drives victoriously through his neighborhood, attracts the envious eyes of his neighbors, and obtains the glorious distinction of starting a fad. Hupmobiles sprout like mushrooms, and the viewer is teased with the possibility that "you might start something too—innocently."

In addition to finding samples of the bandwagon technique on television and radio and in newspapers and magazines, pupils might be encouraged to ask these questions:

1. What does "more" mean? "More than any other company that sells the same kind of product" is far more meaningful than just "more." The term "more" in isolation, can mean "more than we ever hoped to sell of this miserable product" or "more people than last year—thank heavens, we thought we were headed for bankruptcy."

2. Do I need or believe the same thing? Do I need the same kind of bicycle, car, or soap that millions of people are using? Will this product do what *I* need it to do? Even though most of the class wants Fred for president, do I personally think he's the best person for the job?

3. *Why* do more people want it? Because it's cheaper? Because people have discovered it will last longer? Because this company has spent a great deal more money on manipulating wants through advertising? (Children could carry on some interesting surveys and investigations to answer the question of "why?")

A third technique may be termed *transfer*. This technique is probably based on Pavlov's experiments with secondary reinforcement. You remember how Pavlov caused dogs to salivate by presenting them with a piece of meat. At the time of presentation he also rang a bell. Soon the dogs were salivating whenever the bell was rung. The propagandist using the transfer technique also presents two stimuli simultaneously. In some cases the original "saliva-producing" stimuli may be simply a symbol such as a four leaf clover ("Oh, boy—good luck for me"). The secondary stimuli would be the product he wishes to sell, such as margarine. The propagandist hopes, of course, that the positive feelings toward the symbol will transfer to the product. Packard (23) describes one experiment which shows how effective this device can be. The makers of Good Luck Margarine gradually increased the size of the four leaf clover on the margarine package. With each expansion of the symbol there was a significant rise in sales.

Most politicians are masters of the transfer technique. If the President comes to town, the local office seekers try to be seen with him as much as possible (coattail politics). When making speeches politicians will often allude to past glories—how our party saved the country from a depression, or kept the country out of war. Or they may attempt to transfer negative feelings by associating the rival with Communists or Fascists; or by bringing up an extinct issue such as "the depression of '29" or "the Bay of Pigs incident."

Commercial advertisers rely a great deal on transfer in the form of testimonials. Movie stars and other celebrities pick up a good deal of pocket money by mouthing sweet nothings about a product which they may have never tried before and may be content to never experience. Sometimes the stars say nothing about the product, the advertiser being content merely to see his product and the star in the same photograph.

Questions for the student to ask:

1. What is the relationship? Is a movie star qualified to make expert judgments on beverages, or cars, or even soaps? Does the symbol make the product taste better or perform better? Is the local politician competent merely because he was seen shaking hands with the President?

2. Is this a dead issue? Does the Bay of Pigs incident tell us any-

thing important about the way in which our prospective leaders will behave?

3. Why is the relationship made? Who stands to gain by the association? Who is getting paid?

A fourth technique is that of *labeling*. This is also based on Pavlovian psychology. Attach the label of "Communist" to the rival candidate and arouse the fears of the public. Call a soft drink "Zest" or "Zip" or "Zowie" and develop the image of a drink that really picks you up—despite the fact that the subsequent let-down leaves you worse off than you were before (3). Invent euphemisms such as "American advisors" for "American soldiers" or "preventive war" for "aggression" or "liberty cabbage" for "sauerkraut" (during World War II).

Research shows that transfer through labeling is a very effective device. Sargent (25) selected several words or phrases frequently used in a Chicago paper to describe people or programs that the publisher either liked or disliked. He then presented these words and phrases out of context to a group of people, asking each of them if he liked or disliked or had no feeling about the word or phrase. Sargent felt that these words and phrases were used in the paper as labels which would encourage certain attitudes. He found that the labels used positively by the paper were more often liked than disliked by the subjects and the labels used negatively by the paper were more often disliked. Other studies showing similar effects of labeling are described in the chapter on general semantics.

Questions for students to ask:

1. Does the label describe a real thing? (See chapter on general semantics.) Does the soda pop have "zip" in it, or does it contain carbonated water, sugar, and artificial flavoring?

2. What does the label mean? What does "Zowie" mean? What does "Greasy kid stuff" mean? What is a "warmonger"? What does a warmonger do? Does the person who was called a warmonger actually do those things? What does "progressive" mean? What is a "famous" cigarette?

A fifth technique might be called *ego building*. Most of us like to be flattered occasionally, to know that someone thinks a great deal of us, to realize that our uniqueness and high standards are appreciated. That may explain why one cigarette company uses the slogan, "Wherever particular people congregate." It may explain why some ads show a woman or man admiring himself in the mirror while wearing his new clothes or underclothes. (You're supposed to identify with the man or woman, of course.) It undoubtedly explains why both political and commercial propagandists talk so much about YOU.

When studying propaganda of this sort, a counter slogan might be more useful than questions: "Flattery will get you nowhere!" But one question at least ought to be asked: What concrete information is he telling me about the product or his proposals?

A sixth device may be called *identification*. A person using this technique tries to join your in-group by digging up his Irish ancestry or describing his vivid recollection of flying over your town thirteen years ago. Or he might put on his robe of sincerity and his hood of honesty to show that he's a good person like everyone in his audience. Or he may imply that his wife nags him to show how human he is. All of these devices are probably harmless in themselves and are used by most public speakers to some extent. But the unwary may be thrown off guard and become all too willing to accept the rest of the speaker's talk without question.

Commercial propagandists utilize identification by using language which they think is typical of people in the "upper-lower" and "lower-middle" socio-economic classes—their largest group of consumers. Don't say, "Winston tastes good *as* a cigarette should." Say, "Winston tastes good *like* a cigarette should." My only surprise about this is that I have yet to see "ain't" in an advertisement.

Question for students to ask: "So what?"

A seventh device used by propagandists is *oversimplification*. Propagandists often design their statements to appeal to those of us who are sometimes or nearly always too lazy to think. These statements allow for no middle ground and are often in the form of slogans: "Prosperity's just around the corner." "In your heart you know he's right." "When there's no man around, Goodyear should be." "Nothing says loving like something from the oven!" Sometimes the oversimplification occurs in the form of a panacea: aspirin for nearly everything, the Democrats for curing social ills, the Republicans for individual freedom.

Questions for students to ask:

1. What information is given? What corner is prosperity around? You know he's right about what?

2. What are the limitations: Does aspirin cure anything? Does it help all cases of arthritis? If "nothing says loving like something from the oven," what do burnt rolls say, or a packaged cake with more fluff than flavor?

3. See "hyper-generalization" exercises in Chapter 4.

An eighth technique is that of *image making*. Motivation analysis has demonstrated that every product which has been on the market for a while or every politician who is known as more than a name has an image. Tea, for instance, means a sick-bed beverage to many people and prunes are for dried-up old maids, as far as some people are concerned. (23) One make of car may have an image of aristocracy and solid reputation, whereas another car will create connotations of zaniness and a devil-may-care attitude. Producers, therefore, are very concerned about their image and either attempt to promote the image which their company presently owns or try to change it to a more favorable one.

An image is only useful to a propagandist to the extent that people can identify with it. Thus a politician will often attempt to develop a father image, a person who will take care of us children, a good shepherd who will watch over his flock. Or he may decide, upon the advice of his advertising agency, to develp the lovable son image, the young man for whom all mothers would love to cook dinner and of whom all fathers would be justly proud.

Commercial companies generally have no person for people to identify with; therefore, they have to personalize their products. A particular brand of cigarette takes on the image of virility, strength, and masculinity when big, husky, rugged cowboys are shown lighting up after a hard ride. Another cigarette takes on the image of a workingman's cigarette, smoked by "men on the move. Able workers . . . keeping America on the go." A drug company develops an image of protector, of public benefactor, of the dedicated researcher striving unselfishly to improve man's health throughout the world. A beer producer seeks to build an image of expertise by letting the public become familiar with the company's opinionated brewmaster.

The commercial image makers work hard to maintain the loyalty of customers who are buying the image more than the product. They even go so far as to insinuate that the good guys would "rather fight than switch." Their concern is understandable since studies show that most people can't tell their favorite brand of cigarettes or beer from other brands when the labels are hidden (23). The same thing might happen with politicians if they couldn't be seen and their voices were disguised.

Questions for students to ask:

1. What is the image? Would I want to buy it because of its image or because of its usefulness? Do I like his ideas or merely the image he is presenting?

2. Why this particular image? Why does a cigarette company want its product to have a manly image; what customers is the company trying to attract through this image?

A ninth technique used by propagandists is simply *hypnotism* in a variety of forms. The first stage in hypnotism is to induce the subject to fall into a trance (7). Propagandists utilize a variety of gimmicks to induce a mild form of trance. One of these is to use a soothing voice; bathe the listener in soft, glowing, bubble-words; say nothing, but say it smoothly, resonantly. Don't say, "They're made of mild tobacco." Say, "Aaaannd they are mild." Repetition and rhythm help too. Don't say, "Of, by, and for the people." Say, "Of the people, by the people, and for the people." Sing with fervor, "Be happy, go lucky, be happy, go Lucky Strike. Be happy, go lucky, go Lucky Strike today!"

But the most common form of trance inducement is the television show. The idea is to entertain the customer and while he's being entertained slip in a few harmless suggestions, such as, "If you're feeling tired it may be because of iron-poor blood . . . a bottle of this contains more iron than 30 rusty nails." Political propagandists sometimes take advantage of the entertainment trance too. In 1956 the GOP bought the last five minutes of several popular television shows. With the viewers already in a mild trance, it was predicted that the propagandists would have a susceptible, captive audience (23). However, some commercial propagandists have found that it doesn't pay to produce shows which are too entertaining, too exciting, or too thought provoking. These types of shows don't produce the desired trance and viewers don't pay enough attention to the commercials. The mediocre shows are often better for business (23).

Getting people into various states of trances helps to make them more susceptible to suggestion. But arousal of strong emotions accomplishes the same aim. When feelings such as hatred or pride are aroused, the susceptibility of human beings to suggestion seems to increase (7). That's why some politicians consciously or intuitively try to arouse such emotions. Adolph Hitler, as an extreme example, was a master hypnotist. By scraping on the nerve cells of envy, disillusionment, and fear, he was able to turn most of his weird suggestions into a dogmatic creed followed by millions. It's a rare political campaign in our country which does not exhibit at least a modicum of Hitlerian hypnosis. As Estabrooks (7) explains,

> . . . the great orator is generally a great hypnotist using direct or prestige suggestion with far more skill than the psychologist employs when he works with hypnotic suggestion. In general, his appeal will be on an emotional, nonlogical basis since this sensitizes the brain and gives his suggestions far greater strength than can be obtained with any logical appeal.

Packard (23) reports that as early as 1955 commercial ad men were considering the use of hypnosis-trained television announcers. An advertisement in 1965 demonstrated how far they have come in their thinking. This advertisement for a headache tablet was accompanied by a ticking and swinging pocket watch on a chain, an image of a distressed woman, and a deep, resonating, rhythmic voice intoning the word "Pain . . . Pain . . . Pain." So far, at least, political propaganda in our country has not been quite so flagrant, but the day may come.

It is unfortunate that our young people must be informed that some "grownups," in all their wisdom, may attempt to misuse hypnotism (a useful device of medical science) to gain their own selfish ends. But until these practices are abolished, we owe it to our students to advise them to watch for trance inducing gimmicks and over-zealous orators.

A tenth technique, one which is perhaps as treacherous as hypnotism, is that of *sophistry*. The word "sophistry," as it is used here, stands for the use of half-truths, fallacious analogies, and misleading implications. In a West Coast newspaper on November 2, 1964, an advertisement urging people to "Vote No on Proposition 17" had a picture of President Johnson, and under this picture in bold type were the words "President Johnson has denounced the promoters of 17." Now, it's fairly clear, isn't it, that Johnson was against Proposition 17. Or is it? Later in the advertisement, in small type, were *these* words: "President Lyndon B. Johnson has denounced the unauthorized use of his name by the promoters of Proposition 17. These special interests have tried to deceive the public by linking the President's name with their propaganda . . ." Some might say this is the pot calling the kettle black. Of course the first statement, "President Johnson has denounced the promoters of 17," was a half-truth, cleverly designed to lead people into thinking that Johnson was against Proposition 17. (The advertisement *for* Proposition 17 in the same issue was nearly as deceiving—although they did not use a similar form of sophistry but relied instead on associating a "Yes" vote with Eisenhower, Kennedy, and Johnson.)

At the beginning of this chapter was an advertisement which claimed that a nasal spray can think like a doctor. Now everyone knows that nasal sprays can't think like a doctor. They might be able to think like a perfume dispenser, or an elephant spraying people who won't give him any more peanuts, but never like a doctor! "At last, a nasal spray that thinks like a doctor!" You'd think we'd been waiting a thousand years for such a monstrosity to appear. I'd sooner wait for a doctor who thinks like a nasal spray! But, at any rate, it seems evident that some advertisers will stop at nothing when it comes to inventing fallacious analogies.

Nor will they stop at anything when it comes to misleading implications. Consider this advertisement, for instance. "How do husbands react when wives suddenly look years younger? They're a little puzzled but they love it, say 9½ out of 10 husbands interviewed." The advertiser then goes on to reason that since a woman's looks depend so much on her hair she should do something about "washing" that gray away with his special shampoo. Two implications are evident, even though buried in soap suds. One is that 9½ out of 10 husbands liked their wives better after they used the advertiser's shampoo, yet the survey had nothing to do with the shampoo! The second implication is that the woman does not have to stoop to such a practice as dying her hair; in a very natural way she merely washes the gray away. It takes a new kind of thinking to understand this part of the advertisement. When you put blue paint over a white wall, you have to say to yourself, "I'm not painting blue over white, I'm painting the white away." It will take a little effort, but in no time at all we'll be able to substitute advertising lingo for old-fashioned English.

Questions for students to ask:

1. What's the whole truth? Is Johnson against Proposition 17 or against the use of his name in support of a local issue? Has the advertiser given me all of the facts or only enough to mislead me? Am I getting information out of context? (Suppose someone read only the following statement from this chapter: "It will take a little effort, but in no time at all we'll be able to substitute advertising lingo for old-fashioned English.")

2. What's wrong with the analogy? How is a nasal spray *not* like a doctor?

3. What are the implications: Are they justifiable? Can we assume that husbands will like their wives better if the wives dye their hair? (In a television commercial about the same product, the implication is made that as long as the wife's hair is gray, "hubby" will be more interested in listening to a ball game than talking to her; but if she'll only wash that gray away, he'll turn off the ball game.)

## Study of Human Needs

Teaching youngsters to recognize the gimmicks which commercial and political propagandists use is important but probably not enough. Propagandists generally prey upon human needs, and unless people understand their own needs it is likely that they will succumb to propagandistic pressures. Intensive training in propaganda analysis surely should help to fend off the pressures, but a study of human needs along with propaganda analysis should be at least doubly effective.

> First, then, we should ask students to analyze themselves to see what makes them tick and just how they are amateur propagandists in influencing those around them. The next logical reaction will be for the pupil to learn how to protect himself against unwanted persuasion or to accept that which he considers welcome. (8:42)

Maslow's list (20) of human needs would seem to be a focus for study which would be understandable to children, assuming a skillful presentation is made. Maslow suggests that human needs can be placed in a hierarchy, meaning that the first type must be at least partially met before the next type will emerge. His hierarchy includes the following needs: physiological, safety, belonging, esteem, and self-actualization. The lower needs such as those for food, health, and affection have to be partially satisfied before the higher need for self-actualization becomes important to the individual. But, actually none of these needs is ever completely satisfied, and a skillful propagandist makes use of this fact.

Most advertisements aimed solely at the physiological needs of hunger and thirst usually lack subtlety in their deception. A young person soon learns to pay little attention to the picture above the soda counter of a banana split consisting of enormous ice cream volcanoes covered with lava flows of syrup. After his first disappointing encounter with the actual thing—tiny anthills lightly splattered with goo—he learns to take his business elsewhere or to put up with the sham. But advertisements aimed at the physiological need of health are not so straightforward in their deception. Many advertisements play upon our fears of illness or discomfort by presenting us with highly suggestive images of suffering people. We are urged to throw headache tablets or antacid pills into our stomachs at the slightest distress. Unfortunately, the side effects of these pills do not concern the advertiser, whose interest is to get people to gobble his product like popcorn.

The only real weapon which teachers can present against propaganda aimed toward physiological needs is a solid program on nutrition and general health. If nothing else, however, the teacher can introduce skepticism into the picture by indicating the side-effects which can occur with some of the widely advertised non-prescription drugs. For example, aspirin destroys the Vitamin C in the body, and antacid pills neutralize the hydrochloric acid needed for digestion (3). Students can also be made aware of how a strong suggestion can often make a person feel the discomfort (or tiredness) which the commercial propagandist says his product can cure. Have three or four children leave the room and bring them in one at a time. After blindfolding an individual have him hold out one of his arms and tell him with a serious tone of voice that you are going to find out how much heat he can stand. "This may be pretty hot, but I'm sure it won't burn you." The touch his upper arm with an ice cube and watch him jump. Other examples of confusing the senses through suggestion can be found in science and psychology texts. Children can also learn about propaganda directed toward physiological needs by discussing the various ways that they, themselves, use such propaganda. "If you go with me, I'll give you half of my candy bar." "You'll get sick if you eat all of that. Give me some."

Appeals directed toward the need for safety, or security, are made by both commercial and political propagandists. Insurance companies sometimes present a picture of a burning house or the breadwinner in a wheelchair or a dining table with an empty chair, hoping that fear will be aroused and that the name of their company will be imprinted on your mind at the same time. Political propagandists have known for some time that war is the most powerful issue that can be brought into a campaign, and few hesitate to use it as an issue if the other side is likely to lose votes.

The need for safety is no mystery to children. Nor are they unaware of how others may attempt to manipulate them by appealing to this need. "If you don't give me that, I'll hit you." "If you don't stop it, I'll tell Daddy and he'll spank you." "If you don't hurry up, we'll have to leave you behind." "The goblins will get you if you don't watch out." The need for safety, of course, is a very real one and can be partially satisfied by purchasing insurance and electing leaders without a record of warmongering. At the same time, people should be taught to recognize the play upon security needs engaged in by propagandists and to search beyond the fears aroused for solid information. Questions need to be asked: "What evidence do I have that insurance from this company will provide me with more security than insurance from other companies?" "How do I know that this leader will do a better job than the other of keeping us out of war?" Naturally, these are questions which do not concern children directly, but it seems likely that children in the upper grades, by attempting to answer such questions, can develop a mental set against propaganda which preys on the need for safety.

The need for belonging is also no stranger to children. Most children have experienced on several occasions the feelings of being left out, of not being wanted, of not being loved. Through discussion they should be readily able to understand how people sometimes manipulate others by offering to fulfill this need or by threatening to withhold affection. "You can't be in our club if you act like that." "Would you like to come to my birthday party? OK, let's play together at recess today." "OK, you won't be my friend." A study of advertisements which utilize a similar type of manipulation could then follow such a discussion. One insurance company, for example, asked this question, "How come Metropolitan Life insures 45,000,-000 people and can still keep track of you?" Reading between the lines we might find this: "Sure, we have a lot of members in our club, but if you join our club, we'll like you as much as any other member."

Commercial propagandists must be very fond of the technique of appealing to the need for esteem, or status; they seem to use it so often. Their messages follow a simple formula: tell the potential buyer how important he is. Tell him that a person of his stature deserves new clothes, a luxurious car, and should only be seen carrying a new set of luggage. Packard (23) found that successful producers of detergents often spend little time at all describing their product and a great deal of time telling the housewife how important her role is in washing clothes. He also found that a power shovel producer increased his sales by presenting pictures which emphasized the operator more than the shovel.

Children can easily find ads which appeal to the need for esteem. Before studying such ads the children should discuss the need for feeling important and the ways in which people sometimes manipulate others through this need. Children, unfortunately, are given many opportunities to feel that they are not very important, that their parents and teachers couldn't care less about their wishes, that their work is not as good as that of other children. Most of them have also experienced the exhilarating sensation of being recognized positively by adults or peers for outstanding behavior. And they have experienced the process of manipulating or being manipulated via the need for esteem. "Johnny's a big boy; he helped me rake the lawn." "If you won't give it to me, I won't vote for you to be President of our club."

The need for self-actualization might be described as the desire to see one's dreams come true. Most of us recognize that only some of our wishes can be fulfilled, but the need for developing goals and moving toward those goals seems to be universal. The need for self-actualization is the drive toward fulfillment, toward growth, toward the application of developed values.

Perhaps the fact that many people in our society perceive themselves as not achieving self-actualization explains the observation that Packard (23) makes on supermarket buying. It appears that a large proportion of items purchased in supermarkets can be classified as self-indulgence items, and it is likely, although Packard does not say so, that much of this self-indulgence is the result of feeling a lack of fulfillment. Commercial propagandists recognize not only the need for self-indulgence but also the accompanying guilt feelings. Consequently, to sell a self-indulgent product such as candy or cigarettes, they must assuage such guilt feelings. Some cigarette advertisers, for instance, handle this problem by picturing people smoking as a reward for hard work. Appliance advertisements do not tell the housewife that a new appliance will give her more time for bridge or coffee breaks; rather, they tell the potential customer she'll have more time for the children or for intellectual pursuits.

Our need for self-actualization can generate a host of guilt feelings —one for every goal we set for ourselves and do little about. Many of us even have guilt feelings about not brushing our teeth. One toothpaste company capitalized on this fact by claiming that its product was for people who can't brush their teeth after each meal. Two years after this toothpaste was introduced on the market, it was outselling all but one other brand (23). Manufacturers of cake mixes discovered that many women felt guilty about using such mixes: the use of cake mixes kept them from fulfilling their goals of being creative and "giving of themselves" to their family. Consequently the producers quickly put mixes on the market that would allow the producer to add an egg or some other ingredient (23).

Producers of diet products know that the need for self-actualization for many women includes the goal of becoming admirable on the beaches. To mix a little fear with this desire, one advertiser recently came out with a picture of a bathing beauty emerging from the surf with all of her gaiety and slimness showing. The caption above the picture reads, "Only 61 more slimming days 'til summer" —a warning designed to send fear into the hearts of the female masses (and a good portion of the male masses).

Children may find the need for self-actualization more difficult to understand than the other needs, since it is a more subtle and complex one. Nevertheless, the need is real even to children and is manifested in such things as conscience pangs and goal frustration. Children frequently feel guilty when they are not measuring up to expectations—most of which originate with parents and teachers, but many of which become part of the child's self concept. It should be easy for children to recall, moreover, some of the occasions in which other people attempted to manipulate them through these guilt feelings. "Big boys don't cry." "Ladies don't sit like that." Goal frustration is also an everyday occasion for most children—coming in for dinner just when the play gets good; losing a squirt gun to the teacher on the very day that revenge was going to take place. And they can be readily made aware of the concomitant manipulation which sometimes occurs: "If you come as soon as you're called, you'll be able to play after supper until bedtime." "If you show us what a good citizen you can be for the rest of the day, you may have your gun back."

After discussing the common occurrence of guilt feelings and goal frustration and the correlative manipulation that may take place, the children should be ready to understand this type of manipulation in commercial and political propaganda. Propagandists will be very willing to provide examples.

## Training in Critical Thinking

Learning the techniques that propagandists use and the human needs which they prey upon should enable students to build up their resistance toward commerical and social manipulation, and later toward political manipulation. This resistance could be strengthened even further, however, through training in critical thinking. Although Shotka (26) found that certain operations of critical thinking, such as recognizing assumptions and finding biases, could be taught even at the first grade level, it is likely that intensive training in critical thinking would have to be reserved for the upper grades. Critical thinking usually involves a subtlety of thinking which older children can handle much more easily.

Ennis (6) and his colleagues on the Cornell Critical Thinking Project have developed what is probably the most inclusive definition of critical thinking. According to Ennis, critical thinking is the correct assessing of statements, and this assessment involves eleven judgments. These judgments pertain to whether

1. there is ambiguity in a line of reasoning.
2. certain statements contradict each other.

3. a conclusion follows necessarily.
4. a statement is specific enough.
5. a statement is actually the application of a certain principle.
6. an observation statement is reliable.
7. an inductive conclusion is warranted.
8. the problem has been identified.
9. something is an assumption.
10. a definition is adequate.
11. a statement made by an alleged authority is acceptable.

Henderson and Fulton (10), in teaching critical thinking to high school students, utilized a behavioral definition of critical thinking:

1. identifies words and phrases upon whose meaning the whole argument depends.
2. identifies the basic assumptions in an argument.
3. distinguishes between relevant and irrelevant evidence.
4. is not deceived by common errors in straight thinking, such as reasoning after the fact, circular reasoning, reasoning by analogy, assuming the converse or inverse of a proposition, jumping to conclusions, using non sequiturs.

Watson and Glaser (30) have constructed a critical thinking test composed of items that pertain to five operations: evaluation of arguments, recognition of unstated assumptions, deduction, evaluation of inferences, and interpretation. Most people who have studied critical thinking agree with Watson, Glaser, Ennis, and others that critical thinking is a multi-dimensional ability composed of several rather specific skills and that each of the skills can be developed through specific exercises. Here are examples of such exercises.

## Deduction

1. Study the following syllogism. Are the two premises true? Does the conclusion logically follow?
   Premise A:  All people eat food.
   Premise B:  All dogs eat food.
   Conclusion:  People are dogs.

2. Study this syllogism.
   Premise A:   People like to buy from a company they can trust.
   Premise B:   Our company is one that people can trust.
   Conclusion:  You should buy from our company.

## Recognition of Assumptions

1. What assumptions are probably behind this statement? "We will arrive at the airport at 5:00 P.M. Saturday."
   a. We expect to eat dinner at your house.
   b. No accident will occur on our way.
   c. Airplanes are usually on time.
   d. Saturday is a better time to arrive than Sunday.
2. What assumptions are probably behind this statement? "This rancher's wife knows that Drab is better than any other detergent."
   a. A rancher's wife has to wash very dirty clothes.
   b. A rancher's wife should know what detergent is best.
   c. Drab gets clothes cleaner than any other detergent.
   d. Drab works better than old-fashioned soap.

## Evaluation of Inferences

After reading each of the following passages decide which of the inferences are probably true and which are probably false. Are any of them definitely true or false?

1. In Edwardson School a poll of the students was recently made. It was found that most of the students like chocolate ice cream better than any other flavor. Over half of the students buy ice cream at the corner drug store at least twice a week. The main ingredients in ice cream are sugar and milk.
   a. Most of the students in Edwardson School would like sweetened chocolate milk if they had a chance to drink it.
   b. Edwardson students like strawberry milk shakes better than chocolate milk shakes.
   c. Most of the students at Edwardson School have a job or receive an allowance from their parents.

    d. The people who made the poll talked to more than half of the students.

    e. No one at Edwardson School likes chocolate candy.

2. "Now with new Scotch Boy Walplex, you can roll on new beauty in a single coat. It covers so well, one coat looks like two. New Walplex is especially made for rollers. That way there's practically no roller marks or splatter. No unpleasant paint odor, either. When you're finished painting, it's a snap to clean up. Soap and water takes all the paint off the rollers and brushes."

    a. This paint has a "built-in second coat."

    b. A roller would work better than a brush with this paint.

    c. If you apply this paint with a roller, you'll get no roller marks or splatter.

    d. This paint has no odor.

    e. The paint can be washed off the walls with soap and water.

    f. Even if it takes a week to complete your painting job, you don't have to clean your roller until you're finished painting.

## Evaluation of Arguments

Which of the arguments for the following statements are good ones and which are poor ones?

1. "People should drink milk."

    a. Yes, because we have a lot of cows in the world.

    b. No, because some people used to die from a disease carried in unpasteurized milk.

    c. Yes, because milk contains calcium, which is needed for strong bones.

    d. No, because cream is harmful to some people with heart ailments.

    e. Yes, because milk contains many vitamins.

2. "Vote for Pinkston for President."

    a. Yes, he has been a soldier and fought for our country.

    b. No, he has never held any office before.

    c. Yes, he believes in democracy and freedom.

    d. No, he is short, fat, and bald.

e. Yes, he has been a general and has been a leader of men for twenty years.

f. No, he disobeyed a former President.

## Interpretation

After each of the following passages are several conclusions. Decide which ones probably follow and which ones probably do not follow from the information given. Assume that the information is true.

1. In 1960 there were 360 million popsicles sold in the United States. In the same year there were about 180 million people living in the United States.

   a. People in the United States are crazy about popsicles.
   b. In 1960 the average person in the United States ate two popsicles.
   c. People in the United States waste their money.
   d. Popsicles must really taste good.
   e. More than 360 million popsicles were sold in the United States last year, since the population is now well above 180 million.

2. More wars have occurred under a Democratic President than a Republican President.

   a. Democrats like war.
   b. Republicans hate war.
   c. The people would rather have a Democratic President during a war.
   d. No conclusion follows from the statement.

\* \* \* \* \*

People in our country are constantly bombarded with propaganda. Children, in their everyday interaction with adults and peers, are manipulated through social propaganda, and commercial propagandists consider them suitable prey. Teachers are in an excellent position to counteract the thought-stopping influence of propaganda by helping their pupils to analyze propaganda techniques, to understand the human needs which are preyed upon by propagandists, and to develop critical thinking skills.

# REFERENCES

1. Bateman, Richard M. and H. H. Remmers, "A Study of the Shifting Attitude of High School Students When Subjected to Favorable and Unfavorable Propaganda," *Journal of Social Psychology* 13:395-406, May, 1941.

2. Collier, Rex M., "The Effect of Propaganda upon Attitude Following a Critical Examination of the Propaganda Itself," *Journal of Social Psychology* 20:3-17, August, 1944.

3. Davis, Adelle, *Let's Eat Right and Keep Fit*. New York: Harcourt, Brace & World, Inc., 1954.

4. Eller, William and Robert Dykstra, "Persuasion and Personality: Readers' Predispositions as a Factor in Critical Reading," *Elementary English* 36:191-197, March, 1959.

5. Ennis, Robert H., "A Concept of Critical Thinking," *Harvard Educational Review* 32:81-111, Winter, 1962.

6. ————, "Needed: Research in Critical Thinking," *Educational Leadership* 21:17-20, 39, October, 1963.

7. Estabrooks, George H., *Hypnotism*. New York: E. P. Dutton & Co., Inc., 1957.

8. Harter, D. Lincoln, "Helping Pupils Understand Mass Persuasion and Propaganda Techniques," *The Good Education of Youth*, ed., Frederick C. Gruber, Philadelphia: University of Pennsylvania Press, 1957.

9. Hayakawa, S. I., *Language in Thought and Action*. New York: Harcourt, Brace & World, Inc., 1949.

10. Henderson, Kenneth B. and Marian P. Fulton, "Critical Thinking: Geometry Classes Use Radio Programs," *Clearing House* 24:155-158, November, 1949.

11. Hughes, Emmett, "The Impact of TV on American Politics," *Voice of the People: Readings in Public Opinion and Propaganda*, eds. Reo M. Christenson and Robert O. McWilliams, New York: McGraw-Hill Book Company, 1962, 365-371.

12. Huxley, Aldous, "Propaganda in a Democratic Society," *Voice of the People: Readings in Public Opinion and Propaganda*, eds. Reo M. Christenson and Robert O. McWilliams, New York: McGraw-Hill Book Company, 1962, 344-348.

13. ————, "Notes on Propaganda," *Voice of the People: Readings in Public Opinion and Propaganda*, eds. Reo. M. Christenson and Robert O. McWilliams. New York: McGraw-Hill Book Company, 1962, 324-331.

14. Kottmeyer, William, "Classroom Activities in Critical Reading," *School Review* 52:557-564, November, 1944.

15. Lasswell, Harold D., "A Definition of 'Propaganda'," *Voice of the*

*People: Readings in Public Opinion and Propaganda,* eds. Reo M. Christenson and Robert O. McWilliams, New York: McGraw-Hill Book Company, 1962, 321-322.

16. ———, "America's Debt to Propaganda," *Voice of the People: Readings in Public Opinion and Propaganda,* eds. Reo. M. Christenson and Robert O. McWilliams, New York: McGraw-Hill Book Company, 1962, 323-324.

17. Lazarsfeld, Paul F. and Robert K. Merton, "Requisite Conditions for Propaganda Success," *Voice of the People: Readings in Public Opinion and Propaganda,* eds. Reo M. Christenson and Robert O. McWilliams, New York: McGraw-Hill Book Company, 1962, 340-344.

18. Lippmann, Walter, *Public Opinon.* New York: Harcourt, Brace & World, Inc., 1922.

19. Marple, C. H., "The Comparative Suggestibility of Three Age Levels to the Suggestion of Groups vs. Expert Opinion," *Journal of Social Psychology* 4:176-186, 1933.

20. Maslow, A. H., "A Theory of Human Motivation," *Psychological Review* 50:370-396, 1943.

21. Murphy, Mary Kay, "Propaganda—A Part of Students' Lives," *English Journal* 53:445-446, January, 1965.

22. Newcomb, Theodore M., *Social Psychology.* New York: Holt, Rinehart & Winston, Inc., 1950.

23. Packard, Vance, *Hidden Persuaders.* New York: David McKay Co., Inc., 1957.

24. Riesman, David, *The Lonely Crowd.* New Haven: Yale University Press, 1950.

25. Sargent, S. S., "Stereotypes and the Newspapers," *Sociometry* 2:69-75, 1939.

26. Shotka, Josephine, "Critical Thinking in the First Grade," *Childhood Education* 36:405-409, May, 1960.

27. Siepmann, Charles A., "Propaganda Techniques," *Voice of the People: Readings in Public Opinion and Propaganda,* eds. Reo M. Christenson and Robert O. McWilliams, New York: McGraw-Hill Book Company, 1962, 332-340.

28. Snow, Robert H., "The Forces of Miseducation," *Phi Delta Kappan* 41:14-18, October, 1959.

29. Taylor, Warren, "What is Propaganda?," *College English* 3:555-562, March, 1942.

30. Watson, Goodwin and Edward M. Glaser, "Critical Thinking Appraisal, Form Am," Tarrytown-on-Hudson, New York: World Book Co., 1951-2.

31. Wolfe, Evelyn, "Advertising and the Elementary Language Arts," *Elementary English,* 42:42-44, 79, January, 1965.

# Part IV

## Creative Expression through Language

# 7

# *YOUTHFUL WORD-ARTISTS*
## (The Identification of Verbal Magnets)

Imagine a picture which shows a man dressed in a business suit and seated in a reclining seat of an airplane. Which of these descriptions, related to that picture, do you think is the most interesting?

> Mr. Smith is on his way home from a successful business trip. He is very happy, and he is thinking about his wonderful family and how glad he will be to see them again. He can picture it, about an hour from now, his plane landing at the airport, and Mrs. Smith and their three children all there welcoming him home again.

> This man is flying back from Reno where he has just won a divorce from his wife. He couldn't stand to live with her any more, he told the judge, because she wore so much cold cream on her face at night that her head would skid across the pillow and hit him in the head. He is now contemplating a new skid-proof face cream. (4)

What characteristics distinguish writing and speaking which is considered highly interesting in our society from that which is not considered interesting? Why should teachers be keenly aware of those characteristics? The most painfully obvious answer is, "So that we can communicate more effectively with our students!" However, let us assume for one-millionth of a second that teachers are the most effective communicators in the world. Having made this

167

assumption, we could then move on to a second assumption—that teachers are the logical people to instruct children in the art of interesting verbal communication. (If the first assumption was a bit naive, then we might make the less preposterous assumption that teachers can improve their own communication by working *with* children toward more effective speaking and writing.)

But why is it necessary for *children* to learn to speak and write in a more interesting fashion? After all, aren't their shrieks and grunts, their murdered metaphors and snarled similes perfectly suitable for their everyday attempts to manipulate their peers and wheedle their parents? The answer is "Yes," but don't close the book. The goal of our schools is not to produce professional wheedlers and manipulators, although one may wonder about this at times. The primary objective of our schools, at least the one which serves as a preamble to most courses of study and curriculum guides, is to foster the development of each individual's talents and thereby to fulfill both the needs of the individual and the needs of society. The one talent which is fundamental to nearly all occupations in our society is that of verbal communication. Those people who are most effective in their daily occupations are generally those who have learned how to communicate effectively—to interest, direct and understand others. This is true of home management engineers (housewives) as well as presidential aspirants.

Yet there is an even more crucial, present-tense reason for improving children's skills in verbal communication. Improvement in speaking and writing skills leads to the satisfaction of basic psychological needs—needs which must be satisfied in childhood as well as in adulthood. As mentioned in Chapter 6, Maslow (6) has hypothesized six types of needs which all human beings have throughout their lives. These needs are depicted on page 169.

According to Maslow's theory, the "lower" needs must be satisfied before the "higher" needs will serve as motivators. If Maslow's theory is correct, the child's intellectual needs will not motivate him until he has first satisfied—at least partially—his needs for self-actualization, esteem, love and belonging, and the other "lower" needs. Since our schools are predominantly concerned with intellectual understandings, it behooves educators to discover ways of satisfying the lower psychological needs.

How can this be done in such a way that society's needs for

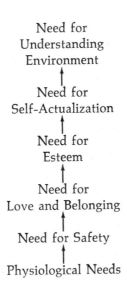

Need for
Understanding
Environment
↑
Need for
Self-Actualization
↑
Need for
Esteem
↑
Need for
Love and Belonging
↑
Need for Safety
↑
Physiological Needs

capable citizens are also met? It is this author's hunch that the answer lies in spending a much greater proportion of time in our schools on the skills involved in verbal exposition and creative expression. A child's need for love and belonging—in a school setting —is naturally going to be thwarted by his inability to interest others through verbal expression. Even the very young student who can express himself in an interesting way usually gets the attention and affection of others (including the teacher). The child whose expression is drab and lifeless has much more difficulty, so it seems, in attracting friends.

The need for *esteem* can also be met through a vigorous creative writing and speaking program. While some children can easily obtain status through athletic prowess and others through scientific, artistic, or musical talents, creative writing and speaking offers another avenue for gaining respect from peers. As for self-actualization, this need is met whenever an individual is given the opportunity to utilize and develop his talents.

It should be evident, then, that the ability to identify and encourage characteristics of interesting speaking and writing is one which most teachers can ill afford to neglect. Future research might well indicate that our entire school program would be enhanced by a more vigourous attempt to help children win the respect of others through verbal communication. It is even feasible, since mental health is so largely a function of effective communication (5, 9), that more attention to our creative speaking and writing programs would help to bring about a lower incidence of mental illness in our society.

## The Search for Criteria

Such programs can only be effective, of course, if the teachers responsible for them are keenly sensitive to high-quality verbal communication. Let us search, then, for those traits which character-ize interesting speaking and writing. Perhaps the two most promis-ing sources of information would be reports of educational research and opinions of professional writers and speakers.

Getzels and Jackson (5) compared creative writing samples of two groups of high school students. The "high-creative" group had scored high on a creative thinking battery but relatively low on an intelligence battery. The "high-IQ" group had scored high on the intelligence battery but relatively low on the creative thinking bat-tery. Judges were asked to examine the creative writing samples to determine the frequency with which six writing techniques were used by the students. (The judges were not aware of the students' scores on the intelligence battery and creative thinking battery.) The six techniques were as follows: stimulus-free theme, unexpected ending, presence of humor, presence of incongruity, presence of violence, and playful attitude toward theme. It was found that the "high-creative" groups employed all six techniques more frequently than the "high-IQ" group. (The first story at the beginning of this chapter was written by one of the "high-IQ" students; the second, by a "high-creative" student.) Statistical analysis, moreover, demon-strated that the differences between the two groups were not chance differences, with the exception of "presence of violence." Therefore, it seems reasonable to suggest that five of the six techniques (omit-ting "presence of violence") can be used as specific criteria for identifying children with talent for writing and speaking creatively.

It is doubtful, however, that those five criteria are sufficient. Some of the five techniques might not be evident in stories written by children who are considerably younger than the adolescents in Getzels' and Jackson's study. It is important, therefore, to examine the work of younger authors. Torrance (11) found that elementary school children who scored high in a creative thinking task produced stories of a different quality from those who scored relatively low on the creative thinking task. The "more creative" children produced longer stories, included a greater variety of words in their stories, and employed first-person pronouns more often. Those three characteristics, then, might be added to our list of identifying criteria.

Torrance (12) has developed two lists of criteria which he and his associates use in deriving a score for samples of creative writing. One list is used for evaluating *originality*. The other list, based on the work of Flesch and Lass (3), is used for evaluating *interest*. The criteria for originality include the following:

1. Picturesqueness: The descriptions are colorful and suggestive of images.

2. Vividness: The story is lively and exciting.

3. Flavor: The writing has a noticeable style.

4. Personal element: The author involves himself in the story or expresses his personal feelings.

5. Original ending: The story contains a surprising conclusion or punch line.

6. Original setting or plot: The story contains an unusual theme or setting.

7. Humor: The author illustrates the absurdity of human behavior or the amusing nature of incongruous events.

8. Invented words: The author combines or creates words to illustrate an idea or object; or he provides his characters with names appropriate to their behavior or occupations.

The criteria for interest include the following:

1. Conversational tone: The author tells the story as if he were conversing with the reader.

2. Naturalness: The language used is informal rather than stilted and artificial.

3. Use of quotations: Whether or not quotation marks are used, the author often presents the direct words of his character.

4. Variations in kinds of sentences: The sentences vary according to use: declarative, exclamatory, interrogative, imperative; or they vary according to form: simple, complex, compound, compound-complex.

5. Variation in length and structure of sentence: The author inter-

mixes short and long sentences; or he varies the position of subjects, predicates, dependent clauses, and independent clauses.

6. Personal touch: This is the same as "personal element" under *originality.*

7. Humor: This is the same as "humor" under *originality.*

8. Questions and answers: The author may present questions and answers in the direct quotations of his speakers; or he may ask the reader a question and then answer it.

9. Feelings of characters: The emotional reactions of the characters are presented through their own words or through the narration of the author.

We have developed several criteria of effective verbal communication by examining the reports of educational investigators. Additional criteria may be generated by noting the opinions of a small sample of professional writers and speakers.

The "Guiding Faculty of the Famous Writers School" in Westport, Connecticut, has prepared a test for detecting writing talents. Although the test cannot be described in detail, the types of qualities the authors attempt to measure are obvious. Two parts of the test are designed to measure *conciseness*—the ability to say something with a few simple words. One part of the test is designed to measure *clarity*—the ability to produce smooth flowing, easily understood sentences. Another part is designed to measure the ability to produce *original and appropriate similes.*

George Orwell and Somerset Maugham are two writers who have recorded their opinions concerning the art of writing. In Orwell's opinion (8) there are two qualities which are common to writing which is not interesting: staleness of imagery and lack of precision. These two faults, Orwell feels, are disgustingly common among English and American writers. Maugham's pet peeve is not *stale* imagery so much as it is *lavish* imagery. In criticizing his own prose which he produced as a young man, he states: "It is wistful, allusive and elaborate. It has neither ease nor spontaneity. It smells of hot-house plants and Sunday dinner like the air in the greenhouse that leads out of the dining room of a big house in Bayswater ..." (7:20) Maugham admired Swift for his "wonderful lucidity, his terseness, his naturalness, his lack of affectation." (7:20) He also greatly admired the prose of Dryden: "It has not the perfection of

Swift nor the easy elegance of Addison, but it has a springtime gaiety, a conversational ease, a blithe spontaneousness that are enchanting." (7:21) In arriving at standards for his own writing Maugham chose "lucidity, simplicity and euphony." In his opinion "to write good prose is an affair of good manners . . . Prose is a rococo art. It needs taste rather than power, decorum rather than inspiration and vigour rather than grandeur." (7:27)

Professional opinions on effective speaking provide us with a few more clues on the nature of interesting verbal communication. Maugham's vote for the most interesting and consistently amusing talker went to Edmund Gosse. "He had read a great deal, though not very carefully, it appears, and his conversation was extremely intelligent. He had a prodigious memory, a keen sense of humor, and malice." (7:7) Taking Maugham's comment as gospel—which he never meant it to be—we might add *informativeness* to our list of criteria. This characteristic should be qualified by the assumption that the wealth of information presented would be spiced with humor or incisive criticism.

According to Dale Carnegie, who has criticized well over 150,000 speeches in the process of training people to speak in public, *enthusiasm* is the most necessary virtue of any speaker who desires to interest others. "Passion . . . Feeling . . . Spirit . . . Emotional sincerity—get these qualities in your talk and your auditors will condone—yes, will hardly be conscious of—minor shortcomings." (1:138)

Crandell, Phillips, and Wigley (2), through their analysis of both accomplished and neophyte speakers, have developed a set of traits which characterize a "good oral style." The reader may agree that these traits are the same traits which characterize a "good" writing style.

1. *Clarity*—using accurate and specific words; avoiding counter words (nice, fine, etc.), technical terms, and jargon.

2. *Conversational quality*—talking to individuals in the audience, using simple phrases, etc. (except at dedications and other formal affairs).

3. *Emphasis*—using forceful words and effective repetition; avoiding redundancies, deadwood, unnecessary qualifiers, and pointless euphemisms.

4. *Aliveness*—avoiding dead metaphors, stock similes, slogans, and cliches; using fresh figures of speech and occasional onomatopoeia and alliteration.

5. *Appropriateness*—using words suited to the occasion, the audience, and one's personality; avoiding labored, studied, self-conscious speaking.

## A Condensed Set of Criteria

The list of characteristics which can be used as criteria for identifying high-quality verbal expression might be extended indefinitely. However, it is likely that a brief list would be more useful to teachers than an exhaustive one with many vague and overlapping criteria. The following list was prepared by your author on the basis of three referents: (1) the research reports and professional opinions recorded above, (2) years of intensive reading and listening, and (3) personal prejudice. This list may serve both as a set of criteria for identifying verbal talent and as a set of specific objectives for teaching creative speaking and writing.

1. *Imagery*—describing a situation or subject in vivid, colorful, concrete language.

2. *Naturalness*—using informal language (except on those rare occasions when formality is expected); maintaining personal contact with listeners or readers; expressing one's individuality.

3. *Inventiveness*—inventing fresh analogies, characters, settings, plots, or words; playing with homonyms, alliteration, and other humorous devices.

4. *Insight*—portraying human strengths and weaknesses by means of satire, humorous incongruity, philosophical generalization, realistic description, and other devices.

5. *Sincerity*—demonstrating keen interest or feeling regarding one's subject, story, or characters.

6. *Flexible Style*—avoiding monotony by altering sentence length, clause position, sentence type, and other elements of style.

7. *Conciseness*—expressing the essence of an idea or situation; avoiding words and details which distract from the main ideas or impressions to be conveyed.

8. *Clarity*—avoiding pronouns with hazy referents, dangling

participles, slang or jargon, mystic phrases, and other habits of speech which are likely to confuse listeners or readers.

It is doubtful that these criteria are met by all speakers and writers whom you and I consider to be "good." It would be impossible, furthermore, for us to agree on the most important criteria. However, I think we can agree that anyone who consistently violates any one of those eight criteria will find it difficult to attract listeners or readers. Thus it is important for teachers to encourage children who do not violate these criteria and to provide special help for those who do. This role, of course, requires a teacher who recognizes effective and ineffective verbal expression.

By careful analysis of children's compositions it should be possible to test and sharpen one's ability to detect individual strengths and weaknesses in writing. This ability on the part of the teacher can then be transferred, without much difficulty, to the evaluation of children's speaking habits. Let us examine, then, several compositions written by third and sixth grade children. In a study by Tabachnick and May (10) compositions by 300 third graders and 300 sixth graders were judged "creative" or "not creative" by twelve judges. Six of the judges were graduate students in English and the other six were graduate students in Education. Since each composition was read by all twelve judges, the "score" for a composition could range from 0 to 12. A score of 5, for example, would indicate that five out of twelve judges considered the story "creative." The compositions which we will consider were written in response to a sketch that included a person, a hill, a tree, and a flying bird. First, we will examine three sets of sixth grade compositions. The first set contains stories which nearly all of the judges considered "creative."

### Grade 6: Story 1: Score 11

"Jack, wake up," called his mother. Jack dove under his blankets. But after a few moments of darkness he raised his head from beneath the blankets. To his horror it was 20 to nine. He sprang out of bed and into his clothes and hustled down stairs. Jack grabbed the piece of toast his mother had set out for him and hurried on to school. On the way it seemed strange and quiet. Then the terrible truth struck him. He had forgotten to set the clock back one hour for daylight saving time. Now he was one hour early for school with nothing to do. Jack kicked a can as hard as he could. To his amaze-ment the can said "Ouch!" He had nothing to do so he investigated further. He slowly lifted up the can and out jumped a leprechaun. Jack had heard of leprechauns in Ireland, but surely not here! The leprechaun whose name was Peter told Jack that he was on a good-will mission here and wanted to help people. "Could you help me?" said Jack. He told Peter the predicament that he was in. At once the leprechaun sent Jack back through time. Jack found himself back in bed. "Jack, wake up." Jack looked up at the clock to find it only 20 to eight. Down at breakfast he looked out the window to see a tin can with a dent in it. He winked at the tin can and it winked back.

This story appears to meet all eight criteria. The author uses abundant *imagery*, e.g., "dove under his blankets," "sprang out of bed." There is a *naturalness* to his expression which most of us adults can never hope to attain, e.g., "Jack had heard of leprechauns in Ireland, but surely not here." His *inventiveness* is evidenced by his ability to breathe life and gaiety into the simple event of turning back the clock. He demonstrated at least a modicum of *insight* into human behavior by portraying a boy who is reluctant to get out of bed, bored with "nothing to do" for a whole hour, and imaginative to wink at a tin can. His composition demonstrates *sincerity, con-ciseness, clarity*, and a reasonably *flexible* style, although his reper-toire of sentence types is naturally limited at this age. In addition to meeting the eight criteria he also shows an ability to introduce a bit of suspense or mystery in a story, e.g., "He slowly lifted up the can . . ." "On the way it seemed strange and quiet."

The next four stories were also judged "creative" by nearly all of the judges. The reader is invited to evaluate them in terms of the eight criteria.

## Grade 6: Story 2: Score 10

The boy runs, swift and light of foot. He is free. He feels as one with the wild. The wind rushes through his hair. It is as if he could run as long and fast as he wished. He wants to be as one with the birds, the flowers, the animals, the wind and the earth. Just as music in perfect harmony blends with rhythm, he blends with the wind. As the birds sing, he sings, as the wind blows, moving ever faster, so he runs, silent and swift. As the wolf hunts, killing for food and fighting to live, as the relentless law of nature "Kill or be Killed." So he hunts, crafty as a vixen with newborn fox cubs. The eagle, dropping swiftly in flight, from far above, the King of the Skies. So he drops, to rest under a tree. The tree, whose spreading branches shelter many animals. And, as he rests, he hears the lonely call of the gull, who just the day before had been happy. Today his mate had died from the poison of man. Man, who ignores the law of nature and kills and destroys. The boy thinks of his grandfather, who lives in Africa. He thinks of the men who come there on vacation. They kill elephants and other animals by the thousands, not thinking that they themselves descended from animals, that they are animals themselves. When dinosaurs roamed the earth and began to die off, small, furry, warm-blooded animals began to appear. Man himself descended from them. The boy begins to grow sleepy from memories of the past. He dreams that someday he will become great and save animals from the destruction of man. Little does he know that 20 years from now he will be nicknamed, "the savior of wildlife." Then, if he had lived, his grandfather would have been proud of him. But for now he will dream and blend with nature, for later years to use his knowledge and wisdom of the ways of nature.

### Grade 6: Story 3: Score 10

This little boy is running away from his troubles. He has no faith in himself. He hates darkness, fear and fate, which every child runs from. He's running to a green valley. Where darkness never comes. Where fear never throbs in the hearts of children. He doesn't want to grow up and face the hate and troubles of this sinful world.

He stops, listens. He wants to hear the birds singing in the valley. But no, silence is upon him. His fears grow greater, and the sun is setting. Darkness is almost here. He runs. He does not bother to stop and listens for signs that he nears the Valley. He has no time for that now! Darkness is almost upon him. He hears a storm coming up. He breaks out with a cold sweat. He can't breathe, he can't see. His eyes are stinging from the hail coming down. The wind is against him. DARKNESS had come! His heart throbs and throbs. Now the rain had come down harder. He was crying. Crying for the valley. Yes, the valley, somewhere out there was the Valley! He saw a cave. But the cave was dark and cold. He hesitated. He could not make up his mind. Finally he stopped and went in. He sat there staring out into the darkness. Shivering with fright. Afraid of what would happen if he never reached the valley. Finally peace came to him as he slept soundly in the cave. His dreams were all about the valley. He saw in his dreams a beautiful lady reach out to touch him. He stepped back. She took him in her arms and said, "I'm the Princess of the Valley." He replied, "Is this the valley I see in my dreams at night?" "Yes, it is," she said in a serious voice. Tears rolled down her eyes as she kissed his forehead. She said, "You are lucky to have seen this valley. Very few people do. But first to live in this valley, you must face the hate, fear and fate of this world. Now go and then come back and then you will live in peace here, forever," she said softly. Then he woke up with a start and started back home. He lived a good life and when he died, he dreamed about the valley. He could see himself walking. I should not be walking, because he was very ill. He had wrinkles and snowy white hair. He walked up to the gate and lived in peace forever. And the valley was never seen again.

### Grade 6: Story 4: Score 9

Once upon a time there was a little eight-year-old boy named Billy. Billy was a lonely boy and was a little shy. Because he was shy the other boys didn't play with him. So, pretty soon Billy played and did things all by himself. He loved to walk alone in the woods playing with the animals and calling to the birds. One day as he walked through the woods he saw a strange object coming toward him. What was it? It looked like a bird but it was much bigger. Faster it came heading straight for Billy. Billy became scared and ran as fast as he could run. But still this strange object followed him. Suddenly, Billy stumbled over a rock and fell to the ground and lay there.

Billy woke up some time later and his head hurt him badly. Suddenly on the ground beside him, he saw the strange object. It was a fierce, large looking bird. Billy was just about to run when the birdlike thing suddenly spoke.

"Hello Billy," said the bird. "You had quite a fall. Are you all right?"

Billy was very surprised but finally managed to say "I-I'm fine, but who are you?"

"Oh, I am what you might call your bird friend," said the bird. "Just call me Birdy."

"All right, Birdy, but how come you talk and know my name?" asked Billy.

"Oh, that's my secret," said Birdy. "I am from a land of sad boys and girls. I know you are sad and that's why I am asking you to come along with me to the land of sad boys and girls where everyone is happy."

Billy stared at the bird for a while and said, "Will I have a mother and father in this land, because I am an orphan?"

Birdy exclaimed, "Of course you will, everything that you can dream of."

Billy said, "I'll go," and away they flew to the land of sad girls and boys where everyone is happy.

Now Billy is happy and never again will he be lonely and shy. He is in the land of sad boys and girls where everyone is happy.

### Grade 6: Story 5: Score 9

This was an important day in the life of John Walters. He sensed it somewhere deep inside him. The impatient voice of his mother, the smell of pancakes for breakfast, all these were in the normal span of his day; yet, somehow, they held an undercurrent of excitement.

"Something's gonna happen today," he announced at breakfast.

"Yes, dear, be sure to drink your orange juice." That was his mother's voice. Sometimes it seemed to John that she had no imagination.

Along the well-traveled road to school he kept thinking, "There's something special going on today." Would it be at school? Yes, John was sure of that. But his Iowa Tests were finished and, surely, what could be more important?

As he fumbled in his pocket for a piece of candy, he felt a grimey, wrinkled sheet of paper. His permission slip for Scout Camp! Quickly he ran home, taking the few blocks as fast as he could. After having his father sign it, he sped again away to school. John was sure then that this "Something" had to do with running. Not the short kind, but a long, grueling trek that was a matter of life and death.

The morning at school passed endlessly. He was terribly absent-minded, and could not for the life of him think of the product of $6 \times 9$.

Then, as Mr. Herwing, the physical education instructor, appeared at the classroom door, he felt his muscles tighten. This Something was about to happen, but, as he trooped outside with the others, a sense of foreboding took hold of him as he saw the colored pennants at each end of the playground.

He was about to burst with curiosity, fear, and excitement, but the voice of Mr. Herwing interrupted his thoughts . . . "Ready all, for the 600 yard walk-run!"

In contrast to the "creative" stories, here are four stories which all of the judges rated as "not-creative." Although each of these compositions demonstrates a tiny spark of talent, all of them seem to lack the imagery, naturalness, and inventiveness of the "creative" compositions.

### Grade 6: Story 6: Score 0

This is a story about a boy who, at the end of the year, got his report card. This boy was very happy because he got five A's and the rest B's.

When the boy got home he told his mother the good news. When his father got home he told him. His father said that for having improved so much he could stay up until 8:30 p.m.

The next morning, as he was going out to play, the phone rang. His mother answered the phone. On the phone was the boy's teacher. His teacher said that the boy's report card got mixed up, that the boy had the wrong card. So the boy's mother, Mrs. Jones, brought out the boy's report card. The boy's teacher gave Mrs. Jones his report card.

When the father came home they told him. Then they opened up the pamphlet and read his grades. They were A's and B's. That night he got 50¢ for every A and 25¢ for every B.

### Grade 6: Story 7: Score 0

One day in May, Kent James got up at 8:00 A.M. He had to get to school and school began at 9:00 A.M. He didn't know that it was so late. Then at about 8:45 he just started to get dressed. So he went to his closet to find out what he was going to wear. Finally, he took a quick glimpse at the clock and then he knew he wouldn't make it to school on time, so he stayed home—(he played hookie).

Then after he ate his lunch he made sure that he went to school. When he was walking along he heard the bell ring, so he started to

run. But then when he got to school, he found it was only the janitor's bell. Then at 1:30 the bell rang, and everyone was seated, so Miss Jones asked Kent why he wasn't in school this morning. "Well, I-I was sick." "Where is your excuse?" "I don't have one," he said shyly. "Why not? I thought we made it clear to everyone that we always have to bring excuses," she said angrily. "You did, but my mother wasn't home," he said. "Where does your mother work?" she asked patiently. "She works at Marx Toy Shop," he answered. "Well, I'll call her and ask her why," she replied.
(20 minutes later)
"Kent, I want to see you after school." "Yes, Miss Jones," Kent said frightened. The bell rang. "Kent," she shouted. "Where do you think you're going?" "Uh, to the lavatory." "I called your mother and she said she didn't know you were home. Why did you stay home?" she asked. "It was too late when I got dressed, so I didn't come," he replied. "In other words, you played hookie. Is that right?" she asked. "Yes it is, Miss Jones. I'm sorry," he apologized. "Well, your punishment is you can't go to the school picnic or the patrol picnic either," she said. "Yes, Miss Jones," he said sadly. "I'm so sorry Miss Jones," he said again. "Yes, Kent. Now you must go home." "Good-night Miss Jones." "Good-night Kent. You be here tomorrow," she answered. "Yes I will," he promised.
The next morning Kent was in school just as he promised. "I'll never do it again," he replied in a low voice.

### Grade 6: Story 8: Score 0

One day the boy got into a fight with some bigger boys. He went home and told his mother and father what had happened to him and they both asked what he did to the boys and why they had beaten him up. He said that he had made fun of them because they couldn't go the county fair and he could. So his mother and father hollered at him a little bit. He ran upstairs and started to cry. The next morning when he woke up he came down to eat and went back upstairs, climbed out of the window, and ran away. He didn't come downstairs to play—or to eat dinner—so they went up and looked in his room to see what was wrong. They found that he was gone. They all thought that he ran away and didn't come back. So they all went outside to look for him but didn't find him. He went way out to the country and in some woods. They had no idea where to look. They were also wondering if he would come back in time for supper because he didn't have anything to eat since breakfast. When it was night time and when it was dark in the house he came and climbed into his bedroom, and went downstairs to look for some food to eat. Just by luck there was something left to eat. He went back upstairs, climbed into bed and went to sleep. The next morning when it was breakfast time he came down and everybody crowded around him and wanted to know where he was. He told them. His father told him to come into the den. He went into the den and his father explained to him that it was for his own good they hollered at him the other day. So every time his mother and father hollered at him he never ran away again. When he was out in the woods he had seen some very pretty things. The next Sunday they all went out to the country to see the woods.

### Grade 6: Story 9: Score 0

One day a boy was walking in the woods. He had a picnic basket under his arm. It wasn't noon so he thought he would sit around and watch the birds and other animals. Soon it was time to eat so he sat by the creek and opened his picnic basket. When he was eating his chicken he heard a noise in the bushes. He looked around but he couldn't see anything. The next time the noise grew louder. Suddenly a big grizzly bear came charging out of the bushes.

Right away the boy knew the bear was after his lunch. He quickly ran and climbed a tree while the bear ate his lunch.

Although it is tempting to analyze these stories in terms of their psychological and sociological implications, the author is deliberately concentrating only on specific characteristics of verbal communication which make it possible to *interest* others. It is his contention that although verbal communication is extremely complex, teachers must select a focal point which is most amenable to classroom management. This is not to say that teachers should ignore the psychological and sociological implications of children's compositions, but to say, rather, that teachers who concentrate on improving children's communication in very specific ways can make a tremendous contribution to the welfare of individual children. (With some children it will be relatively impossible to help them improve their communication skills without first helping them with more basic psychological or sociological problems.)

The average score for the sixth grade compositions was approximately 4. The following are three stories which might be considered "average." Although imagery and inventiveness are used more often in these stories than in the stories rated 0, these characteristics are not used as consistently throughout the composition as they are in the stories rated 9 and above.

## Grade 6: Story 10: Score 4

Jimmy Jackson lived in Maine along the ocean with his grandparents. Jimmy was nine and very curious with a mind of his own.

The day was sunny. He walked along the high banks overlooking the ocean. Ahead he saw his destination, Pine Mountain. Pine Mountain was hollowed out with many caves and caverns. He walked and walked until he stepped into a large hole. He looked into the hole and there saw a large, monstrous dragon with six eyes and ten legs and two feet on each leg. The dragon had a large arm on the top of its head and pulled Jimmy down into the hole. He ran around dodging the twenty feet. Soon he found a door. He opened up the door and ran down a long hallway. On the sides of the hallway were cages. In the cages were little purple men with pink feet. Soon he got outside and ran home. A seagull cawed loudly overhead.

## Grade 6: Story 11: Score 4

It was a beautiful summer morning when a little boy named Jimmy Adams was walking down the street. He heard a lot of noise. The next thing Jimmy knew there was a big, black dog chasing him. Jimmy ran up a street and down a street, through many people's back yards. Once a lady was hanging her wash out and Jimmy ran right through her yard and knocked her over, wash and all. But Jim didn't stop for anything. He kept right on running till he was in a great big forest. The dog really didn't mean any harm. All he wanted to do was play with him. Now Jimmy was very sorry he ran like that. He knew he was left alone in a big forest with nothing but a dog.

The dog wanted to play with Jimmy very much, so Jim decided to play with him. Jimmy had very much fun with this dog. Jimmy made an expression while sitting on a log. He said "We sure are having oodles of fun." So Jim decided to call the dog "Oodles." Now Oodles and Jimmy had been in this forest one week. All they ate were strawberries and other foods.

One day a strange thing happened. All the animals came out by Jim. They wanted to have fun too. So all that day the mice, rabbits, raccoons, and even skunks came to play.

After the day was over Jimmy and Oodles went to sleep in a log. Jimmy was dreaming about his mother and father. He wished he could go home again by his brothers and sisters. The next morning he said goodby to all his animal friends. You would think he would let Oodles stay there too but no, he thought he would take his nice companion along. They walked through the forest looking for a way to get out. But it was terrible. All they were doing was walking in many circles.

Jimmy climbed a tree to see if he could see anything. He thought he saw a bunch of smoke and many red trucks. So Jim ran very fast to see what had happened. He fell a couple of times but he got up and ran. When he got there a man with a red cap was there asking me if I saw the fire and everything. I just told him what had happened. When he heard this he told me to wait in the truck.

Jimmy was very happy now because he knew this man would take him home where he belonged. But all of a sudden he wanted to know where Oodles had gone. Jimmy snuck out of this truck and tried to find Oodles. Yes, he found Oodles. But when he got back there were no big red trucks. Jimmy sat on a nearby log and cried. Oodles wanted to make him happy.

Suddenly a lady dressed all in white appeared and told Jimmy she would take him home if he promised never to run away like that again.

Jimmy was very happy when he got home. His parents let him keep the dog too.


### Grade 6: Story 12: Score 4

One day as I was running home because I was late, as usual, a tree stopped me. Here is our little chat that we had:

"Hey, little boy. Why are you in such a hurry?" said the big tree.

The little boy said, "I am running because I am late for supper!

And if I don't get home soon my father will yell at me so much people in Siberia will hear him."

"I see," said the tree, "but I am sure another ten or fifteen minutes won't make any difference!"

"I guess you are right," said the boy.

"Let us talk awhile about things of interest to us both, but please not saw mills!" said the tree.

"Say, Mr. Tree, what should I call you?" said the boy.

"Just call me Jars. That is short for Jarslove. Everybody does. What should I call you?"

"You can just call me Butch. That is short for Butcher Rosebud Hinklemeyer. Everybody calls me that, so be my guest!"

"Thank you very much, Butch. I like the name Butch a lot more than Jarslove!"

"Jars, I'd better be going now," said Butch.

"Okay. See you again soon, I hope," said Jars.

Everybody lived happily ever after.

Having examined sixth graders' compositions at three levels of creativity, let us now look at three sets of stories written by third graders in response to the same stimulus that was given to the sixth graders. The first set contains four stories which were considered "creative" by nearly all of the judges. All four of these stories seem to meet especially the criteria of naturalness and inventiveness. Although there seems to be less imagery in the stories written by third graders than in those written by sixth graders, this is probably due to the relatively limited vocabulary which third graders generally have in comparison to sixth graders.

### Grade 3: Story 1: Score 10

One day there was a little boy named Johnny Ring. He lived in a village by the meadow. His mother and daddy were very cruel to him. One morning he crept out of his bed. He had a window in his bedroom, so he crept out of it. When he got outside he ran and ran and ran. When Johnny got to a big oak tree he stopped. Something was strange about the tree. It had golden leaves on it. He saw a little man painting with golden paint. He said hi to the little man. The little man heard it and he jumped out of his pants because he thought Johnny was a giant. After that they made friends. He was a magic elf man. He turned Johnny down to his size. They played and played together and Johnny was so happy he lived happily ever after. His mother and father never saw him again.

### Grade 3: Story 2: Score 9

Once there was a boy who went to the top of a mountain, to an uncommon tree. It was an enchanted apple tree. But the one thing that he was afraid of was a wild eagle which was at the top of the mountain. One time long, long ago, before you were even born, a lady judge came to this town to rule the country. After a couple of months the lady became queen of this town. She was honored with a seed. Then she planted it at the top of the mountain. She bought an eagle to take care of her tree, all her life and even after she died. It did too. Well, anyway, that's how the tree got there. The boy got to the top of the mountain to get the tree. When he got there he was so afraid that he almost fell back down the hill. He got his shovel out of its case and snuck to the tree so that the eagle would not get clobbered. He dug the enchanted apple tree up and took it to the bottom of the mountain. When he got there he found that there were millions of people. They all wanted to know why. And he told them "Why, I am the queen's son" he said. "She died when I was born. And my daddy said that I was old enough to climb the mountain, so I did." Everybody congratulated him. He took the tree home and planted it and the eagle came and took care of it until the end of the world. He is still there taking care of the tree. People still come to see it.

### Grade 3: Story 3: Score 9

Once there was a tree that would do many odd things. One time when it was rainy, he thought that he would catch cold so he went and built a house and went inside the house and was warm. Another time when there was a fire, he thought he would burn, so he bought a sprinkler and set it up so that water would be on him all the time. Another time the street lights didn't go on. It was too dark for him, so he bought a light bulb and a socket and a cord. He put them together and plugged the cord in the ground, and the light bulb went on, and there was a lot of light. Another time there was a lot of ants around. He thought they would eat him up, so he went to the store and bought some insect killer. So he sprayed himself with it. He got sick and called the tree doctor of Tree Village. The tree doctor fixed him up, but he got all the ants. Another time there was a robber around the tree and he thought he might take his top branch, which was his head, so he called the tree policeman to guard him. Another time he was falling apart. Nobody could help him, so he fell apart.

### Grade 3: Story 4: Score 9

This story is going to be one I think you will like. One day there was a boy who liked to run a very long time. Once he was running in the field when he came to a place he never saw before. It was not like other places he saw.

Then he saw something, it was a flying creature that was very ugly. It started after him. He got very scared and started to run. All of a sudden a very strange tree grew arms and tried to catch him. Luckily he could run fast, but the tree started after him too. Then he got even more scared. The sand beneath his feet got hotter.

The boy thought he might be finished. The sun was getting hotter and hotter. He was slowing down, but a cool wave was coming from a cave. He ran into the cave and found some unknown animals.

He said, "Where am I?" The animals all said together, "The lost desert." The boy asked still another question. "Where does this cave lead to?"

"It leads to a beautiful place where flowers grow and a nice pink house." The boy said, "That's my house!" He followed the tunnel, and sure enough it was his house.

The second set of compositions by third graders includes four stories which were judged "not-creative" by all twelve judges. The first story in this set lacks not only imagery and inventiveness but also consciseness and clarity. Maybe you can decipher it better than your author could. (It's doubtful that the judges had much luck.)

### Grade 3: Story 5: Score 0

Once upon a time there was a boy named Tom.

One day he ran up to a tree and climbed up it and got a red apple from the tree. He went down the tree and ran into the house and got a drink of water, and ran outside and played with his friend Bill and

Jack, and went to his mother and asked if he could go to Bill's house.

Mother said, "Yes, you can go to Bill's house but be back by seven o'clock."

Bill asked if he could have Tom and Jack at his house until 7 o'clock.

His mother said, "Yes, you can have Tom and Jack here until seven o'clock."

Bill said, "Jack and Tom here."

And then it started to rain and Jack and Bill and Tom ran to Bill's house and Jack called his mother. And his mother came to Bill's house. And Tom called his mother and his mother was not home. So he went to Jack's house. He called his mother and she was home. She came and got him. And she called the doctor and he came and he said he had gotten a cold in the nose. He was sick for 19 days.

### Grade 3: Story 6: Score 0

There was a boy that was asking his mother if he could run through the park and his mother said he could run through the park but he should not go too far or he would get lost so he said, "O.K. Mom," and he went through the park and then he went too far and he got lost and then he started to cry.

Then a policeman came along and he saw the boy crying and the policeman said, "What's wrong?" and the boy said, "My mother told me not to go too far," and the policeman said, "Come with me," and the boy said, "What are you going to do with me?" and the policeman said, "I'm going to take you home."

The policeman said, "What's your fire number?" and the boy said, "It is 104," and the policeman took him home. And he was glad to see his mother and his mother was glad to see him too.

### Grade 3: Story 7: Score 0

Once there was a boy. The boy ran up and down the hill. He ran up and down there to get some exercise. He ran about two, three or four miles. One morning he said he would never run again.

### Grade 3 : Story 8: Score 0

Once upon a time there was a little boy. His name was Pete. Pete liked to run. He always ran to school and he ran back. One day when he was in school his teacher asked him what he was going to be when he was big. He said, "I'm going to be a runner. I like to run a lot." When he got home, he started to run in the field. He saw the green grass and trees. He said to himself, "I want to be a farmer like dad." And a great farmer was he. He still could run very fast.

The average score for the third grade compositions was approximately 3. The following are three stories which might be considered average:

### Grade 3: Story 9: Score 3

One day a boy was running up the street. When he got by the big tree he saw a big bird coming after him. The boy ran, ran, ran, ran, ran and ran. He wasn't getting any place. The bird had the boy in his claws. The bird flew away with the boy. On top of the tree the bird stabbed the boy and the boy's soul went up to heaven, and the bird went down to hell. The boy was happy up in heaven, but the bird was not happy down in hell.

AND THE BOY LIVED HAPPY IN HEAVEN.

### Grade 3: Story 10: Score 3

Once there was a boy who walked past a tree. The tree said "Hello" to the boy. The looked and looked but he could not find a person in sight. The tree said "Hello" again. He looked again. Then he looked at the tree. The tree said "Hello" and then the boy said "Hello." The boy said "Are you the person who talks?" The tree said "yes." Then the tree said "Where are you going?" The boy said "I am going to my grandmother's house." Then a bird came. The bird said "Hello." The boy said "Hello" to him. Then the bird said "What is your name?" "My name is Gregg." The boy said to the bird "Where did you learn to talk?" Then the tree said "He learned from me."

### Grade 3: Story 11: Score 3

One day a little boy named Bill went out to play in the hot sun. There was a little tree by his house that would walk away from the house. Then little Bill would take him by the trunk so that he wouldn't get away from him. A big bird came to eat it all up. Then little Bill would cry and cry. It was an apple tree. He could take an apple off the tree and eat it. Little Bill went to crying to his mother.

His mother said she would come outside and hit the big bird with the stick and open his mouth and get the tree out. So she did. The little boy named Bill was so happy that he cried. Then the little boy named Bill lived happy with the tree and his mother and father.

*     *     *     *     *

We have briefly examined why it is important for teachers to be able to recognize characteristics of high-quality, oral and written composition. Research reports and a small sample of professional opinions have been used to develop a list of such characteristics, and the list has been condensed by the author to make it more useful to teachers. Several compositions written by third graders and sixth graders were shown in order that we might test the usefulness of the condensed set of criteria and in order that we might add to our perspective on the various levels of creative ability demonstrated in children's writing.

The intention of this chapter has not been to encourage teachers to turn themselves into talent scouts. There is considerable danger involved in "pushing" talented youngsters too early. When, for example, the prestige of teachers and parents becomes irrevocably attached to the performance of children, the jaws of frustration and demoralization are open to children and adults alike. The intention of this chapter, rather, has been to point to another way that teachers can facilitate the processes of effective communication among *all* youngsters, namely through recognizing and encouraging those characteristics of speaking and writing which make people interesting to each other.

# REFERENCES

1. Carnegie, Dale. *Public Speaking and Influencing Men in Business.* New York: Association Press, 1945.
2. Crandell, S. Judson, Gerald M. Phillips, and Joseph A. Wigley, *Speech: A Course in Fundamentals.* Chicago: Scott, Foresman & Company, 1963.
3. Flesch, Rudolph and A. H. Lass, *The Way to Write.* New York: McGraw Hill Book Company, 1955.
4. Getzels, J. W. and P. W. Jackson, "The Study of Giftedness: A Multidimensional Approach." *The Gifted Student.* Cooperative Research Monograph No. 2. U. S. Department of Health, Education, and Welfare, 1-18; 1960.
5. Hayakawa, S. I., *Language in Thought and Action.* New York: Harcourt, Brace & World, Inc., 1949.
6. Maslow, A. H. "A Theory of Human Motivation." *Psychological Review* 50:370-396, 1943.
7. Maugham, W. Somerset. *The Summing Up.* New York: New American Library, 1938.
8. Orwell, George. *A Collection of Essays.* Garden City, New York: Doubleday & Company, Inc., 1954.
9. Rogers, Carl R. "Communication: Its Blocking and Its Facilitation." *ETC:* Winter, 1952.
10. Tabachnick, B. Robert and Frank B. May, *Effects of Three Different Stimuli on the Creativity of Children's Compositions,* Report to U. S. Office of Education, March, 1965.
11. Torrance, E. Paul. "Creative Thinking of Children." *Journal of Teacher Education* 13:448-460; December, 1962.
12. ———. "Supplementary Scoring Guide for the Evaluation of Originality and Interest." *Scoring Manual for Evaluating Imaginative Stories* by Kaoru Yamamato: 40-48; University of Minnesota: Bureau of Educational Research, 1961.

# 8

# CREATIVE TEACHERS
## (The Identification of Pedagogical Schemes)

*Teacher:* Fred, why aren't you writing a story?
*Fred:* Aw, I don't know how to write.
*Teacher:* Why sure you do, Fred. All you have to do is think of something to write about.
*Fred:* I can't think of anything.
*Teacher:* Surely you can think of *something* to write about.
*Fred:* Nope. Can't think of a thing.
*Teacher:* How about writing about your pet.
*Fred:* Ain't got one.
*Teacher:* Well then, write about your hobby.
*Fred:* Ain't got one of them neither.
*Teacher:* Well, write about something you like to do more than anything else.
*Fred:* I don't like to do nothing that much.
*Teacher:* Then write about something you *hate* to do more than anything else.
*Fred:* Can't
*Teacher:* Why not?
*Fred:* I hate writing the most.

Depending on the personality of the particular teacher involved, a boy like Fred is capable of inducing feelings ranging from dreary despondency all the way to hateful hostility. The middle range of feeling might be classified as FRUSTRATION. In general, there have been two methods which teachers have used to combat this frustration. One method is to deny that creative expression is very important—"so why teach it, anyway." The other method is to search continually and frantically for "motivating" gimmicks such as mood music, curtain pullers (stories half read), and stimulating titles: "The Fun I Had Minding Baby Sister" or "The Case of the Missing Pencil Sharpener."

Examination of the *Education Index* reveals that while the quantity of articles on creative *speaking* is nearly weightless, the large mass of articles on creative *writing* is heavily loaded with gimmicks for inducing children to write. Most of the gimmicks are probably useful. Yet, by themselves they are weak foundation stones for a creative writing-creative speaking program. Instead, the program should rest on two pillars: the classroom *atmosphere* which fosters creativity and the *processes* involved in writing and speaking creatively.

## Creative Atmosphere

A creative atmosphere must pervade the total school program, and it must prevail during the entire school year; without this pervasive atmosphere, the attempt to teach children to speak and write creatively will probably be no more successful than flying a kite in a vacuum. But how does a classroom teacher develop a creative atmosphere? A creative atmosphere in the classroom requires at least two conditions. The first condition is a teacher whose own behavioral goals are at least moderately creative. A study by Torrance (19) demonstrates the importance of creative motivations on the part of the teacher. Several groups of intermediate grade children were given specific training in creative writing for a period of three months. All of the groups carried on approximately the same activities. Before the training began, the teachers of the groups were given a "Personal-Social Motivations Inventory," designed to measure creative motivation. The inventory requires true and false responses to such items as the following: "I enjoy work in which I must keep trying out new approaches." The pupils of teachers with strong creative motivations showed gains that were significantly higher than those pupils whose teachers had weak creative motivations. The latter group of pupils showed *almost no gain* despite the fact that the training time was the same for all groups.

The second condition of a creative atmosphere in the classroom is a teacher who reacts positively toward children with highly creative personalities. Psychologists have long emphasized the importance of reinforcement in causing behavior to become habitual. Teachers who do not reward, or at least tolerate, the characteristic behavior of highly creative children cannot expect to have a creative atmosphere in the classroom.

What are the typical personality characteristics of highly creative people? Research (1, 3, 7, 10) has shown that a highly creative individual can usually be described with the following adjectives:

1. Autonomous—Makes judgments without relying very much on the opinions of others; has a high degree of self-confidence; goes against the crowd in the interest of seeking truth.

2. Visionary—Has a sense of personal destiny; desires change and perceives change as possible.

3. Goal-oriented—Has many ideas for keeping occupied; applies considerable effort to projects which interest him.

4. Flexible—Shows a high degree of adaptability in problem situations; has a keen sense of humor.

5. Perceptive—Demonstrates abundant curiosity; shows reluctance to apply judgment too quickly; seldom uses mechanisms of suppression and repression; tolerates and seeks new ideas.

6. Adventurous—Takes risks; likes to try something new; prefers complexity.

Unfortunately, a few teachers might perceive those six characteristics as follows:

1. Autonomous—stubborn; brash; conceited; can't follow directions.

2. Visionary—rabble rouser; daydreamer.

3. Goal-oriented—can't apply himself to school work.

4. Flexible—unprincipled; annoying sense of humor.

5. Perceptive—always asking silly questions; too introverted.

6. Adventurous—trouble maker; poor judgment.

It is unlikely that a teacher with those perceptions would be capable of developing a creative atmosphere in the classroom.

Some studies demonstrate that not all teachers find it easy to reinforce the characteristic behavior of creative students. Getzels and Jackson (6) found that most of the high school teachers involved in their study preferred the "high-IQ" students to the "high-creative" students. Torrance (19) found that the elementary school teachers involved in his studies also preferred the high-IQ children to the high-creative children. Furthermore, the teachers admitted that they "knew" the high-IQ pupils better than the high-creative pupils. The previous studies do *not* indicate that most teachers are incapable of reinforcing creative behavior. They do indicate, however, that some teachers may have to change their perceptions of what constitutes a "good" student before they can achieve greater success in motivating creative composition.

To repeat an important idea, the two conditions of a creative atmosphere in the classroom are a creatively motivated teacher and a teacher who reinforces the characteristic behavior of creative individuals. Can teachers become creatively motivated? A study by Meadow and Parnes (11) shows that they probably can. Is it possible for teachers to change their reinforcement patterns? Again, this change can occur only when teachers change their perceptions of what constitutes a "good" student. It is encouraging to find that teachers *have* changed their perceptions once they were taught to recognize the characteristics of creative individuals (20).

## Creative Processes

In addition to establishing a creative atmosphere in the classroom, the teacher should instruct children in the specific processes or elements of creative writing and speaking. The teaching of creative expression has one thing in common with the teaching of any other skill; if there are specific abilities which one wants to see developed; then he had better teach them in a specific way and not hope for them in a general way. Some educators argue that the best procedure for encouraging creativity is to get out of the child's way. This argument probably has merit if one is referring to the actual act of creating. But *prior* to the act of creating, children need help in learning to use the tools, media, and processes of the creative act. Like a painter who needs knowledge of his media as well as a sensitivity to his own creative urges, a writer or speaker must understand his media of words and the processes which induce the creative product. There are at least three different frameworks which might be used in teaching those processes to children.

## Stages in Creative Thinking

One framework is that of the stages which are often experienced in creative thinking. Wallas (22) describes the stages as preparation, incubation, illumination, and verification. Foshay (5) describes them as openness, focus, discipline, and closure. Sessions (15) delineates them as inspiration, conception, and execution. For purposes of teaching creative writing and speaking, however, I would recommend that the teacher keep in mind the following stages of creative thinking.

*Preparing:* This stage often involves careful, open-minded observation of a person, an event, an object, or any other subject of one's investigation. A mind which is relatively free of bias and one which is willing to be surprised is more capable of insightful description than a mind which habitually classifies its environment too soon or screens out unusual, disturbing phenomena. Sometimes this stage involves the sensing of problems, gaps in knowledge, or other deficiencies in one's environment. The "soul cries out" for something better—something more just, or more elegant, or more truthful. This is the stage during which a writer sees the need for a *new* organization of his society, a *new* concept of human nature, or a *new* form of poetic expression. At times this stage involves the act of seeking inspiration—through music, through beautiful poetry or prose, through nature, through the memory of past glories, through daydreaming. And at times this stage involves the more mundane operation of gathering facts through reading, interviewing, or observing.

*Focusing:* This stage involves the act of perceiving a solution to a problem, a procedure to follow, or an end product. "Oh, I've got it!" "Say, how about doing it this way!" "Now I know how to say it!" Sometimes the perception or insight comes during the process of conscious reasoning. Frequently, however, the insight comes after a period of incubation, during which time the mind has been seemingly concentrating on problems which are unrelated to the creative task (14). Some people have their greatest insights while taking a shower, or riding on a bus, or playing cards. Some people induce insight by leaving their creative task for a period and returning to it later. All methods of inducing insight, however, involve the necessity of listening to oneself, and this is one point, among many, at which the preparing and focusing stage merge (none of the stages is discrete). Focusing also involves commitment on the part of the creator to a particular form, procedure, or product. Sometimes it is very difficult to reach the point of commitment since alternative ideas may plead for attention. At times the alternatives may be so forceful in the would-be creator's mind, he cannot make a decision, and the next stage of creativity is never entered upon.

*Executing:* This stage requires hard work! It might be called the "sweat and tears stage," and many embryonic creators haven't the perseverance to last through it. This is the stage at which the sins of procrastination are most tempting—time to sharpen all of one's pencils, clean one's desk, or chat with a friend. A tremendous amount of resolution is often required at this stage just *to begin* the pencil work. At least as much resolution is needed to prevent premature closure; the temptation to rush it through, to get it in its "final" form, to cut it off too soon, is stronger than many can withstand. On the other hand, there are some writers who would fuss until doomsday on every little word if some kind teacher or editor didn't snatch the product from their hands and push them on to the next stage. Knowing when to stop, then, is also part of the executing stage.

*Communicating:* Although some people may create with no desire to share their product, such a mode of operation is hardly typical. Most of us can hardly wait to share our marvelous ideas with others. Not that this stage is always pleasurable. On the contrary, it may be quite painful and even traumatic. It's a rare public speaker who feels no pain in the delivery room. How few the writers must be who can toss their products to the wolves without fear and trembling. Yet, despite the visceral imbalance and other neurological disturbances, the desire to communicate to a sympathetic audience remains.

How can a teacher encourage those four stages as they apply to creative writing and speaking? *Here are some ways of aiding the preparing stage:*

1. Encourage children to observe with as little bias as possible; to avoid immediate structuring of perceptions; to accept all of the data even though some of it might be threatening.

Possible types of experience for children:

a. Examine a familiar object as if you are seeing it for the first time. Discuss or write about your observations.

b. Write about (or discuss) things that frighten you.

c. Write about (or discuss) a person that you dislike, but describe only his good points.

d. After viewing a skit or film with moral overtones, describe what happened without making any judgment or using emotional words.

e. Describe a landscape without using any value words such as "beautiful" or "glorious."

2. Encourage children to use the "deferred judgment" technique. (12) Parnes and Meadow (13) have found that this technique is conducive to original and useful ideas. The essence of the technique is simply to accept, for a period of time, any idea which comes to mind.

Possible types of experiences for children:

a. Before deciding upon a writing topic, list as many ideas for topics as you can; defer judgment of your ideas until you have created a long list. Then select one topic to write on.

b. Use the deferred judgment principle to develop a list of names of the characters in your story.

c. Use the deferred judgment principle to develop a list of sources that might be used to get more information on your topic.

3. Encourage children to use all of their senses whenever possible during observation.

Possible types of experiences for children:

a. Look at an object in the room; describe it orally or on paper. Then, touch the object, shake it, and listen to the noise it makes. Smell it, and even taste it, if the situation is sufficiently sanitary. Describe the object again. Discuss the differences in the two descriptions.

b. Describe another object in the room after some children have only looked at it; some have only felt it (eyes shut); some have only smelled it; some have only listened to it while the teacher shakes it; some have only tasted it. (The class will have to be divided into small groups in different parts of the room.) Discuss the differences in the descriptions.

4. Encourage children to be sensitive to deficiencies in their environment.
   Possible types of experiences for children:
   a. List as many ways as you can of improving the chalkboard in this classroom. Discuss several of the ideas in a complimentary rather than critical way.
   b. Write about (or describe orally) an "ideal" school—one which you would like to go to. Share your ideas.
   c. Describe (or write about) a means of transporting people which would be better than the way we do it in our town. Discuss your ideas; send some to the Mayor.
5. Encourage children to develop imaginative foresight.
   Possible types of experiences for children:
   a. What would happen if people stopped drinking milk because they thought it was poisonous? List as many things that might happen as you can. Discuss.
   b. Make up more "What if" problems.

   *Here are some ways of aiding the focusing stage:*

1. After the preparing stage has occurred, encourage children to decide on their own way of making sense out of their observations.
   Possible types of experiences for children:
   a. Write a story, poem, or play (or give a talk) based on the previous observations during the preparing stage.
   b. Write an essay expounding a theory based on the previous observations.
2. Encourage children to utilize the process of incubation.
   Possible types of experiences for children:
   a. After deciding on the means of focusing, concentrate for several minutes on the anticipated project; then take time off for recess or some other easy task; return to the creative task.
   b. Make an "idea" notebook for your school desk and also one for home. Write down ideas as soon as possible after they occur. Expand these ideas during your spare time and during the time set aside by the teacher for this purpose.
3. Encourage them to commit themselves in the presence of others to a definite product (after adequate time has been given for the preparing stage).

*Here are some ways of aiding the executing stage:*

1. Provide a period each day for uninterrupted work—perhaps during the end of the school day so that children might carry on a project at home while their pens are hot.

2. Provide adequate materials so that children are not tempted to quit because of lack of resources (paper, pencils, tape recorder for the child who wants to think out loud, "stenographers" for children who have difficulty writing, time).

3. Reward persistence through individual praise.

*Here are some ways of aiding the communicating stage:*

1. Permit children to choose among several alternate ways of sharing their work with others, e.g., classmates guess "student author" after teacher reads aloud; student places his creative writing product in an "anonymous author file" or a "teacher only file"; student gives a spontaneous talk or reads his paper.

2. Develop a classroom newspaper, magazine, or book to share with parents, children in the same school, children in another school, children in another city, or children in another country.

3. Refer to children frequently with terms such as "authors," "writers," "poets," and "reporters."

## Mental Abilities Involved in Creative Thinking

A second framework which might be used in teaching the processes of creative speaking and writing is that of the mental abilities involved in creative thinking. Guilford and his associates (8) have defined creative thinking, by means of tests and factor analysis, as a composite of several abilities. These abilities include fluency, sensitivity to problems, spontaneous flexibility, adaptive flexibility, redefinition, and originality.

According to Guilford *et al.*, (9) there are four types of fluency. These will now be defined; also related activities for teaching creative writing and speaking will be described.

*Word fluency:* the ability to think rapidly of words which have particular structural characteristics. This ability is helpful, for example, in writing poetry which requires a definite rhythm or rhyme.

Sample activities:

1. In two minutes think of several words which end with the syllable "ate," e.g., refrigerate.

2. In one minute think of several words which rhyme with "rusty."

3. In two minutes think of several phrases which have the same rhythm as "down the dustry road."

*Ideational fluency:* the ability to think rapidly of ideas which are appropriate to a given situation.

Sample activities:

1. In three minutes think of several titles for the following plot: A perfume peddler ran out of gasoline on a deserted road. He poured several bottles of perfume in the gasoline tank and managed to drive to the nearest town. Example: "An Odorous Solution."

2. In three minutes think of several titles for this cartoon (selected by teacher).

3. In three minutes think of as many uses as you can for a broom.

*Associational fluency:* the ability to think rapidly of words which have a specified relationship to a given word. This ability is useful, for example, when repeating an idea in a variety of ways, or in expressing vivid images.

Sample activities:

1. In two minutes think of several words which mean the same as "sly."

2. In two minutes think of several words which mean the opposite of "heavy."

3. In two minutes think of several similes for this sentence: He ran down the hall like a _____.

*Expressional fluency:* The ability to think rapidly of phrases or sentences which have a restricted structure. This ability is necessary, for example, in producing newspaper headlines or a rhythmic line.

Sample activities:

1. In three minutes make several five-word sentences. Each word must begin with the given letter. No word may be used twice. (8)

Example:

M_____ g_____ a_____ r_____ f_____.
Marjorie's granny ate rotten figs

2. In three minutes describe the following situation with several three-word headlines: Mrs. Smith left her purse on a bus. She later caught a bus which she assumed was the one on which she had left

her purse. Mrs. Smith found her purse, but another woman, named Mrs. Hammer, was holding it. Mrs. Hammer insisted it was hers, whereupon Mrs. Smith slapped Mrs. Hammer and retrieved the purse.

Example:

*Smith Beats Hammer*

Spontaneous flexibility, adaptive flexibility, and redefinition are defined as separate creative-thinking abilities by Guilford, *et al.* (8) However, because those three abilities seem to have overlapping characteristics, they will be considered here as a composite ability called "redefinition." *Redefinition* will be considered as the ability to restructure a problem situation in order to produce a variety of solutions. In creative writing and speaking, redefinition is most noticeable when a person produces a humorous remark by using words which have several meanings. In each of the following activities the child must consider more than one meaning of a key word.

Sample activities:

1. In three minutes write several short sentences in which the word "hand" is used in different ways.
   Responses which show a lack of redefinition:
   a. I hurt my hand.
   b. I cut my hand.
   c. Your hand is cold.
   d. His hand is small.
   Responses which show that redefinition has taken place:
   a. I hurt my hand.
   b. Hand me that book.
   c. He was a hired hand.
   d. The audience gave her a hand.
2. Make up a funny remark for each of the following:
   Example: Why didn't you catch the train? *I forgot my butterfly net.*
   a. Does your father smoke?              _____
   b. Did the bull charge?                 _____
   c. Do you have a rubber band?           _____
3. Make up a riddle with each of the following words:
   Example: <u>flies</u>
   Question: What has four wheels and flies?
   Answer: <u>garbage truck</u>

a. *change:* ___ _____

b. *spring:* _____

c. *light:* _____

4. Make up some "Tom Swifties."
   Examples:
   "There's a ghost town," he said, spiritedly.
   "I'm looking out the window," he said, painfully.
   "This coat is definitely not made of lambs wool," she said with a sheepish grin.

Sensitivity to problems is the ability to perceive deficiencies, gaps, or weaknesses (8). Without such an ability an inventor would have no impetus to invent; nor an author to improve his writing. With respect to creative writing and speaking, there are probably several components of the ability called sensitivity to problems. Sensitivity to gaps in descriptions could be considered as one of the components. Sensitivity to weak imagery could be considered as another component.

Sample activities:

1. Sensitivity to gaps in descriptions: After the description list several questions which, if answered, would help you to understand the situation better.
   a. The mountain lion sniffed the air. The branch of the tree began to crack. The sound of a shot was heard.
   Sample question: Who heard the shot?

2. Sensitivity to weak imagery: For each sentence think of two words that would sound more interesting than the underlined word.
   a. The snake gave a loud warning as we came near.

   _____        _____

   The child who has learned to be sensitive to weak imagery might substitute two onomatopoetic words, such as hissed and rattled.
   b. The stars moved across the sky.

   _____        _____

The child who has learned to be sensitive to weak imagery might substitute two metaphors, such as *slid* and *rolled*.

*Originality* is the ability to respond to a situation in an unusual, remote, or clever manner. (8) The originality of a response can be most easily determined by the relative frequency of its occurrence within a particular population, such as a classroom group, or all sixth-grade students in one school. A response which occurred only once or twice in a class of 30 youngsters would be considered original. A response which occurred several times would not be considered original.

Sample activities:

1. Time <u>goes</u> on and on.                    _____        _____

The teacher should have the students substitute more interesting words for the underlined word. After determining the most common responses, such as "marches" or "travels," give the students the exercise again at a later date. This time direct them to use interesting words *other than* "marches," "travels," or whatever words are common for the group of children.

2. Invent a new ending for "Goldilocks and the Three Bears." Try to create an ending which you think no one else in the class will think of.

3. Invent similes of this sentence: After working all day, he felt as weak as a _____. After determining the most common responses, such as "kitten" or "new-born babe," the teacher should give the exercise at a later date. This time direct the children to invent similes *other than* "kitten," "new-born babe," or whatever similes are common for the group of children.

## Characteristics of Creative Speaking and Writing

A third framework for teaching the processes of creative speaking and writing is the characteristics considered important by experts. In the previous chapter several criteria of interesting writing and speaking were discussed. These criteria were distilled by the author into a brief list of traits which characterize interesting speaking and writing, recognizing, of course, that no list of this nature can be inclusive or final. With those limitations in mind, the following list of eight criteria is recommended as a third framework for teaching creative speaking and writing:

*Imagery:* describing a situation or person in vivid, colorful, concrete language.

Sample activities:

1. Compare these two verses. Which one creates the most interesting picture in your mind? Why?
   a. Once there was a teddy bear
      Poor little thing had no hair
      Yes, had no hair I did declare,
      But actually, he didn't care.
   b. Teddy is bald from head to toe.
      His skin is smooth as a leather purse.
      But he's not feeling sad and low,
      For after all it won't get worse.
2. Describe how a relative or friend of yours looks when he is angry. Invent some metaphors and similes to make your description interesting. (It is assumed that the teacher will first teach the children how to use metaphors and similes.)

*Naturalness:* using informal language; maintaining personal contact with the listeners or readers; expressing one's individuality.

Sample activities:

1. Compare these two stories. Which one is the most interesting? Why?
   a. Once there was a rabbit by the name of Herman. This rabbit was a very happy rabbit. Also, he wasn't very bright. Now most of you would think a rabbit would live in woods and eat green things, but not Herman. Herman lived at the South Pole, of all places, and ate fish all the time! Herman had a mother, a father, and a sister whose name was Kadiddily. One day, Herman had to take Kadiddily for a walk. This he hated very much. He didn't want to be a sissy! . . .
   b. Herman was a rabbit who lived at the South Pole. His daily diet consisted of fish. Although Herman was very happy, he was a rather ignorant rabbit. He lived with his mother, father, and sister, Kadiddily. Each day he took his sister for a walk. Herman did not care for this job. . . .
2. Try writing a short story as if you were writing a letter to a good friend who knows how you feel about things.
3. Give a five-minute talk on any topic you choose. Talk to the class as if you were telling your story to your best friend.

*Inventiveness:* inventing fresh analogies, characters, settings, plots, or words; playing with homonyms, alliteration, and other humorous devices.

1. Compare these two descriptions. Which one seems more fresh and interesting? Why?

    a. Bill fought like a tiger. As quick as a wink he threw Jim to the ground. Jim's glasses broke on the sidewalk. This made him so mad he started kicking like a steer. Bill was kept busy as a bee dodging Jim's thrashing feet.

    b. Bill fought like a robin having a tug of war with a worm. With one swift tug he threw Jim to the ground, shattering Jim's glasses on the sidewalk. Jim swelled up with anger and began kicking his feet as if he were running upside down after Bill. Bill dodged Jim's feet by inventing a new dance.

2. Make up a story about an animal which is different from any animal you have ever heard of. Have him do things which no other animal would do. Make up a name for the animal.

3. Create a short dialogue, using words with double meanings.

    Example: From "Panic in the Palace" by Martha Swintz

    PAGE:   (Reading from large scroll: By order of the King! This day shall be celebrated throughout the land of Eidelwitz as a holiday in honor of the first birthday of our fair Princess! So be it!

    ALL:   Long live the Princess!

    KING:   That's a very good proclamation. Who wrote it?

    PAGE:   You did, Sire.

    KING:   Oh, I can't be bothered with writing proclamations. I hire ghost writers. All the famous dignitaries have them.

    QUEEN:   I've never seen any of your ghost writers around here.

    KING:   CERTAINLY NOT. I have a new angle. I'm the only king in the world who uses real ghosts.

    QUEEN:   Real ghosts?

    KING:   To be sure. Think of the saving. No food—no shelter. Just an occasional sheet now and then.

    QUEEN:   But don't they make the proclamations too grave?

    KING:   Oh no. As writers they are out of this world.

4. Make up an alliterative phrase for each description:
   a. large wads of dirty grease—*great gobs of grimy grease*
   b. little bright shoes— _____
   c. a half dozen sick Navy men— _____
5. Think of "unlikely spots" for:
   a. a man to have a sneezing attack: *when "swearing in" on the witness stand.*
   b. a woman to put on lipstick: *in a men's barber shop.*
   c. boys to play baseball: _____
   d. girls to jump rope:  _____
6. Rewrite a familiar story; keep the same characters and setting, but make several important changes in the plot.
7. Rewrite a familiar story; keep the same plot and characters but make several important changes in the setting.

*Insight:* portraying human strengths and weaknesses by means of satire, humorous incongruity, philosophical generalization, realistic description, and other devices.

Sample activities:

1. Which of the following situations would probably make the funniest story? Why?
   a. A monkey who was caught by a zoo keeper, or a man who was caught by a dog catcher.
   b. A child who gets spanked by his father or a father who gets spanked by his child.
2. Describe a person getting out of bed in the morning. Try to make us understand how many people *feel* about it.
3. Same as 2; using other situations which would make it possible to depict human nature, e.g., spilling milk on the tablecloth, practicing the piano, helping a younger person learn how to do something, saving another person from being hurt.
4. You have probably noticed that boys generally argue a great deal while they play baseball. You can write a humorous satire of this situation by exaggerating such arguments. For instance, in your satire you might have the game begin by having one boy hit the ball down the third base line; then the entire recess is spent arguing about whether the ball was foul or fair. In what other ways could you satirize this activity?
5. Write a humorous satire about other situations, e.g., girls dis-

cussing their hair and clothes, fathers getting ready for a fishing trip, mothers shopping for a pair of shoes.

6. Make a list of "Things I've Learned About People," e.g., Some mothers like to _____.
   When a person gets excited he's likely to _____
   _____. (After a list has been made, have the children write a short story about one of their statements.)

*Sincerity:* demonstrating keen interest or feeling regarding one's subject, story, or characters.
Sample activities:

1. Listen to a tape recording (made by the teacher) of a story or talk—given once with enthusiasm and feeling, and a second time in a drab and lifeless manner. Discuss the difference: Why is the first way of speaking more interesting than the second?

2. Before giving a talk or reading a story in front of the class, practice it with the tape recorder. See how much feeling you can get into your presentation.

3. Give a talk or write a chapter for a class book about an animal in which you are particularly interested. Be sure to find some facts about this animal which you have never known before and which probably no one in the class knows. For instance, did you know that lions are good swimmers?

*Flexible Style:* avoiding monotony by altering sentence length, clause position, sentence type, and other elements of style.
Sample activities:

1. Which of these is the most interesting description? Why?
   a. Mr. Simpson flew down the hall. He grabbed Jerry by the back of the collar. He pushed Jerry against the wall. Mr. Simpson commanded Jerry to tell why he had done it. Jerry was feeling very much ashamed! He didn't want to tell Mr. Simpson the real reason.
   b. Mr. Simpson flew down the hall. He grabbed Jerry by the back of his collar and pushed him against the wall. Shaking his finger in Jerry's face, Mr. Simpson demanded to know why he had done it. Jerry felt so ashamed! He didn't want to tell Mr. Simpson the real reason.

2. Rewrite this sentence several times without changing the main idea. Verb forms may be changed and words such as "while"

and "as" added. Phil ran quickly down the street, leaving a trail of gumdrops behind him.
Example: Quickly, Phil ran down the street, leaving a trail of gumdrops behind him.
3. After writing a story or tape recording a talk, count the number of times you used each of these four types of sentences: declarative, interrogative, imperative, and exclamatory. Did you overuse any type? Did you underuse any type?

*Conciseness:* expressing the essence of an idea or situation; avoiding words and details which distract from the main ideas or impressions to be conveyed.
Sample activities:
1. Which set of directions is more interesting and easier to understand? Why?
   a. So as to understand something about magnetism, one might perform an experiment. Get some paper clips from your teacher or your parents. Or, purchase some from an office supply store. Place the paper clips on a table or desk. Ask a science teacher to loan you a magnet. Some magnets are called horseshoe magnets because they are in the shape of a horseshoe. Some magnets are called bar magnets. Some bar magnets are bent to form a U-shaped magnet. Any type of magnet will work in this experiment. Place the end or ends of your magnet on the paper clips. Now try to pick up other materials, such as paper, glass, or wood, with your magnet.
   b. What kinds of material will a magnet pick up? Try as many materials as you can.
2. Rewrite the following passage in twelve words or less.
   I think that it might be necessary to find a way of covering the hole in this boat so as to keep the boat from becoming so full of water that it will sink.

*Clarity:* avoiding slang or jargon, dangling participles, mystic phrases, pronouns with hazy referents, and other habits of speech which are likely to confuse listeners or readers.
Sample activities:
1. Which of these sentences is easier to understand? Why?
   a. Having finished his sketch, we began to ask the artist questions.

  b. After the artist finished his sketch, we asked him questions.
2. Rewrite these sentences to make them easier to understand.
  a. Being painted in a color he did not like, Mr. Snow did not wish to buy the car.
  b. Running after him as fast as we could, the dog got away.
3. Find a way to make this paragraph easier to understand.
  "Joan took her sister over to Aunt Mary's house. She was dirty and her clothes were torn, but she didn't mind. She had a good time, and she was glad she had brought her."
4. What's wrong with these sentences? Can you find any mystical phrases?
  a. He knew that somewhere in the great unknown he would find the mystery of the mysterious and the wonder of the wonderful.
  b. And if we do this we can be sure of continual progress toward the fulfillment of life's dreams and the revelation of better days ahead.
5. Underline the words and phrases which are hard to understand. Then rewrite the paragraph so that it is both interesting and clear.
  "The thingamabob on this steering gismo doesn't work. I tried to make with the music down the street when a man-child ran out in front of me, but the music was dead, man, dead. If the brakes weren't so nifty-keeno, the man-child would have been dead too."

## Stimulating Written and Oral Compositions

  In the previous section it was suggested that a successful creative writing-creative speaking program cannot be based on gimmicks. A successful program requires a teacher who knows how to develop a creative atmosphere in the classroom and one who understands the processes of creative thinking. Three frameworks and related activities for encouraging creative thinking were suggested. Most of those activities, however, were designed for purposes of specific training toward specific abilities. Another aspect of the creative language program should be that of providing children with ample opportunities to prepare oral and written compositions—compositions which are not stimulated by specific training exercises. Most of the training exercises suggested in the last section were designed to develop specific skills. These skills should then be utilized in written and oral compositions of broader scope. (At least the children should be given the chance to utilize them.)

What, then, should the teacher use to stimulate such compositions? Literally thousands of articles and books have been written on this subject. The number of different stimuli dreamed up by teachers approaches infinity.

Although ideas for stimuli are abundant, experimental research in this subject has been meager. Witty and Martin (23) found that a symbolic film without narration motivated children to write stories of high quality. The film stimuli, however, was not compared with other stimuli. Carlson (2), on the other hand, compared a series of eight multisensory stimuli with the common stimulus of allowing children to choose a topic from a list of topics. Her subjects consisted of 217 children in grades four through six from 18 classes in six cities. Carlson found that four out of the eight stimuli—interesting toys, pictures, unusual experiences, and daydreams—encouraged more original stories than the choice of topics did. Nevertheless, it is difficult to isolate the factors which contributed to the stimuli's effectiveness in Carlson's study. One cannot say, for example, that pictures, per se, are effective stimuli. Their effectiveness would surely depend on their subject matter, color, and other qualities. (Carlson found that one series of pictures was effective and another series was not.)

Sofell (16) attempted to discover whether assigned or chosen topics are more effective in stimulating high quality writing. A group of 304 children in grades four through six were asked to write compositions at two-week intervals. While the first, third, and fifth topics were assigned, the second and fourth topics were chosen by the children. A panel of judges rated the compositions written on the chosen topics as better on writing mechanics, organization, and literary quality than the compositions written on the assigned topics. Again, however, it is difficult to isolate the specific factors responsible for the difference in stimulus effectiveness. Were the assigned topics interesting enough? How were the two types of stimuli presented by the teachers? (The teachers in Sofell's study were told to begin the non-assigned sessions with the statement that choosing one's own topic is "more fun." How significant was this statement in producing better results?)

Edmund (4) gave 140 fifth graders and 90 seventh graders 45 minutes to write on any topic. A questionnaire was administered afterwards which made it possible to divide the children into two groups—one group wrote stories based on direct experiences and the other group wrote stories based on vicarious experiences. The stories based on vicarious experiences included more words and a greater number of descriptive words and were rated by a panel of judges as more creative. Edmund concluded that teachers may need to do more in developing children's abilities to interpret their first-hand experiences, since an understanding of direct experiences is probably quite significant to the growth of an individual. (Edmund found that only 20 per cent of the fifth graders made use of their general interests as topics for compositions.)

Ujlaki and Macdonald (21) compared the effectiveness of four different types of stimuli on the interest value of fourth graders' compositions. The four types of stimuli were (a) an abstract painting, (b) abstract music, (c) free choice of topics, and (d) a motivational paragraph designed to invite reactions to scientific adventures. A group of 24 children produced 192 stories in eight sessions (two sessions for each type of stimuli). Three judges independently grouped the stories into seven forced-choice categories ranging from "1" as the least interesting to "7" as the most interesting. The total scores for the four stimuli were as follows: Free Choice 619, Assigned Topic 574, Abstract Pictures 554, and Abstract Music 548. Some of these differences, however, could have occurred by chance; only the difference between Free Choice and Abstract Music was considered statistically significant. Ujlaki and Macdonald concluded that self-selection of topics may be the most effective means of encouraging creativity in children's writing. Nevertheless, we are still left in the dark as to the effectiveness of other types of stimuli. No comparison was made between the two different abstract paintings, the two different pieces of abstract music, and the two different assigned topics. So far, researchers have developed no framework which will help teachers choose one picture, musical composition, or topic over another.

None of the research cited above has been concerned with the specific characteristics which distinguish one stimulus from another. Yet research indicates that creative people may be attracted to particular types of stimuli. MacKinnon's study (10) of creative writers, architects, and engineers suggests that creative people are challenged by complex, unfinished, and unordered stimuli. Barron's study (1) of Air Force Captains demonstrated that creative people tend to like and construct things which are not simply ordered. Stein and Meer (17) used Rorschach ink blots to measure creative thinking abilities and found that the Rorschach measurements correlated significantly with supervisory judgments of creativity.

The studies by Stein and Meer, MacKinnon, and Barron indicate, therefore, that an appropriate device for inducing creative writing or speaking would be an unorganized stimuli. Drews (3), however, found that highly creative adolescents are fond of making original interpretations of common phenomena. Furthermore, although the Rorschach ink blot test is often used in an attempt to measure creativity, the Thematic Appreciation Test is also used for this purpose. While the Rorschach test would require the creative individual to synthesize an unorganized stimulus in an uncommon way, the TAT would require him to make an original interpretation of an organized, common stimulus. Moreover, the investigations of creative thinking by Guilford and his associates (8) have led them to define creative thinking with such terms as spontaneous flexibility, adaptive flexibility, and redefinition, implying that creativity involves an ability to restructure common stimuli in order to produce something new.

Research indicates, then, that although creativity may be stimulated by an organized stimulus, it might also be stimulated by an unorganized stimulus. Research does not indicate, however, the relative effectiveness of the two types of stimuli in promoting creative writing and speaking. With this problem in mind, Tabachnick and May (18), in a study partially funded by the U.S. Office of Education, compared the results of three different stimuli on the written compositions of 600 third and sixth graders. These children were randomly assigned to one of three groups. Each group, consisting of one-third of the population, received a different stimulus—organized, unorganized, or a choice between the organized and unorganized. The organized stimulus was a sketch which included a person, a hill, a tree, and a flying bird. The unorganized stimulus was an abstract sketch, arranged in a meaningless order. All children in the study received a mimeographed sheet, at the top of which was the organized sketch or the unorganized sketch or both of these stimuli.

Those receiving either the organized or unorganized sketch were asked to write an imaginative story about the sketch. Those who received both the organized and unorganized sketches were asked to choose between the two stimuli and then to write a story about their choice. All subjects were given 40 minutes in which to write their stories. (The choice group was given an extra five minutes in which to make a choice.) The stimuli were administered by the regular classroom teachers, who participated in a short training session and received a standardized administration guide. The teachers informed the children that they were involved in an important research project. The stories were collected and typed, with spelling and gross grammatical errors corrected. The stories were then judged "creative" or "not creative" by six graduate students in English and six graduate students in Education. Since each composition was read independently by each of the twelve judges the score for a composition could range from 0—12. A score of 5, for example, would indicate that five out of twelve judges considered the story "creative." (The third-grade and six-grade compositions were judged separately.)

Table 1 shows the mean scores on the third graders' creative compositions. None of the differences among or between means were considered statistically significant.

TABLE 1

Mean Scores on Creative Compositions by 270 Third
Grade Children*

*Stimuli*

|         | Organized | Unorganized | Choice | Total |
|---------|-----------|-------------|--------|-------|
| Boys    | 2.80      | 3.18        | 2.96   | 2.98  |
| Girls   | 3.47      | 3.31        | 2.84   | 3.21  |
| Total   | 3.13      | 3.24        | 2.90   | 3.09  |

* Cells were equalized by random deletion of subjects.

Table 2 shows the mean scores on the sixth graders' creative compositions. The difference among the three stimuli was not considered statistically significant. However, the difference between boys and girls and the interaction between sex and stimuli were considered statistically significant. In general, the girls performed better than the boys on this task—a finding which is consistent with the general superiority which American girls develop in verbal fluency. On the other hand, the girls' superior performance in this situation was largely due to the very poor showing which the boys made in the group which had the organized stimulus. The girls performed considerably better than the boys in the "organized" and "choice"

TABLE 2
Mean Scores on Creative Compositions by 258 Sixth
Grade Children*

|  | *Stimuli* | | | |
|  | *Organized* | *Unorganized* | *Choice* | *Total* |
|---|---|---|---|---|
| Boys | 2.07 | 4.09 | 3.12 | 3.09 |
| Girls | 4.09 | 3.16 | 4.30 | 3.85 |
| Total | 3.08 | 3.63 | 3.71 | 3.47 |

* Cells were equalized by random deletion of subjects.

situations. Yet the boys performed much better than the girls in the "unorganized" situation. Evidently the boys blossomed and the girls wilted when asked to respond to the unorganized stimulus. In the choice situation both girls and boys performed well, relative to their overall means, but again the girls' performance was quite superior to that of the boys.

Table 3 shows the mean scores of only those children who were in the "choice" group. In both the third-grade and sixth-grade groups

TABLE 3
Mean Scores on Creative Compositions of Children
in Choice Group

|  | *Chosen Stimuli* | | | |
|  | *Organized* | | *Unorganized* | |
|  | *Mean* | *N* | *Mean* | *N* |
|---|---|---|---|---|
| Grade 3 | 2.96 | 85 | 3.46 | 13 |
| Grade 6 | 3.37 | 76 | 4.83 | 24 |

those who chose the unorganized stimulus tended to perform better than those who chose the organized stimulus. (However, only with the sixth grade group was the difference between means considered statistically significant.) Tabachnick and May (18) suggest three possible reasons for this phenomenon: (1) Highly creative children may have been more prone to select the unorganized stimulus than their less creative peers. (2) The unorganized stimulus may have encouraged a slightly better performance than the organized stimulus. (There is some evidence for this in Table 2.) (3) The *combination* of choice and unorganized stimulus may have been more motivating than any one of the stimuli by itself. Notice in Table 3 that the sixth-grade mean related to the unorganized stimulus is considerably higher than any mean in Table 2.

Table 4 shows the frequency of stimulus preferences of the children in the third-grade choice group. The organized stimulus was obviously more popular than the organized stimulus for both girls and boys.

TABLE 4
Frequency of Stimulus Preferences of Children in Third
Grade Choice Group

|  | Organized | | Unorganized | |
|--|--|--|--|--|
|  | f | % | f | % |
| Boys | 44 | 88 | 6 | 12 |
| Girls | 41 | 85 | 7 | 15 |
| Total | 85 | 87 | 13 | 13 |

Table 5 shows the frequency of stimulus preferences of children in th sixth-grade choice group. The organized stimulus was the obvious favorite of the sixth graders. The difference between the

TABLE 5
Frequency of Stimulus Preferences of Children in Sixth
Grade Choice Group

|  | Organized | | Unorganized | |
|--|--|--|--|--|
|  | f | % | f | % |
| Boys | 44 | 73 | 16 | 27 |
| Girls | 35 | 81 | 8 | 19 |
| Total | 79 | 77 | 24 | 23 |

sexes was not considered statistically significant, although the tendency for boys to choose the unorganized stimulus more than the girls is consistent with the boys' superior performance in the "unorganized" group (see Table 2).

Tabachnick and May's study indicates that the stimuli used to motivate creative speaking and writing should include the opportunities to respond not only to organized stimuli but also to unorganized stimuli. An experimental approach by the teacher would be that of mixing the stimuli—using an organized stimulus on one occasion, an unorganized stimulus on another occasion, and a choice on another.

For teachers who are not used to using "unorganized" stimuli to motivate creative compositions, here are several suggestions:

1. Abstract paintings (reprints or slides) such as Mondrian's "Horizontal Tree" or Kandinsky's "Black Lines."

2. "Modern" music such as Bloch's "Schelomo" or Prokofiev's Symphony No. 5.

3. Abstract drawings or paintings produced by the children.

4. Scrambled words—the teacher reads a list of five or six unrelated words or writes the words on the board. (The children should not be encouraged to use the words in their composition; the words are used only to get them started.)

5. Scrambled objects—unrelated objects are hung up or placed on a table in front of the room, e.g., fly swatter, hat, knife, book.

6. Scrambled odors—children walk up to a table four at a time and smell the contents of four cans concealed by cheesecloth on top. (Discussion should be discouraged at this point.) The cans should contain very unusual spices, etc.

7. Mysterious objects—children walk up to a table four at a time and feel the contents of four boxes without looking into the opening of the boxes. (Discussion should be discouraged at this point.) The boxes should contain very unusual objects such as an irregular piece of smooth wood or a ball of wet paper. Objects should be selected which will not leave tell-tale marks on the hand.

8. Abstract sculpture produced by the children or by local artists.

## Two Basic Issues

Regardless of the stimulus used (and a stimulus is always used even if it is nothing more than silent consent to let Betty write during the arithmetic period), there are still two basic issues which confront the teacher. These issues have been discussed in innumerable articles and books and will be only touched upon here.

One of the issues concerns the mechanics of writing and speech: Should teachers correct the usage, spelling, and punctuation of children's creative expression? Some say, "Yes!" Some say, "No!" Some say, "Yes, but do it nicely, nicely." Perhaps a sensible, middle-ground position can be taken here, in which the purpose for writing or speaking determines the degree of stress on mechanics. If a child is writing creatively and intends to submit his product to the class magazine, for example, he will have a purpose in considering stand-ard spelling, usage and punctuation in his *final* draft. If, on the other hand, he is giving a spontaneous talk or is writing a story which he may or may not read to the class, the teacher certainly should not hover over him with a red pen or use him as a living grammar lesson.

The other issue is whether time for creative composition should be scheduled; or should it be allotted as the desire to create arises spontaneously? This issue, however, is related to a more basic one: Should creative composition be considered a way of capturing emo-tions and experiences or should it be a separate experience in itself? Many of the stimuli which we teachers have used to encourage crea-tive composition tend to make this process a separate experience. Of course, time for this kind of experience can be easily scheduled. If, on the other hand, creative composition is encouraged as a means of capturing emotions and experiences, it is obvious that time cannot be scheduled in advance, especially for capturing emotions.

Here, again, it seems sensible to take a middle-ground position. Why not include both types of composing situations in a school program? Those children who seldom find pleasure in "capturing" their emotions and experiences by means of creative composition might enjoy immensely the type of composition instigated by inter-esting devices. Those who feel hampered by the latter approach might prefer the former. This dual approach to creative composition would certainly allow more for individual differences than a single approach.

\* \* \* \* \*

In this chapter the thesis has been presented that a teacher cannot succeed in motivating children to write and speak creatively by gimmicks alone. Such motivation demands a creative atmosphere which is based on the teacher's desire to be personally creative and also on his respect for the personality characteristics of creative individuals. It also demands a teacher who understands creative processes.

Three different frameworks for encouraging creative processes were suggested. These frameworks consist of the stages which are often experienced in creative thinking, the mental abilities involved in creative thinking, and the characteristics of creative composition considered important by experts. Appropriate exercises for each framework were described. These exercises were designed for the purpose of teaching specific skills involved in creative composition. It was suggested, however, that such exercises are not sufficient for a creative writing and speaking program; that children should be stimulated to produce oral and written compositions of greater scope; and that both organized and unorganized stimuli should be used.

Finally, the issues of writing mechanics and of time allocation for creative composition were discussed. A middle-road position was taken in each case, with purpose determining the degree of emphasis on mechanics, and individual differences determining, to some extent at least, the appropriate time for creative composition to occur.

# REFERENCES

1. Barron, Frank, "The Psychology of Imagination." *A Source Book for Creative Thinking,* Edited by Sidney J. Parnes and Harold F. Harding: 227-237; New York: Charles Scribner's Sons, 1962.

2. Carlson, Ruth K., *Stimulating Children in Grades Four, Five, and Six to Write Original Stories,* Doctoral Dissertation, University of California, Berkeley, June, 1959.

3. Drews, Elizabeth M., "The Four Faces of Able Adolescents." *Saturday Review:* January 19, 1963.

4. Edmund, Neal R., "Writing in the Intermediate Grades." *Elementary English* 36:491-501, 1959.

5. Foshay, Arthur W., "The Creative Process Described." *Creativity in Teaching,* Edited by Alice Miel: 22-40; Belmont, California: Wadsworth Publishing Company, Inc., 1961.

6. Getzels, J. W. and P. W. Jackson, "The Study of Giftedness: A Multidimensional Approach." *The Gifted Student.* Cooperative Research Monograph No. 2, U. S. Department of Health, Education, and Welfare: 1-18; 1960.

7. Gough, Harrison G., "Imagination—Undeveloped Resource." *A Source Book for Creative Thinking,* Edited by Sidney J. Parnes and Harold F. Harding: 217-226; New York: Charles Scribner's Sons, 1962.

8. Guilford, J. P., R. C. Wilson, and P. R. Christensen, "A Factor-Analytic Study of Creative Thinking II. Administration of Tests and Analysis of Results." Reports from the Psychological Laboratory: No. 8. University of Southern California, 1952.

9. ——— and P. R. Christensen, "A Factor-Analytic Study of Verbal Fluency." Reports from the Psychological Laboratory: No. 17. University of Southern California, 1956.

10. MacKinnon, Donald W., "What Makes a Person Creative." *Saturday Review:* 15-17; February 10, 1962.

11. Meadow, Arnold and Sidney J. Parnes, "Evaluation of Training in Creative Problem-Solving." *Journal of Applied Psychology* 43:189-194; 1959.

12. Osborn, Alex E. *Applied Imagination.* New York: Charles Scribner's Sons, 1963.

13. Parnes, Sidney J. and Arnold Meadow, "Effects of 'Brainstorming' Instructions on Creative Problem-Solving by Trained and Untrained Subjects." *Journal of Educational Psychology* 50:171-176; 1959.

14. Poincare, Henri. "Mathematical Creation." *The Creative Process,* Edited by Brewster Ghiselin: 33-42; New York: New American Library Inc., 1955.

15. Sessions, Roger. "The Composer and his Message." *The Creative Process*, Edited by Brewster Ghiselin: 45-49; New York: New American Library, Inc., 1955.

16. Sofell, C. "A Comparison of the Use of Imposed with Self-Chosen Subjects in Conjunction with Elementary Children." Masters Thesis, University of Pittsburgh, 1929 (Summarized by Neal R. Edmund in *Elementary English* 36:495, 1959.)

17. Stein, Morris I. and Bernard Meer, "Perceptual Organization in a Study of Creativity." *Journal of Psychology* 37:39-43, 1954.

18. Tabachnick, B. Robert and Frank B. May, *Effects of Three Different Stimuli on the Creativity of Children's Compositions*, Reports to U. S. Office of Education, March, 1965.

19. Torrance, E. Paul. *Guiding Creative Talent*. Englewood Cliffs, New Jersey: Prentice-Hall, Inc., 1962.

20. ———. "The Minnesota Studies of Creative Thinking: 1959-62." Laboratory Report; University of Minnesota: Bureau of Educational Research, 1962.

21. Ujlaki, Vilma and James B. Macdonald, *A Study of Children's Creative Writing in Relation to Various Stimuli*, Research Bulletin No. 62-3, Campus Elementary School, University of Wisconsin, Milwaukee, 1962.

22. Wallas, Graham. *The Art of Thought*. New York: Harcourt, Brace & World, Inc., 1926.

23. Witty, Paul and William Martin, "An Analysis of Children's Compositions Written in Response to a Film," *Elementary English* 34:158-163, March, 1957.

# INDEX